INTERNATIONAL PERSPECTIVES IN HIGHER EDUCATION

THE EDUCATIONAL INNOVATIONS SERIES

The Educational Innovations series explores a wide range of current school reform efforts. Individual volumes examine entrepreneurial efforts and unorthodox approaches, highlighting reforms that have met with success and strategies that have attracted widespread attention. The series aims to disrupt the status quo and inject new ideas into contemporary education debates.

Series edited by Frederick M. Hess. Other books in this series:

The Strategic Management of Charter Schools
by Peter Frumkin, Bruno V. Manno, and Nell Edgington

Customized Schooling
Edited by Frederick M. Hess and Bruno V. Manno

Bringing School Reform to Scale
by Heather Zavadsky

What Next?
Edited by Mary Cullinane and Frederick M. Hess

Between Public and Private
Edited by Katrina E. Bulkley, Jeffrey R. Henig, and Henry M. Levin

Stretching the School Dollar
Edited by Frederick M. Hess and Eric Osberg

School Turnarounds: The Essential Role of Districts
by Heather Zavadsky

Stretching the Higher Education Dollar
Edited by Andrew P. Kelly and Kevin Carey

Cage-Busting Leadership
by Frederick M. Hess

Teacher Quality 2.0: Toward a New Era in Education Reform
Edited by Frederick M. Hess and Michael Q. McShane

Reinventing Financial Aid: Charting a New Course to College Affordability
Edited by Andrew P. Kelly and Sara Goldrick-Rab

The Cage-Busting Teacher
by Frederick M. Hess

Failing Our Brightest Kids: The Global Challenge of Educating High-Ability Students
by Chester E. Finn, Jr. and Brandon L. Wright

The New Education Philanthropy: Politics, Policy, and Reform
Edited by Frederick M. Hess and Jeffrey R. Henig

Educational Entrepreneurship Today
Edited by Frederick M. Hess and Michael Q. McShane

Policy Patrons: Philanthropy, Education Reform, and the Politics of Influence
Megan E. Tompkins-Stange

Convergence of K–12 and Higher Education: Policies and Programs in a Changing Era
Edited by Christopher P. Loss and Patrick J. McGuinn

The Every Student Succeeds Act: What It Means for Schools, Systems, and States
Edited by Frederick M. Hess and Max Eden

Letters to a Young Education Reformer
by Frederick M. Hess

Bush-Obama School Reform: Lessons Learned
Edited by Frederick M. Hess and Michael Q. McShane

International Perspectives in Higher Education

Balancing Access, Equity, and Cost

Edited by

JASON D. DELISLE

ALEX USHER

Harvard Education Press

Cambridge, Massachusetts

Paperback ISBN 978-1-68253-267-6
Library Edition ISBN 978-1-68253-268-3

Library of Congress Cataloging-in-Publication Data is on file.

Published by Harvard Education Press,
an imprint of the Harvard Education Publishing Group

Harvard Education Press
8 Story Street
Cambridge, MA 02138

Cover Design: Wilcox Design
Cover Image: bgblue/Digital Vision Vectors/Getty Images

The typefaces used in this book are Adobe Garamond Pro for text and Myriad Pro for display.

Contents

Introduction

Jason D. Delisle and Alex Usher

Higher education in the United States has reached a turning point. A decade ago many students, parents, and policy makers could point to Ivy League schools or public research universities such as the University of California at Berkeley as evidence that the US had the world's greatest higher education system. In this conventional view, the only major drawback of the American system was that some students might struggle to pay for their education, although this problem could be solved with limited, targeted student aid programs.

In recent years, however, the consensus around higher education has been shaken, and a view has taken hold that Americans should look abroad for education policy solutions. This change has been driven by concerns that college prices have increased to such a point that even middle-class families are shut out. Stories in the media that ask whether a postsecondary education pays off in higher earnings are ubiquitous.[1] Many observers see rising student loan debt and stories of students struggling to repay as symptoms of unaffordable prices and the diminishing payoff prospects from overpriced degrees.[2] Others worry that the US has fallen behind other countries in competitiveness because of high dropout rates, or that other countries better match their higher education systems to needs in the labor market and therefore achieve higher job placement rates.[3]

As a result, observers of higher education in the US are increasingly inclined to cite systems and policies in other countries to make the case for reforms they support at home. The implication is that other countries have solved some of the big challenges that still plague the higher education system in the US, and if only we were to import their solutions, we could achieve similar results.

It is true that the US has much to learn from other higher education systems. However, advocates and researchers rarely examine the broader context in which such policies are embedded, how they evolved, or the inherent trade-offs of adopting a particular approach. Too often, alternative policies are presented as silver-bullet solutions that can simply be lifted from one country and grafted onto the US system. Unintended consequences that may arise from such a shift are glossed over or even ignored. In some cases, proponents are unaware of these shortcomings or trade-offs; in others it is implied that the US somehow can avoid negative consequences by taking only the "good parts" from international models.

This book attempts to provide a more balanced and honest perspective on how different countries approach key higher education policies. Specifically, it attempts to highlight the trade-offs that these policies entail and makes the case that similar trade-offs emerge across many countries with different types of higher education systems, suggesting that competing priorities and unintended consequences are not easily avoided. In contrast to those who present international policies as silver-bullet solutions, the authors point to a natural tension between access, cost, quality, equity, student affordability, and administrative feasibility. Different higher education policies are not off-the-shelf solutions that can be transferred from one country to another; rather, they represent a balancing of competing priorities in response to specific conditions, circumstances, and values. Taking a broader view of international models highlights how the implicit values on which the US higher education system is based make borrowing policies from abroad more difficult than reformers suggest. Similarly, American readers may be surprised to see how our own system offers some unique advantages over international models and designs.

WHICH ISSUES BENEFIT MOST FROM INTERNATIONAL COMPARISONS?

Tackling a topic as broad as international higher education creates some editorial challenges. With 192 countries, vastly different government structures, and continuously changing higher education sectors, there are undoubtedly more topics of interest to US audiences than can fit into a volume that maintains some level of thematic consistency. With such a broad topic, a natural response is to focus narrowly on higher education in only one country or region. Such an approach, however, raises the same "cherry-picking" problems (i.e., pointing to specific systems or policies that appear to "work" without examining the larger context) that this volume hopes to address. Instead, the volume takes a dual approach. First, it focuses on a set of cross-cutting policy topics that are central to all higher education systems, such as tuition policies, the role of private institutions of higher education, and college access policies, and it provides a broad examination of the range of different policy approaches to each topic. Three single-country case studies then illustrate the policy trade-offs from higher education systems and reforms in a particular country.

The topics featured throughout this volume were chosen because they are particularly salient for contemporary debates in the United States. Not surprisingly, the book therefore places a heavy emphasis on issues of higher education finance and access to education: free tuition and cost-sharing policies; student loan systems; policies that determine who has access to higher education and who enrolls; and what role, if any, private nonprofit and for-profit institutions play in higher education systems abroad. The emphasis on financial issues is intentional for two reasons: (1) because it is often the starting point for many of the contemporary debates in the US that invoke international comparisons and (2) because many observers in the US view finance as the most obvious and consequential way in which US higher education policy differs from those in other countries. But the chapters in this volume also feature discussions of accountability, regulation, governance, vocational education, and even the role of research in higher education systems, as it is difficult to examine financial models for higher education without taking these factors into account.

COMPETING PRIORITIES IN INTERNATIONAL MODELS

A brief discussion of the topics and case studies in this book shows why examining international higher education policies through the framework of trade-offs can inform the most salient debates in the United States. Consider the debate in some US states, and to a lesser extent at the federal level, over making public college tuition-free. Some state and federal lawmakers (as well as some presidential candidates) have responded to concerns about access, equity, and affordability by calling for the federal and state governments to adopt free college policies. They frequently highlight countries—Sweden, Denmark, and Germany, for example—that provide publicly funded, tuition-free college as evidence that these policies are not only desirable in the US but feasible as well.[4]

While such advocates acknowledge that providing access to public universities without charging tuition is costly for governments, they rarely discuss how these costs lead lawmakers to sometimes limit enrollment and how this in turn leads universities to become more selective. The restrictions on capacity that therefore often accompany free tuition policies usually mean that only the most academically prepared students, most of whom tend to come from upper-income families, have access to public universities, which is precisely the outcome that free tuition advocates seek to avoid.

Trade-offs between access, quality, and the price of college arise frequently in this volume. Debates in the US that sidestep this tension miss one of the more counterintuitive trends in international higher education. In an effort to ensure both access and quality, many countries have moved away from tuition-free models in favor of charging students and families at least some of the cost of their education and have used the proceeds in part to meet the rising demand for higher education.[5] In the United Kingdom, adopting a cost-sharing model (i.e., charging tuition) in the 1990s increased overall college enrollment rates, including from traditionally underrepresented and low-income student groups.[6] Contrary to some popular narratives in the US, experience elsewhere teaches that tuition can help *increase* access to higher education. Conversely, some countries—notably Germany and Chile—that previously had fees have recently reverted back to free tuition. This volume shows how such examples offer complicated lessons for those interested in adopting such policies in the United States.

Similarly, popular media accounts commonly note that US institutions need to do more to ensure that low-income students can access high-quality public universities.[7] Advocates are quick to point to policies in other countries that increase access and argue for their implementation in the United States.[8] While such policies may indeed make higher education more available to underrepresented groups, they are often accompanied by unintended consequences.

For example, in Australia, as chapter 7 explains, policy makers' decision to eliminate enrollment caps at public universities expanded access, but per-student funding levels have not kept pace with the enrollment growth. Lawmakers have not boosted funding to accommodate the influx of students, nor have they allowed institutions to charge more in tuition. Some of Australia's most elite public universities now argue that they have had to sacrifice quality. Other chapters in this volume show that Australia is not alone in this regard: countries that aggressively pursue enrollment increases often struggle to stretch limited university resources to cover the additional costs of adding students. As higher education systems continue to "massify" around the world, more countries are having to wrestle with similar trade-offs that come with adopting more open-access policies, as the US has done for a long time.

This book is also intended to address another blind spot in many policy discussions regarding international models: namely, that most focus only on public universities.[9] Yet many countries, including Japan, South Korea, Brazil, and Chile, have relied on robust private higher education sectors to expand access. They have often done so partly to achieve cost savings, especially in Brazil, where tuition is free at public universities. Providing students with government aid to attend fee-charging private institutions increases access to higher education without the high costs for the government of enrolling more students in tuition-free public universities. In some circumstances, at least, the private sector may be better equipped to address the increasing demand for access to higher education.

Additional lessons in the role private providers play abroad are also featured in this volume. Many in the US education policy community view for-profit institutions skeptically, and that has fueled calls for tougher quality assurance policies. Other countries with large private sectors have adopted their own approaches to accountability policies. Chapter 8 of this volume examines Brazil in detail because that country shares some elements of the US system but breaks from it in others with respect to for-profit institutions. In general, Brazil has been able to maintain a for-profit sector comparable in quality to its public institutions by keeping relatively high enrollment standards. Even so, Brazilian policy makers still worry that many students fail to repay their loans from these institutions and have adopted other policies to address such concerns. Some of the policies implemented in Brazil will look familiar to US audiences, but others may prove surprising.

The policy debate around the US student loan system includes frequent calls to import policies from abroad.[10] In response, this volume brings in an extensive discussion of why the features of a country's student loan system should not be viewed in isolation, as they often are in US policy discussions. For example, the Australian student loan system is routinely lauded by US reformers, including the economist and Nobel laureate Joseph Stiglitz, who prominently called it "a model for the rest of the world."[11]

Here again, vital information on the context and trade-offs of such policies is left out when supporters make the case for implementing a similar policy in the United States. Australia's income-contingent loan system, which historically did not require borrowers to repay until they earn over approximately AUD 55,000 (or roughly USD 47,500), worked well because until recently the program was restricted to bachelor's-level education and above, and the number of students that universities could enroll was capped at a level that was low compared to that of the United States. Since universities primarily enrolled only the most academically prepared students, who graduated into a labor market in which the constrained supply of college degrees ensured they would earn a premium wage, students were likely to repay their debts. The program also limited borrowing to tuition, while the US allows borrowing for living expenses as well.[12] This underlines a more general point: when other countries' policies appear both more generous and affordable than American ones, it is often because they are being offered to a much more restricted and elite population than they ever could be in the United States.

Carefully considering the opposing priorities in higher education systems abroad can also change the way reformers view the US system. Policies that other countries might adopt to solve a particular problem or achieve a certain goal can sometimes be at odds with implicit values on which the US higher education system rests. Other countries may not place as much weight on these values, therefore making it easy for them to structure their systems in ways that would be widely unpopular in the United States. That the US system implicitly makes trade-offs in terms of fundamental values may not be obvious to policy makers until they consider the merits of borrowing a policy from abroad.

For example, many students in Brazil's higher education system are enrolled in for-profit institutions, and policy makers there have worried whether students who receive government-issued student loans to attend these institutions will repay the debt. This is quite similar to the current policy environment in the US. But unlike the US, Brazilian policy makers imposed stricter eligibility criteria on *students* in addition to the colleges themselves in order to bolster quality assurance. Students can receive the federal aid only if they score above a certain level on a national high school exit exam. In other words, the policy seeks to prevent certain students from receiving loans to attend a for-profit college. The US would be unlikely to adopt such a policy, because it runs contrary to the view that access to college should be open, should not be contingent on test scores or merit, and should offer a "second chance" for students who attended low-quality elementary or secondary schools. In the US, it is institutions of higher education, not students, that should be subject to quality assurance standards.

This case illustrates that sometimes the "looking abroad" approach shows that a public policy from another country is a poor fit for the values that undergird the US system. That is, the problem identified in the US higher education system exists not because policy makers are unaware of the successes another country achieved by adopting a particular policy; rather, US policy makers are unwilling to adopt the policy solution despite its success, because it runs counter to deep-seated values.

Other contributors to this book discuss access policies, such as tracking in Germany or lotteries in Denmark and France, that would likely not sit well with US policy makers. German students are placed in an academic track that leads to a university education at age ten, and while, in theory, students can change tracks later, few actually do. Tracking tends to break down along socioeconomic lines, perpetuating educational stratification. Denmark and France ration access to some programs or professional training, such as medicine, by awarding slots to qualified students via lottery. This volume helps to explain why US policies stand in such contrast to some of those abroad. The US tends to place a higher priority on choice, second chances, and broad access to higher education regardless of test scores and academic achievement than many other countries. Examples like this are illustrated throughout the book.

THE CHAPTERS AHEAD

Part 1 of this book addresses the trends and policies that have shaped higher education systems in non-US countries. The first two chapters focus on tuition and "cost-sharing" policies in other countries. In chapter 1, education journalist Jon Marcus of the Hechinger Institute covers some of the challenges that European countries have historically experienced related to access, quality, and student debt, despite their free tuition policies. For example, in Germany, free college has increased enrollment but has overstretched resources and is threatening quality. Marcus also explains how Denmark, a country with one of the highest tax rates in the world, is scaling back its free tuition and living stipends as a growing share of the population seeks access to higher education. He goes on to cover some surprising similarities between the US and the European countries that offer free tuition. Only 14 percent of children from the least-educated families in Norway go to college compared to 58 percent of children from the most-educated families. Those figures are nearly identical in the United States. It turns out that free college is not an antidote to student debt either. In Sweden, which is perhaps the most commonly cited country among free college advocates in the US, approximately 85 percent of students incur debt, and the average debt level is approximately $20,000 due to cost-of-living expenses not covered by the government. Marcus juxtaposes these cases with the success the UK has had using an aggressive outreach strategy to boost enrollment among underrepresented groups.

Marcus points to not just the policy challenges of free tuition but also how those policies are coming under increasing political scrutiny. In chapter 2, Bruce Johnstone of the State University of New York at Buffalo charts the global trend toward more cost-sharing in higher education. While US audiences might think the US is an outlier for its ever-rising college tuition, many countries have scaled back generous tuition subsidies over the past two decades as they seek to cover the cost of providing higher education to larger shares of their populations (a process that goes under the somewhat unwieldy term "massification"). Johnstone explains that developed countries face another set of pressures on subsidized tuition: aging populations and the programs that provide for their health and income security in retirement.

Chapter 3, by Daniel C. Levy of the State University of New York at Albany, breaks from the focus on tuition policies to examine the role of private institutions in other countries. He explains how, historically, higher education systems in other countries relied overwhelmingly on public universities, but that has changed in the past several decades. Private institutions collectively enroll about a third of students globally. The chapter explains what led policy makers to expand private higher education and how they have managed the different challenges that private providers entail.

Anna Mountford-Zimdars of the University of Exeter writes in chapter 4 about the different ways countries determine who has access to higher education. She argues that there may be no single best access policy and that systems that use different approaches to admissions and outreach can end up with similar results, good or bad. She also details how countries with different access policies have a limited impact on breaking down economic and class barriers that are reinforced in the elementary and secondary school systems.

In chapter 5 Alex Usher of Higher Education Strategy Associates takes a close look at different structures for student loan programs and how these designs can reflect and influence other policy goals such as access, affordability, and equity. Much attention has justly been given to those countries that have coalesced around a model of income-contingent loans collected through the tax system. While these systems are undeniably interesting because of their efficiency, Usher cautions that these models are predicated upon certain features of these countries' tax systems that are not easily exportable to the United States. But while loan collection policies are important, there are a host of other policy design issues related to loan eligibility that have equally if not more important effects on access, and on these measures the US system stands out as being relatively generous.

Part 2 presents three case studies. Each features a country that has experienced significant change in its higher education system and offers a concrete example of the many themes discussed in the previous chapters. The first case study, by Andrés Bernasconi of the School of Education at the Pontificia Universidad Católica de Chile, analyzes the recent free college policy adopted in that country in the wake of massive student protests. The promise proved ambitious, and policy makers ultimately settled on providing free college to students from the bottom half of the income distribution, many of whom received generous aid before the new policy.

The second case study profiles the Australian higher education system and recent reforms. Vicki Thomson, chief executive of the Group of Eight in Australia, offers insight into the trends and pressures that led the country to adopt a "demand-driven system" for its public universities in 2012. That change increased enrollment as intended but with many unintended consequences.

The final case study returns to Latin America to trace key policy developments in Brazil's higher education system. Dante J. Salto, a fellow at the National Scientific and Technical Research Council (CONICET) Universidad Nacional de Cordoba (UNC-Argentina), discusses what led Brazil to rely so heavily on private institution of higher education. He notes that policy makers on the political right and left have historically subsidized the private sector to expand enrollment. This is despite the fact that the private providers are dominated by for-profit institutions. While some in Brazil worry about the quality of these institutions, the fear of reducing access to higher education for lower-income students tends to take precedence over tough oversight. Moreover, many for-profit providers produce student outcomes that are on par with public institutions.

In the concluding chapter, editors Jason D. Delisle and Alex Usher outline a number of ways that the US higher education system produces results that are in line with, or even superior to, those in other countries. This provides an important reality check on the motivation that many reformers have to examine policies from other countries: that other countries are outperforming the US. The remainder of the concluding chapter is devoted to applying the lessons and themes from the chapters in this volume to specific policy debates in the United States.

PART 1

Trends and Policies Shaping Higher Education Systems Abroad

CHAPTER 1

The Limitations of Free College in Europe

Jon Marcus

In some European nations, higher education has always been largely free. In others, where it was once offered without charge, there is now tuition. Still others have added and then removed fees. These examples make Europe a sort of accidental laboratory of the effects of university tuition policies. What are the results?

Contrary to the view from outside, there is not popular consensus about the absolute right to free university tuition, even in largely socialist Scandinavian nations. Financial pressures have governments looking for ways to speed students to degrees and pay for their own living costs and, in some cases, graduate courses. As an example of the extent to which politics is tangled up with university tuition policies, political aspects have even begun to overlap with the hot-button issue of immigration. Some critics want to scale back free higher education for immigrants, but those who advocate for such programs say that immigrants comprise only a tiny fraction of university students benefiting from the policies. So contentious have these debates become that they have resulted in protests as large as those in the turbulent era of the late 1960s.

Such tensions have resulted in the counterintuitive reality that even in countries where the cost of a university is "free," students graduate with debt. That's because governments have slowly and quietly added ancillary charges, making "free college" a semantic fiction while students' living expenses comprise an equally unanticipated but even more substantial cost. Grants to cover living expenses, where available, are shrinking, failing to keep pace with inflation, or being converted into loans. That's a particular drag on attending college among the children of parents with the fewest resources.

There are other reasons, too, that free tuition turns out to have less of an effect on low-income students than might have been expected. Primary- and secondary-level preparation and whether a prospective student's parents went to college also remain stubborn and prominent influences distinct from the question of cost. Nor does imposing tuition necessarily discourage low-income, first-generation, and ethnic and racial minority prospects from attending university. In England programs were dramatically expanded to recruit and support these prospective students even as tuition was increased dramatically, and their enrollment numbers actually went up.

Behind the public quarrel is the high and growing cost to countries of providing higher education. Universities find their budgets increasingly stretched thin, affecting quality and raising questions about whether free tuition is sustainable. On the other side of the equation, students are resistant to surrendering the privilege of free university education once they have it.

THE POLITICS OF FREE COLLEGE IN EUROPE

The battle over free tuition in some European countries has come to speak directly to the age-old philosophical divide over whether higher education is a personal or public good. On one side of this argument is the idea that if graduates benefit financially from their education, they should pay their own way. The other side argues that an educated citizenry benefits society. Students, understandably, prefer the second point of view. Student entitlement, political pushback, budget constraints, and other factors are among the sometimes unexpected consequences of free higher education experienced by European countries that have either imposed tuition or eliminated it.

Consider the trend in Denmark. For more than a decade, successive governments have tried to whittle away at the benefit enjoyed there and elsewhere in Europe by the citizens of Norway, Sweden, Germany, and Finland: a free university education. A seemingly minor proposed change to that prerogative in Denmark sparked demonstrations on campuses nationwide. Professors were blocked from getting into classroom buildings. Angry crowds besieged the Christiansborg Palace in Copenhagen, where parliament was about to open. Danish journalists described it as the most raucous protest in their country of five million since the 1960s.[1] The proposal? Shortening the time students could remain in school without paying for it.

Danish students take an average of 6.1 years to finish combined bachelor's and master's degrees, which the government says should take no more than 5. That makes these so-called eternity students among the slowest in Europe to graduate.[2]

The cost of guaranteeing up to six years of free college has become so great that even in a country with one of the highest tax rates in the world, the government says it has to be cut. Denmark invests 6.5 percent of its gross domestic product in education, the second-highest proportion (after the United Kingdom) among the thirty-six members of the Organisation of Economic Cooperation and Development, or OECD. The most politically vulnerable policy has been the government grants that students receive for living expenses, equal to about DKK 5,100 (USD 760) a month, in addition to their free tuition.[3] Those grants, and the extended time students remain enrolled enable a tradition called the *fjumreår*, or "year of goofing around."[4] Even in this generous country, such an expensive perk was costing the Danish treasury an estimated DKK 2.3 billion (roughly USD 410 million) a year and delaying students from graduating, joining the workforce, and paying taxes. So lawmakers approved the *fremdriftsreformen*, or study progress reform, gradually reducing the amount of time the state will subsidize post-secondary education by 7.6 months to a year, depending on the university and course of study.[5]

Attempts to chip away at free tuition in countries that already have it, said the Danish Students Council, should concern "all those who believe that better-educated citizens are, as a starting point, a future gain for society."[6] The idea of charging for a university education "is based on the ideological/economic belief of dividing higher education into public and private benefits," echoed the European Students Union. "Such a division is popular in some economic theories, but it directly contradicts the societal norms and values of higher education as a basic institution of civilization and a human right."[7]

That's a division that may never be resolved. But European models do provide a window into not just the philosophical implications of adding or removing fees but also the practical—and often unanticipated—outcomes.

The freshest case of this is Germany, where public university tuition fees were introduced and then eliminated in quick succession. This occurred when several of the *Länder*, or states, successfully challenged a federal ban on tuition in 2005 on the grounds that underwriting higher education—or, for that matter, charging for it—was their role and not the federal government's. After the court ruling, annual fees of up to EUR 1,000 (about USD 1,200 at today's exchange rate) were imposed at public universities in seven *Länder* beginning in the fall of 2007. Loans were made available, but most students relied on their parents to help them pay.

As in Denmark, chipping away at free higher education fueled a massive backlash in Germany, where students had been accustomed to free higher education. In Bavaria alone, 1.4 million Germans signed petitions to eliminate the fees, and students refused to pay them; some occupied campus buildings in protest.[8] As the political cost of returning to fees became apparent, parties along the ideological spectrum competed with one another to return to free tuition at the public universities that educate the vast majority of German students, beginning just one year later in the state of Hesse and ending in Lower Saxony, where tuition fees were ultimately dropped in 2015.[9] "We do not want higher education which depends on the wealth of the parents," pronounced the Lower Saxony minister for science and culture, Gabrielle Heinen-Kjajic.[10]

But while Germans seemed so passionate that university education should be free, an exhaustive survey shows that since such a policy was adopted, they have become ambivalent about it: 46 percent remain in favor of free college, but 40 percent say they would reimpose tuition.[11] When told by the pollsters at the ifo Center for the Economics of Education at Ludwig-Maximilian University's Center for Economic Studies in Munich that university graduates earn more than those with only vocational training, the proportion of Germans who support making students pay for their own education jumped to 48 percent and the percentage against fees fell to 37. An even higher 62 percent liked the idea of requiring students to pay for their tuition after graduating, as a portion of their incomes, in a model similar to those in place in England and Australia.

"The general feeling was that 80 to 90 percent in Germany were opposed to tuition fees, which is just not the case," says Ludger Woessmann, professor of economics at the University of Munich and director of the ifo Center. "Those who profit from this very generous scheme are so devoted to it that they turn out in the hundreds of thousands for these protests. All the rest aren't so sure about it, or are quite opposed to it."[12]

Making people pay for their own education, if degrees will help them earn more than they would without them, is a populist idea that parallels political shifts as much as it portends a threat to public support for universities. With Germany's strong tradition of vocational apprenticeships, a comparatively low 16 percent of twenty-five-to-sixty-four-year-old Germans have the equivalent of associate or bachelor's degrees. That's half the proportion of American and British twenty-five-to-sixty-four-year-olds who do.[13] But free tuition, combined with a rising earning premium, has prodded more Germans to go to colleges and universities. Since 2000, Germans with university degrees have widened their earning premium from 45 percent more than their countrymen with lesser education to 74 percent more, compared to the OECD average of 59 percent.[14] People who go through apprenticeship programs earn about 84 percent as much as those who go to universities, enough of a gap to lead to a shortage of qualified tradespeople while putting still more pressure on institutions of higher education to accommodate demand.[15] For comparison, Americans with associate degrees earn, on average, 18 percent more than those with only high school educations, the Bureau of Labor Statistics says, and with bachelor's degrees, 67 percent more.[16]

Woessmann speculates that resentment over the wage benefit enjoyed by university-goers may drive German nonstudents to oppose free tuition, "or they just feel in general that if you get a higher education and later on you're going to earn much more, why should the state give away this education for free?"[17]

In a country with one of the highest tax rates in the OECD—nearly 48 percent of income—Germans appear to bristle at the thought of paying for degrees for other people who may eventually earn more than they do.[18] Opinions about tuition were comparatively unaffected by other variables, including whether keeping higher education free might help increase the small proportion (in Germany 25 percent) of first-generation students who go on to college. Most Germans surveyed also oppose the *Exzellenzinitiative*, a federal and state program just getting under way to funnel more resources to the top universities. Only 6 percent think funding for higher education should be increased at all.[19]

"In the nationalist populist movement, there is a sentiment against the intellectual elite," says Hans de Wit, director of the Center for International Higher Education at Boston College, who has consulted for organizations including the European Parliament and the World Bank. He says people whose political opinions are inclined that way think, "'Why should we subsidize that?'"[20]

BUDGET PRESSURES AND QUALITY CONSTRAINTS

The German experience shows how expensive it can be for governments to provide free college. But the costs are not all budgetary. There are consequences for quality and capacity as well.

In the last ten years the annual cost to German taxpayers of subsidizing higher education has gone up by 49 percent to EUR 35.1 billion (roughly USD 42 billion), and there are questions about how long this can be sustained.[21] German *Länder* started running up funding shortfalls for higher education almost immediately after axing fees in the late 2000s.[22] Universities, for their part, say that even this infusion of support is too little to keep up with the growing demands on them that free education triggers. Administrators and faculty complain that they are blocked from an important source of revenue—tuition—at exactly the same time they are being asked to educate more students. As enrollment has increased, spending per student by universities has declined, doctoral students instead of full-time faculty often teach courses, and classrooms have become more crowded.

Even while eliminating fees, the federal government and the *Länder* made provisions for enrollment to increase by ninety-one thousand but gave the universities EUR 5,500 (about USD 7,000) for each of these additional students when the German Rectors' Conference—an association of German higher education institutions—says each student actually costs at least EUR 7,300 (USD 9,000) to educate. (The United States spends, on average, USD 27,900 per student in postsecondary education. [23]) Even so, more seats are still scheduled to be added at EUR 6,500 (USD 8,000) each. That's a slight increase but still less than the universities say it costs to serve each student, meaning they will continue to face budgetary shortfalls and pressures.[24] German universities perform a bit lower than expected in international rankings and measures of research output.

Government allocations are a far less predictable source of funding than tuition, since state subsidies typically depend on such factors as which political parties are in power. The German Rectors' Conference has declared that adding needed faculty and staff "is just as infeasible as long-term investment decisions on the basis of such funding." This, it said, has created an "intolerable situation" in which "the continuous task of teaching can increasingly only be covered by temporary staff" and "construction, renovation, equipment and digitalization have been neglected. The equipment of higher education institutions has in no way kept pace with the increase in capacities."

Declines in funding levels have helped create a need for EUR 29 billion (USD 36 billion) in building renovations, for which existing allocations will fall EUR 8 billion (roughly USD 10 billion) short, and the universities association estimates that growing enrollments require an additional EUR 35 billion (USD 43 billion) for expansion—also as yet unfunded.[25]

Germany is not the only place in Europe where universities are struggling under the strain of offering free higher education. In Scotland, a 2016 audit found that the cost of making higher education free for Scottish and European Union students has created "underlying risks" to its financial stability. The audit also found that Scottish and European Union undergraduates were underfunded by 6 percent, even as further cuts in spending were planned, and that capital funding for buildings and equipment had declined by 69 percent, when adjusted for inflation, since 2010.[26]

The twin issues of cost to the government and support for university finances are what drove England away from largely free higher education to a system that allows its institutions to charge tuition fees. Universities have been given the right to set varying levels of tuition, beginning with GBP 3,000 per year in 2006 (roughly USD 4,200).[27] That maximum has since quickly risen to GBP 9,250 (almost USD 13,000).[28] As a way of imposing those costs on only higher-earning graduates, students finance these fees with government-issued loans repaid as a percentage of their post-enrollment incomes once they reach an annual threshold of GBP 25,000 (about USD 35,000).[29]

The relatively high tuition in England means that students earning bachelor's degrees there rack up more student loan debt than those in any other major English-speaking country, including the United States—more than GBP 44,000 apiece (USD 61,000) on average.[30] By comparison, Americans who earn such degrees from public or private nonprofit universities and colleges owe an average of USD 30,100.[31] But the generous income-based repayment schemes in England and the US, both of which include loan forgiveness after a period of time, complicate the process of comparing how much students will actually repay. Uncollected student debts, political pressure to increase benefits, and implementation snags have resulted in higher than expected costs for nearly all governments that have adopted income-based repayment plans.

Not all university heads in countries with free higher education say it starves them of resources. "Because of my job, I'm required to say, 'Well, of course we need more money,'" says Curt Rice, the American-born rector, or president, of Norway's Oslo and Akershus University College.[32] "Of course, every sector of the public economy, including higher education, is constantly lobbying the government for more money."[33]

But unlike in the United States, Scandinavian countries don't spend enormous sums on recruiting. Norwegian universities, like most of their counterparts in Europe, also don't have dorms or other ancillary services that drive costs. According to Rice:

> I see these massive tuition increases in the US, and my [American] colleagues in the industry say that's because the guys down the road built a new science building, so I had to build a new science building; or the parents want suites in the dormitories; or I have to have an office for recruitment with five hundred people. None of those things apply here. I'm only marginally in the business of preparing students for working life, because the unemployment rate is just so low that students all get jobs. And, of course, I don't have sports teams. So those things that are really cost-drivers in the US aren't happening here. . . .
>
> On the one hand, it's true that Norwegian universities don't rank highly on the standard international rankings, in part because US universities are so much richer, and now Chinese universities are richer. Sure, if I had more money I could have more world-class groups of researchers. So from that perspective, yes. But the quality of the education that a student receives is okay here. I think I can get more out of the money I do get before I ask for more.[34]

Still, by providing free university educations, governments have clearly already assumed enormous costs, and many have sought to impose restrictions to save money, or shift some of the expenses back to students. For example, students in

Germany are charged "administration fees" of EUR 300–500 (about USD 350–600) a year—almost as much, when accounting for inflation, as the tuition that was briefly levied by some of the *Länder* in the late 2000s. Those administrative fees bring in about EUR 2.8 billion (USD 3.5 billion) annually.[35] By the fall of 2017, the southwestern state of Baden-Württemberg had become the first to reintroduce a tuition fee of EUR 1,500 (about USD 1,800) per semester for students from outside the European Union, including immigrants, who had started flocking to free German universities; German lawmakers said they couldn't afford free education for everyone.[36] This introduced another spark to the tinderbox that European university tuition has become and was immediately denounced by the European Students Union. "Education is a human right and should be accessible to everyone," the association said. "To use the nationality of individuals as criteria to determine if one has access to higher education deserves condemnation."[37] (The Norwegian government has also repeatedly pushed universities in Norway to charge tuition fees to students from outside the EU to save NOK 162 million per year (about USD 24 million), but the parliament and universities have so far refused to go along.[38])

Another way Germany cuts down on the cost of keeping higher education nominally free is by requiring students to pay for master's degrees in subjects that don't follow on from their undergraduate majors. As has now also become the case in Denmark, most *Länder* also essentially penalize students for taking too long to graduate.[39]

Norway is also pushing students to finish college more quickly, especially since the 1999 Bologna Process standardized—and, in most cases, shortened—the time to complete courses for a degree. "When that happened, that forced us all from four- to three-year bachelor's degrees. The institutions all saw a quarter of their revenue from the government disappearing," Rice says. So "there is an economic push here to get people through the system."[40]

Denmark is responding to budgetary pressures as well. Its *fremdriftsreformen* strips funding from universities that let their students linger. Danish students complain that being rushed to a degree allows them less time to do such things as decide on a major, study abroad, or take an internship, and many have pushed back to the changes by saying they're sick and avoiding their exams—but more changes have followed.[41] Those, too, have been accompanied by protests. First, students were prohibited from enrolling at state expense in other academic programs after getting their initial bachelor's and master's degrees. That was estimated to save DKK 300 million (about USD 50 million) per year. "We can admit that, if we had unlimited money, we would probably not restrict this," former education minister Christine Antorini said. "As we don't have unlimited money, we think it is fair."[42]

The tension in these countries is characteristic of the debate between policy makers' desire to reduce spending and, as students see it, sacrificing the quality of educational programs and offerings.

LIVING EXPENSES: DIMINISHING GRANTS, MORE LOANS, AND WORK

Living expenses are a significant but often unacknowledged part of the free tuition story. As in the United States, costs outside tuition are being recognized in European countries as substantial barriers to college-going, especially for the lowest-income students. Even in countries where tuition is free, living costs aren't covered, or government subsidies fall short of what's needed or fail to keep up with inflation. This means students still struggle to pay for rent and food and often graduate in debt.

More support for living costs has become a new rallying cry for students; fully funding them, the European Students Union has proclaimed, "will enable wider participation in higher education, as well as enable students to finish their studies on time as they will be able to focus on their studies."[43] Instead, countries struggling to maintain free or low-cost higher education have been whittling away at living grants, often replacing all or some of them with loans. This puts the greatest burden on the lowest-income students, whose families cannot afford to help them pay for rent, food, books, transportation, or supplies, while wealthier students get free degrees they have the means to pay for.

In addition to pushing students to graduate more quickly, the Danish government proposed a 20 percent reduction in the living grant that students receive, in favor of an interest-free loan. The grant is the same whether students study part time or full time, which policy makers say is another reason why they take so long to finish.[44] (There, too, the government partly blames immigrant students for driving up the cost of helping university-goers pay for rent and food, though the European Students Union counters that international students get just 1 percent of the money and that their share is going down, not up.[45])

An estimated forty-three thousand students went back into the streets again to protest. They and their political allies argue that the living grant is what inspires them to go to college in the first place. Many of the Danish students who came out to demonstrate against the changes were still in high school.[46]

As hard as students have fought to preserve it, the monthly living grant in Denmark falls well short of covering their typical expenses. It comes to about

DKK 5,100 (USD 760) a month, in a country where the monthly cost of rent, food, transportation, school supplies, and incidentals is estimated by the Ministry of Higher Education and Science itself at around DKK 7,450 (about USD 1,200).[47]

And the Danish grant is generous compared to what students get in neighboring Sweden, which gives them grants equivalent to about USD 325 a month and low-interest loans of up to USD 820 a month from the Centrala Studiestödsnämnden to pay the rest of their expenses. Although tuition is free in Sweden, 85 percent of Swedish graduates (compared to half of US graduates) finish with an average debt of SEK 124,000 (nearly USD 20,000).[48]

In Norway living costs are covered by loans exclusively. As a way to incentivize students to graduate faster and ease the burden on taxpayers, those loans are partially refunded if students finish their degrees on time.[49] The gap between cost-of-living grants and their expenses means that students in these countries often also work to pay for rent and food, especially those who have no other means of support. This has been shown worldwide to slow the progress to completing degrees or even altogether end it. Working twenty hours a week or more, whether on or off campus, reduces students' grades and level of academic engagement, according to research in the United States.[50]

This has also left students in Germany less enthusiastic about the return to free education than might be expected. There, living costs are also covered by a combination of grants and interest-free loans through the *Bundesausbildungsförderungsgesetz* (*BAföG*), or Federal Education and Training Assistance Act. About a quarter of students receive *BAföG* loans, which are repaid after graduation when the borrower reaches a given income threshold. A ceiling ensures that the total repayment doesn't exceed EUR 10,000 (about USD 12,000). The maximum *BAföG* award is EUR 735 a month (close to USD 900), and the average award is EUR 441 (the amount depends on the students' parental income) in a country where the German Academic Exchange Service estimates that the monthly cost of living is EUR 819 (about USD 1,000).[51]

Sixty-eight percent of German students work, according to the Free Federation of Student Unions, or FZS, which argues that the cost of living forces lower-income students to compress their education and choose majors they think will pay off quickly, such as marketing and human resources, over higher-paying fields that take longer, such as medicine or law.[52] (If they're lukewarm about free tuition for other people's children, Germans are equally split on whether to increase the *BAföG* for all students, regardless of their socioeconomic status: 47 percent are in favor of the idea, 45 percent against, according to the ifo Center for the Economics of Education survey.[53])

"It's a big problem," says Nathalie Schäfer, a student and a member of the FZS board. "In cities where students live, often rents are very high and take almost half of the grants or more just for the housing, and then you don't have food or other living costs covered." As a consequence, she says, many students drop out.[54]

That's what happened in Scotland. To underwrite the cost of eliminating undergraduate tuition for Scottish and European Union residents, some money was shifted from living benefits that previously went to lower-income students. That transferred GBP 20 million (more than USD 25 million) a year from grants to cover their rent and food to their higher-income classmates who could afford to pay tuition but no longer do, according to research conducted at the University of Edinburgh. Since there, too, the difference in living expenses now must come either from family support or loans, the lowest-income students graduate with the highest levels of debt.[55]

HOW FREE TUITION CHANGES WHO ENROLLS (OR DOESN'T)

Money is far from the only factor that influences university-going. The European experience suggests that getting rid of tuition doesn't necessarily encourage first-generation, low-income, and nonwhite students to go to college, and that adding it doesn't necessarily discourage them. "That's a trend everywhere, that free-tuition movements benefit the wealthier," says de Wit, the Boston College specialist in international education. "It is an illusion of those movements to think that this would be increasing access and equity. On the contrary, it benefits higher-income groups."[56]

Still, the greater fear was that imposing fees would discourage lower-income students from seeking university degrees. To quell political opposition in the UK, which included an attack by angry students at a London rally on a wayward Rolls-Royce carrying Prince Charles and the former Camilla Parker Bowles, universities were required to meet goals for enrolling more low-income, racial and ethnic minorities, and first-generation students as a condition for raising their prices. These so-called access plans are reviewed and approved by a government agency called the Office for Fair Access, or OFFA.

A counterintuitive result occurred when England raised its fees to be among the highest in the world: full-time undergraduate enrollment has grown by 31 percent, according to Universities UK, a representative organization of British universities. Postgraduate enrollment has also increased.[57] The proportion of underrepresented students on campuses overall has not declined. In fact, it has increased to its highest level ever, thanks in part to aggressive recruitment programs that begin in primary school and also in part to tough oversight by OFFA, which often rejects universities' access plans and demands more focused effort. The outreach programs cost the higher education institutions millions, but the expense is more than offset by the additional revenues that come from larger fees.

Students from areas that are considered affluent, the measurement used by UK policy makers, are still 2.4 times more likely to enter university and 6.3 times more likely to go to the most selective institutions than those from areas considered low-income.[58] But those figures are down from nearly four times as likely ten years ago.[59] Outreach efforts start in primary and secondary schools, which are invited to bring classes regularly to university campuses and get their students accustomed to the idea of higher education—and often so familiar with the universities that kids as young as nine years old can give directions. The odds that UK students from the most disadvantaged areas will enter full-time higher education are now 43 percent greater than they were in 2009, according to the Department for Education.[60] "The expectation in this country was that [fees] would be a disincentive to people from disadvantaged groups, and instead we've seen an increase in the poorest groups since fees were introduced," says Les Ebdon, director of OFFA.[61]

Even if it might have been intended as one, Ebdon's agency has turned out to be much more than a formality designed to mollify the opposition to increased tuition. In some years it has rejected the access plans of as many as two-thirds of all universities, because the goals weren't high enough, they didn't commit to spending enough money to attract more students from low-income neighborhoods, or for other reasons.[62] Even if the government wasn't watching, universities have an incentive to recruit all students, including those from low-income families; because they now depend on fees for the balance of their revenues, each new student means more money. "That has been important," Ebdon says of how institutions' self-interest helps propel the process.

It is also important to persuade parents, says Ebdon. "You can talk to young people relatively easily—about how the system works and you don't have to pay up front and everyone can afford to go, and the maintenance loans and the fee loans, and the advantages of the higher salaries, and the way lower-skilled jobs are disappearing in the economy—and they understand it. Then they go back home and the parents say, 'Where are we going to get nine thousand pounds per year?'" When he himself was a university vice chancellor or president, Ebdon says, "I knew I had to reach [parents], perhaps even more than the students. Sometimes it took quite a bit of explaining to them."[63]

Unlike universities in Norway, Denmark, and Germany, where recruitment offices are rare or nonexistent, huge departments at English universities are devoted solely to recruiting young people from low-income neighborhoods, showering them with branded merchandise and even comic books about higher education, fanning out into communities to speak with parents who themselves didn't go to university, offering scholarships (called *bursaries*), and teaching low-income students how to apply for admission and register for courses. Once students are enrolled, they receive enhanced academic advising and support.[64]

Such efforts have not been cheap. The cost of access programs has ballooned from GBP 444.1 million (about USD 600 million) in 2011–2012 to more than GBP 833 million (USD 1.1 billion) in 2017–2018, Universities UK reports.[65] Nor have the results been perfect. At the most selective universities, the proportion of low-income students has fallen slightly, an analysis by the British Press Association found. About 10 percent of students at Oxford and Cambridge are from disadvantaged groups, down from a peak of 12 percent.[66] The ranks of people from low-income neighborhoods enrolling part time have also plummeted by 47 percent, as has the number of all part-time students, since the new funding system now requires part-time entrants to pay up front.[67]

But unlike Oxford and Cambridge, other top universities that are part of the Russell Group (the British counterpart to the Ivy League) have slowly increased their percentages of low-income students from under 20 to as high as 37 at some schools. Among all British universities, the percentage of students from low-income backgrounds has increased over the last ten years to 33 percent, up from 28 percent a decade ago.[68]

Researchers from Columbia University, the University of Texas at Austin, and University College London have found that England's move to charging high tuition fees has brought "increased funding per head, rising enrollments, and a narrowing of the participation gap between advantaged and disadvantaged students. . . . Tuition fees, at least in the English case, supported their goals of increasing quality, quantity, and equity in higher education."[69]

Of course, not charging tuition seems an easier way to get students into college. For instance, according to the Scottish Parliament Information Centre, the number of undergraduates in Scotland is up by 17 percent since 2007, when tuition fees were dropped.[70] But without tuition revenue, Scottish universities have been forced to cut per-student spending levels.

It might appear at first that not charging tuition boosted enrollment in Germany as well. Indeed, enrollment is up 16 percent since tuition was rolled back.[71] But because tuition was first reintroduced in Germany, before being once again eliminated, the German experience offers something of a test case through which to study the results. And that leads to another surprise: during the period when

German universities charged tuition, there was no discernible impact on enrollment, according to research by the Higher Education Policy Institute at Oxford. The lesson is that the *existence* of tuition fees does less to drive university-going in one direction or the other than the *amount* of tuition fees, and other factors, the Oxford analysis concluded.

"The supposition of such a negative effect was the main argument for abolishing tuition fees," researchers wrote. "Our results suggest that this argument had little empirical basis. . . . The German experiment suggests that deterrence does not occur if, first, tuition fees are rather low, second, tuition fees are combined with an appropriate public student loans program, and third, tuition fees are not imposed if certain social criteria such as a low-income-family background apply."[72]

Making tuition free has also not created any noticeable change as far as whether students from low socioeconomic levels find their ways to universities in Germany. That depends less on the cost than on whether or not their parents went and how much their families earn, research has found.[73] "What you generally see is that people are really concerned that if they are from a nonacademic background their kids can still go to universities. The fact is, they never do," says Woessmann, the Munich economist.[74]

Three-quarters of children of parents who have university degrees in Germany go to university themselves, compared to just a quarter of those whose parents don't.[75] This is partially a result of the German tracking system, which places students on college, vocational, or apprenticeship tracks, except in Berlin and Brandenburg. Because of the differential and uneven quality of primary and secondary education, fifteen-year-olds from families with the lowest 10 percent of income are four years behind in math compared to fifteen-year-olds from families with the highest 10 percent, putting those from lower-income families at a disadvantage for postsecondary education.[76] "Those factors that are in place are as important as the money factor," says de Wit. "Money in a direct way probably is overstated. In an indirect way, it's much more difficult for students from lower-income groups to go to the right universities."[77]

That is particularly clear in Norway. Like its neighbor Denmark, Norway offers tuition-free access to college, plus living expenses for students while they are enrolled. In spite of this, only 14 percent of children from the least-educated families in Norway go to college.[78] And although that has eked up from 6 percent in 1991, those levels are as low as in the United States, where higher education is generally far from free. This demonstrates a critical point that some higher-education experts say is widely misunderstood: family college-going experience and the presence of college-educated role models have as much of an impact as tuition, or more, in keeping first-generation prospects from enrolling.

Just as children of parents in Norway without college education tend not to pursue degrees themselves, nearly 60 percent of the children from the most educated families do enroll.[79] That's not only the result of parents' expectations or the potential to earn more but also because of an unlikely class system in this most egalitarian of societies, says Rice. "A lawyer and a carpenter probably make the same amount of money," Rice says. "But there's still a class difference. And to keep your extended family in the lawyer class, you have to take higher education."[80]

There have been other effects of tuition policy in Europe. In Germany, for instance, the number of students opting for vocational education through the nation's vaunted apprenticeship system has declined as tuition for conventional universities has been dropped.[81] This has raised fears of shortages in some vocations. In England, where tuition fees were reintroduced gradually beginning in 1998 and then raised in 2006 and again in 2012, the universities themselves say students have become more demanding than they were when fees were largely free, encouraging consumer-driven innovations such as flexible delivery and teaching and personalized learning.[82] As they face increasing debt, English students also have been shifting to majors that lead to higher-paying jobs, such as biological sciences (up 36 percent), engineering (up 21 percent), and business and administrative studies (up 9 percent), while enrollment in education and language departments has declined.[83]

Of course, there are also lots of other, competing reasons for university-going behavior. One is the wage premium enjoyed by graduates. In Norway it's unusually small, meaning students see less of a financial incentive to spend as long as six years forgoing income while studying toward degrees—even though university educations there are free.

"For somebody that comes from a non-educated family, having twenty-five thousand dollars in student debt is massive. And you have to evaluate the alternative. You could buy a car for that kind of money, and maybe having the car when you're twenty-one is much more important to you than having a university degree," says Elisabeth Hovdhaugen, a sociologist and senior researcher at the Nordic Institute for Studies in Innovation, Research, and Education.[84]

A bachelor's degree bumps up the wages of a typical Norwegian by just 14 percent, even less than the extra 19 percent earned by students in Norway with the equivalent of an associate's degree.[85] Salaries remain almost equally high for blue-collar workers, such as plumbers or electricians, as for university graduates.

And students who opt for vocational apprenticeships begin to be paid as early as the second year.

"Even if education makes a difference for where you are in the [wage] scale, the scale is so compressed that it doesn't really mean that much," says Rice. "That has to be combined with our understanding of the cost of education. What the Norwegian case in fact shows is that it's not just about cost. It's about cost versus benefits, and maybe that's the heart of the issue."[86] In England, by comparison, the return is more dramatic; people between the ages of twenty-five and sixty-four with the equivalent of bachelor's degrees earn 51 percent more than their counterparts without them, encouraging a growing number of people to seek higher education even as the price continues to increase.[87]

CONCLUSION

Tuition policy in Europe is far from set in stone. Political volatility is beginning to extend beyond comparatively small tweaks in living grants and duration of study. The Labour Party in the UK has pledged to once again remove tuition fees, for instance. And de Wit expects to see tuition reimposed in Germany because of universities' eventual inability to continue to do more with less. "There's increasing pressure," he says. "If you want to keep up the competition and quality, you have to do something, and they don't have the money to do that. There's a concern about the investment in higher education and the quality of the higher education sector. You see that everywhere—attempts to increase tuition fees."[88]

There are growing signs of taxpayer impatience, too, de Wit says. "It doesn't exist—'free' higher education," he says. "Someone has to pay for it." That is leading these countries to consider how to pay for higher education—by reinstating tuition, sharing the cost, or mimicking such ideas as income-based repayment for student loans.

CHAPTER 2

The Expanding Role of Tuition and Other Forms of Cost-Sharing in Higher Education

Bruce Johnstone

Higher education in the United States and the world over has become a large and growing enterprise. It is thought to be the key to national as well as individual economic prosperity and to a stable and inclusive democracy and a vibrant civil society. Higher education is also increasingly costly: to individual colleges and universities, to national and multi-campus systems, and, in most countries, to parents and students.

This chapter explores what in international higher education parlance has come to be called *cost-sharing.* Cost-sharing is, in part, a statement of fact: that the instructional costs of higher education and the costs of student living are shared mainly by governments, parents, students, and philanthropists. Cost-sharing has also come to signify a nearly worldwide shift of these costs from being borne by governments (principally taxpayers) to being borne increasingly by parents and students. Such a shift, which seems reasonably accepted in America, is bitterly contested, politically and ideologically, in much of the world, even when it is reluctantly conceded to be a financial imperative.[1]

THE SHIFT OF COSTS FROM GOVERNMENTS TO PARENTS AND STUDENTS

Among these principal bearers of instructional costs, philanthropy is a widespread source of revenue for higher education only in the United States, where it generated some USD 37.7 billion in 2013–2014 and where public and private colleges and universities in fiscal 2014 had endowments totaling more than USD 535 billion.[2] Philanthropy has also been significant to the universities of Oxford and Cambridge in Britain, and it has played important but limited roles (generally in a handful of elite universities) in Canada, Japan, Turkey, South Korea, South Africa, Chile, Colombia, and a few other countries. But widespread philanthropic giving to colleges and universities, especially annual giving from alumni, is expensive to initiate and requires a culture of giving to colleges and universities that other countries do not yet enjoy.[3]

Another source of higher education revenue that is sometimes included in a cost-sharing paradigm is faculty and institutional entrepreneurship. Such entrepreneurship may occur through externally supported research or training grants, renting spaces in university facilities, or providing nondegree courses and certificates in such popular subjects as English language, accounting, or information systems. However, such entrepreneurship is mainly feasible only for certain faculties and departments and generally contributes little to a university's core instructional expenditures. Moreover, these activities divert faculty from the primary activities of teaching and scholarship. For these reasons, although institutional entrepreneurship is an important supplement to governmental appropriations in some countries, it is generally not viewed as a long-term solution to limited governmental appropriations.

Finally, some would add businesses or corporations to the parties that can share the costs of higher education and supplement revenue from government or families. However, at least arguably, donations from businesses or corporations can be thought of as a form of philanthropy and borne either by the owners or the shareholders (and partially subsidized in some countries by government through the deductibility of charitable donations from otherwise taxable income). Or such contributions may be viewed as an expense of doing business and borne by the end consumers of the products or services—and these consumers are nearly indistinguishable from the general citizenry or taxpayer.

Thus, the principal bearers of higher education costs in most countries tend to be some combination of governments (or taxpayers), parents, and students—the latter mainly through part-time employment, student loans, or deferred tuition fees.[4] The shift of some portion of instructional costs from governments to parents and students takes a variety of forms and raises complex policy issues and questions in all countries.

For example, what are the appropriate levels of tuition and other fees, especially for public colleges and universities?[5] Should tuition fees vary by sector—that is, by research universities, bachelor's or master's colleges, or two-year or certificate-granting institutions? Should university tuition fees vary by lower or upper divisions of a bachelor's degree or by undergraduate, graduate, or advanced professional levels? Should fees vary according to the instructional costs associated with different majors or programs—for example, higher for engineering and chemistry but lower for the social sciences and humanities? Should fees vary by market demand—higher fees for business and law but lower for theoretical physics and linguistics? Or should the financial needs of colleges and universities be met not on the *revenue side* through greater governmental appropriations, increasing tuition fees, or other ways of shifting instructional costs to parents and students, but rather on the *cost side*, by slowing or even reversing the rising costs and revenue needs of institutions with cost-cutting, labor-saving technology, or some kind of radical restructuring of the higher education enterprise?

Cost-sharing also raises issues of equity. Virtually all countries profess an aim to make higher education opportunities accessible to deserving students regardless of family income or ethnic, racial, or linguistic status. Clearly, any shift of instructional costs to parents and students thus raises questions about the effect of tuition fees on higher education access, persistence, and success. Do higher tuition fees, for example, discourage young people from low-income families from aspiring to, or even preparing for, higher education while they are in secondary school? Do these fees directly affect access, persistence, and college choice? At what levels of family or independent student income do such consequences materialize? Do the deleterious behavioral effects of higher tuition fees include decisions not to pursue graduate or advanced professional levels of education, or to apply to and matriculate in more costly colleges or universities? Finally, such questions raise a host of issues regarding financial assistance: the cost-effectiveness of various forms of student aid, the trade-off between grants and loans, and the different behavioral effects of the many varieties of repayment terms and effective interest rates associated with student loan schemes.

This chapter mainly addresses the issues of tuition fees and other forms of cost-sharing, both worldwide and as presented to US policy makers at the state and federal levels of government. These issues also arise with college and university leaders and governing boards as they balance the needs of institutional finance, marketing, and accessibility, and with parents and students as they face trade-offs among saving, borrowing, part- or full-time employment, choice of institutions, and student living standards.

THE BASIS FOR A SHIFT OF HIGHER EDUCATION COSTS TO PARENTS AND STUDENTS

Fundamentally, cost-sharing in its several forms—most notably the imposition of, or sharp increases in, tuition fees—is about higher education's seemingly ubiquitous quest for additional revenue and its search for nonpublic revenue to meet the costs that in most countries seem to rise faster than available revenues from government. Underlying the rising costs are three primary forces.[6]

The first reason why per-student instructional costs increase is due to the addition of new programs and academic specialties and from the rising costs of materials and scientific equipment. Unlike the application of technology in agricultural and manufacturing industries, adopting new technologies at institutes of higher education usually increase unit costs rather than lower them.

A second factor behind rising per-student costs is the productivity-resistant production function in higher education. Simply put, most colleges and universities lack the kinds of continuous productivity enhancements typically associated with the goods-producing sectors of the industrialized economies that are able to outsource labor-intensive components to low-wage jurisdictions or to substitute capital and technology for labor in order to enhance productivity. On the other hand, the great expansion of technology in higher education, although it replaces some clerical staff and may, by some measures, enhance the quality of learning and research, tends to add to the per-student costs. Thus, in the United States as elsewhere, unit costs in higher education—as in basic education, symphony orchestras, nursing homes, and other labor-intensive enterprises—faces a *default* per-student cost trajectory that reflects mainly its cost of faculty and staff labor, which generally exceeds the prevailing rate of inflation.

The third factor accelerating the already rising instructional costs in most countries is rapidly increasing enrollments. Massification of higher education is driven by rising birth rates and accelerated by larger cohorts of students being prepared for (and expecting access to) higher education. These trends are most visible in the less-developed world, where birth rates remain high and participation in secondary education is rapidly increasing. In these countries, young people are graduating from schools expecting access to universities that are already overstretched.

Magnifying the dilemma of these increasing higher education costs is the declining ability in almost all countries to keep up with the rising revenue needs thorough their public treasuries alone. In higher-income countries, the limitations may be the rapidly rising and competing costs of health care, pensions, and security as well as demands for tax cuts. In low- and middle-income countries, the competing needs may be for public infrastructure, public health, basic education, and a more adequate social safety net. And in all of these countries—especially in low-income countries that are facing the most rapidly rising revenue needs—taxation can be as difficult technically as it is unpopular politically (particularly taxation that is both progressive and not detrimental to the economy).

FORMS OF COST-SHARING

In response to these diverging trajectories of annually increasing costs and revenue needs and flat or declining resources from governments, higher education institutions throughout the world are turning to revenue sources other than governments to fill a portion of the gap.[7] Cost-sharing, as introduced above, refers mainly to a shift of some of the burden of instructional costs from governments to either parents or students or both. The student contribution is occasionally from savings or trust accounts, but more commonly it comes from summer or term-time employment or from borrowing (sometimes euphemistically called deferred tuition, graduate taxes, income share agreements, or other terms describing innovative repayment schemes).[8]

Cost-sharing in a worldwide perspective can take several quite different forms. One of the most obvious forms of cost-sharing occurs when countries introduce tuition or fees (or both) in areas where higher education was formerly free. For example, China introduced tuition fees in 1997, followed by the United Kingdom in 1998, Austria in 2001, and some of the German *Länder* (states) in 2006. Similarly, some countries have sharply increased fees in areas where public sector tuition already exists, thus enlarging the share of costs financed by students and families and shrinking the proportion of costs financed by government. In England the maximum allowable tuition fee increased to over GBP 9,000 (more than USD 12,000), which is triple what was previously allowed. Sharp increases in tuition have also occurred across the United States and in many Canadian provinces.

A second form of cost-sharing occurs when countries introduce a tuition-paying track alongside a regular non-tuition-paying track reserved for state-supported students. This two-track system maintains the political appearance of free higher education (which is socially and culturally important in formerly Marxist countries) yet allows universities to raise revenue from non-state-supported and international students. Separate tuition-paying tracks have been introduced in Russia, East Africa, most of Eastern and Central Europe, and countries that were formerly part of the Soviet Union.

Another method of cost-sharing is the addition of new fees to cover expenses that were formerly financed by the government, such as residence halls, dining halls, and common study areas. Living costs in countries that were formerly communist were highly subsidized. This practice absorbed increasing shares of higher education budgets as more students attended college. Introducing fees to recover expenses formerly financed by the government has become a popular cost-sharing mechanism and typically meets less political resistance than raising tuition prices.

Student aid reforms have become another popular area for implementing new cost-sharing mechanisms. For example, governments have shifted main forms of student aid from grants to loans in order to save limited resources while maintaining open access to higher education. This has occurred largely in the United States, where need-based grant aid has remained flat while federal loan programs have rapidly expanded in light of increasing higher education costs. A similar situation occurred in the United Kingdom, where cost-of-living grants have been replaced by an assortment of loan programs. Some countries have decreased or cancelled student aid altogether, increasing costs incurred by the students. The United Kingdom froze its cost-of-living grants in the late 1980s and then later cancelled the program altogether.[9] Additionally, most of the former communist countries have capped or rolled back the amount of maintenance grants offered to students.

Declining government subsidies on student loans and other publicly funded programs is a final form of cost-sharing that almost always increases the proportion of costs that students pay. Raising interest rates, reducing interest-free grace periods, and reducing the number or amount of loans for which repayments can be forgiven are all methods that shift the cost burden from the government to students. Governments can also indirectly decrease subsidies by elevating cost-collection efforts (such as reducing and limiting the amount of student loans that can be discharged in bankruptcy), which occurred in the United States in the late 1990s.

Finally, some governments have reduced subsidies by supporting demand-absorbing private sectors at the expense of the traditional public options. Countries such as Japan, South Korea, the Philippines, Indonesia, Brazil, and other Latin American countries have limited or avoided significant governmental expenditures on public higher education institutions by encouraging, subsidizing, or expanding the fee-dependent private sector. As governments encourage private sector growth, traditional forms of aid may be channeled away from public institutions to those of the tuition-dependent private sector that rely on high fees.

THE SPECIAL SIGNIFICANCE OF TUITION FEES

Of the several forms of supplementing flat or declining governmental revenue, tuition fees have the greatest potential to shift a portion of the cost burden away from governments and taxpayers on to parents and students. Tuition fees can be financially significant—that is, they are able to generate substantial net revenue in support of public colleges and universities. Fees can be annually recurring—

unlike grants or charitable gifts that need continuous and, often, problematic renewal. Tuition and other mandatory fees compete less with faculty instructional responsibilities—unlike entrepreneurial noncredit teaching or the diversion of faculty having to continually seek new grants while conducting related research and producing the needed reports. And finally, to some proponents of cost-sharing, fees bring to public higher education the attributes of a market, presumably making students and families more discerning consumers and the colleges and universities more responsive and cost-effective suppliers.

Tuition fees internationally take three distinct forms: up-front, deferred, and dual-track. The most common are *up-front* tuition fees, found in the United States, Canada, Japan, China, and most of the rest of the world where tuition fees exist. The up-front fees are paid upon matriculation (sometimes monthly for a slight additional fee), generally by the parents of traditional college-age undergraduate students to the extent of the family's financial ability. Students also contribute by obtaining loans or part-time employment. Parents may or may not assist financially with tuition fees or living expenses for adult or legally emancipated students, or for graduate or advanced professional students.

Dual-track tuition fees, another form of cost-sharing, are up-front fees that differ according to two distinct tracks of students: (1) state-supported students, selected by examination, paying no or very low tuition fees, and limited to the number the state can afford to accommodate; and (2) privately supported students, who pay full or near the full cost of fees. Devised after the collapse of Soviet communism and the centrally planned economies, the dual-track system is commonly employed in transitional, postcommunist, or post-socialist countries that have a powerful and often legally mandated legacy of free higher education that the state can no longer afford to sustain.[10] The dual-track system allows the state to profess conformance to free (or nearly free) higher education to those labeled "regular students" while raising substantial levels of revenue from the fee-paying tracks.

An objection to dual-track system is that it tends to privilege students who have had the best secondary schooling and tutoring (which often requires paying high tuition fees) and who pass the entrance exams at a high enough score to obtain free higher education.[11] Low-income students who score just below the cutoff may be unable to afford the high tuition fees either in the fee-paying tracks or in private colleges or universities. On the other hand, although it may be less equitable than a system of moderate public tuition fees plus means-tested financial assistance, the dual-track system may be the only way for countries that are unable to rely on direct up-front fees in public higher education to obtain the much needed supplemental revenue from the tuition fees of the fee-paying tracks. Public higher education capacity (and possibly quality) is then enhanced, and more middle-income students have access to the regular public institutions. Furthermore, as the size of the fee-paying tracks relative to the state-supported tracks grows larger, the additional revenue might support some means-tested financial assistance—and the diminishing free, or state-supported, tracks then begin to resemble American colleges and universities with generous merit-based grants and discounts.

Finally, *deferred* tuition fees are found in Australia, New Zealand, and within the United Kingdom in England, Wales, and Northern Ireland (but no longer in Scotland, which abandoned up-front fees for deferred fees in 2001 and then in 2007 abandoned tuition fees altogether).[12] Deferred fees are actually interest-bearing student loans that are repaid not on a fixed schedule but as a percent of income, making the repayments more manageable and forgiving remaining debts after so many years of repayment. Allowing all students to defer their tuition fees has proven to be popular with students, even though a change from up-front fees that were means-tested to deferred fees (as happened in England in 2006) shifts a share of the burden of instructional costs from middle- and upper-income parents—who were no longer required to pay tuition fees—to all students, including students from low-income families who had not been required to pay the means-tested up-front fees.[13] The popularity among students of deferred fees may be due in part to their being treated as independent adults rather than financially dependent children and being offered a university education that is at least free at the time of enrollment. And the income-contingent repayment obligation is not only more manageable for borrowers but is often perceived (and sometimes portrayed) as fundamentally different from, and even less costly than, a conventional student loan.[14]

RATIONALES UNDERLYING COST-SHARING

There are three rationales underlying the spread of cost-sharing. The first and most common is the sheer need to counteract the diverging trajectories of increasing costs and flat or declining governmental revenues experienced by colleges and universities throughout the world. This gap is especially felt in low-income countries that typically experience the most severe enrollment pressures as well as the most politically and socially compelling competition from other public needs, such as public health, basic education, and public infrastructure.

A second rationale for tuition and fees is based less on financial need than on the notion of equity. In virtually all countries, and especially in low-income countries, a disproportionate number of the beneficiaries of higher education are from middle-, upper-middle-, and upper-income families who could and would pay at least a portion of the costs of instruction if they had to. Such willingness on the part of both parents and students demonstrates the private value of the higher education opportunities they seek. The alleged unfairness of this disproportionality is exacerbated by the fact that so-called *free* higher education is largely financed by the government, and it can be argued that all taxpaying citizens pay for it regardless of whether they receive any benefit or even perceive they have been taxed. And in many countries, most taxes—public policies or intentions to the contrary—are collected through tax systems that are regressive or at best proportional, or fall mainly on individual incomes that cannot be hidden or diverted. Governments may also acquire their claims on public goods and services less through taxation and more through the confiscation of citizens' purchasing power brought on by the inflationary printing of money. In this sense—again, especially in low-income countries—the higher public subsidy required by a policy of low or no tuition can be said to resemble a transfer payment from the average citizen mainly to middle-, upper-middle-, and upper-income families.

A final rationale for cost-sharing is to introduce market principles to the system of higher education, which may increase the efficiency of suppliers and responsiveness of consumers. In the higher education marketplace, the price a consumer pays is represented by tuition, and postsecondary education is a good that is increasingly growing in value and demand. As cost-sharing increases, students and their families should become more discerning consumers and universities should become more cautious about future price increases. When universities increase tuition, they should, by the principles of markets, become more responsive to individual and societal needs. When universities decide to increase tuition to raise supplemental revenue, they will be more responsive to individual and societal needs. Cost-conscious education providers will look to provide the services that are in the highest demand and delay projects and programs that are less desired by consumers.

Following the above rationales, an increasing shift of higher education costs from governments to parents and students may be most compelling in countries that combine the following:

- a formidable backlog of politically and socially compelling needs that are likely to be funded before additional public funds for higher education;
- a limited capacity for additional taxes, especially taxes that are at all progressive;
- overcrowding and other forms of a worsening austerity in public higher education, often aggravated by surging demand for places;

- a current student population that is comprised disproportionately of children of parents who are themselves university-educated and able to afford at least a modest tuition fee; and
- a financial assistance system that provides some targeted, or means-tested, assistance to deserving students who would otherwise be unable to access higher education.

RESISTANCE TO COST-SHARING

Resistance to shifting the burden of higher education costs from governments and taxpayers to students and families, particularly through tuition fees, is widespread. The extent of, as well as the rationales for, opposition varies greatly depending on a country's dominant political and ideological orientation, the rationales employed by the proponents of cost-sharing, the current configuration of sharing—such as tuition fees, user fees, dual-track or deferred fees, or the reliance on a demand-absorbing private sector—and the forms and sufficiency of financial assistance available to maintain accessibility in the face of whatever additional shift may be on the political table.

Resistance to cost-sharing may take any (or more than one) of the following forms. A first is self-interest: students and parents, regardless of ideology or even affluence, tend (understandably enough) to resist the first imposition of, or later sharp increase in, tuition fees. A second source of resistance is more ideological: cost-sharing may be resisted—quite apart from family socioeconomic status or the ability to afford tuition fees—by those who view higher education, like basic education, health care, or clean air and water, as benefits that should be provided by the government without cost (other than the need for taxation). Self-interest and ideology reinforce each other, and student opposition to cost-sharing, especially to tuition fees, can be a formidable political force, especially when allied with a general political opposition to a government pursuing business-friendly, conservative, or neoliberal policies.

Similar to an ideological opposition is a resistance to cost-sharing out of a concern for access. This opposition, prevalent among current students and many on the political left, is based on a concern that cost-sharing, and especially increases in tuition or other fees, will lead potential students not to apply to—or even to prepare for or aspire to—a college or university because of a belief that higher education is unaffordable.[15] The concern for access extends to a concern that costs, including student living costs, may also lead a student to take only the most affordable option, possibly forgoing more costly alternatives, including living away from home or attending a private institution, either of which might be a better option. An increase in tuition fees might increase the odds of a student's dropping out before receiving a degree or deciding to abandon plans for graduate or advanced professional education.

A wealth of research in many countries has shown most students and families to be relatively insensitive to modest increases in tuition fees.[16] In fact, in some middle- and low-income countries, budget shortfalls in public higher education have made a lack of capacity—not the expense to students and families—the major barrier to higher education access for many students. Thus, the additional revenue made possible by the initiation of tuition fees in some countries has increased capacity and thus actually increased access, at least for some students. However, research has confirmed that increased tuition fees can indeed have a negative effect on students from low-income families, from weak secondary schools, or from marginalized groups, such as ethnic and linguistic minorities and those in rural areas. Some of the research has also shown that decreases in financial aid have similar effects as increases in fees: minimal for most students but a deterrent to low-income, marginalized, and those students who otherwise may be ambivalent about their college experience.[17]

A less ideological and more nuanced source of resistance is a concern for the potential (some would say likely) future erosion of financial assistance. The fear is that financial assistance, while possibly adequate for the present to maintain accessibility in the face of rising fees, requires constant and probably increasing governmental appropriations that may well diminish over time or be replaced by student loans. (This fear is borne out by the experiences of many African and transitional countries, and even in the United States and the United Kingdom, where once generous support for student living expenses has been frozen or transitioned from grants to loans.) This view can be held by those who fully accept the theoretical rationales for cost-sharing but are concerned that higher tuition fees are likely to remain and that increases in financial assistance must compete annually with all of the other competing public needs and thus may not be feasible.

A related concern in many countries is not simply over tuition fees, or even over accessibility per se, but over the deleterious effects of rising student indebtedness. These mounting debt loads are a rising concern in England, China, Australia, and elsewhere. This concern extends to the Nordic countries, which have maintained free higher education but, because of high student living costs and the absence of any officially expected parental contributions to these expenses, have experienced high average student debt loads. In the United States, average student loan balances have also increased. Between 1996 and 2012 the median student loan balance among students who borrowed for a bachelor's degree rose from USD 14,475 to USD 26,500, after adjusting for inflation. At the 75th percentile, balances among these students increased from USD 22,248 to USD 40,000 over the same time period.[18] However, some of the largest growth in student debt in the US has been for those students who pursue graduate and professional degrees, not undergraduate degrees.[19]

A final source of opposition to the increasing shift of costs from governments to parents and students is essentially strategic: a concern that the theoretical revenue supplementation from tuition and other fees may in practice do little either for improving the quality of instruction or for advancing access and affordability. This view can also be held by those who fully accept the theoretical rationales for cost-sharing but who are concerned that the supplemental revenue from an increase in tuition fees can just as easily permit a commensurate withdrawal of public revenue from higher education and a transfer to some other pressing public need—or simply to enable a cut in taxes.

In summary, cost-sharing is increasing around the world, taking many forms, with tuition fees being the most common, the most financially significant, and the source of the greatest political opposition. The rationales for cost-sharing are several, the most compelling being the need for revenue due to rising instructional costs and revenue needs that exceed the likely or even possible increase in public revenue. Opposition and resistance to cost-sharing, especially to rising tuition fees, are also worldwide and take many forms. Table 2.1 illustrates some of the variations in cost-sharing and student assistance for a sample of countries from around the world.

COST-SHARING IN THE UNITED STATES

Cost-sharing in the United States is best understood by first considering those factors that, in their totality, are unique to the financing of higher education in the US. These unique factors affect both the extent and the form or forms of cost-sharing. The following practices are among the distinctions that have bearing on cost-sharing and tuition fees in the United States.

The Delegation of Authority over Higher Education to the Fifty States

According to the US Constitution, policies concerning higher education—including the appointment of presidents or chancellors, faculty, staff, members of public college and university governing boards, and matters of finance, including the setting of tuition fees—belong to the governments of the fifty states.

TABLE 2.1 International sample of tuition fee policies

Country	*Tuition Fee Policies*
Australia	Students are either Commonwealth supported (CSP) or full fee paying. In 2016, maximum tuition fees for CSP students vary depending on program costs and demand. All can be deferred through the Higher Education Contribution Scheme (HECS-HELP) income-contingent loans at a zero percent real interest rate.
Chile	Cost-sharing has vacillated with changing governments: from neoliberal high tuition fees to a 2014 leftist promise of free university tuition to meet student demands where low-income students are mainly in private for-profit and short-cycle institutes.
China	Tuition and other fees for all first-time degree students, approved in 1997, have helped finance great expansion of enrollments and institutions, including in the private sector. A 2012 devolution of policies to provincial authorities saw further increases in fees and differentiation by program. The average total cost for first-time degree-seeking students was estimated to be USD 1,500 in 2012, with access for loans and grants.
Wales, Northern Ireland	The UK was the first European country to have more than free or near-free higher education. Scotland separated in 1998 with deferred fees and income-contingent repayments (later abandoning all fees). England followed in 2001 with very high but deferred tuition fees (now near USD 14,000).
France	No tuition fees but modest other fees, although short of real cost-sharing. All academic secondary school graduates qualify for universities, but many of the most able elect the very selective Grandes Écoles, some of which are private with tuition fees.
Germany	No tuition fees in 2017, but individual *Länder* have authority to impose fees, which several did in the 1990s and 2000s. Parents are legally obligated for students' living costs. Access is through means-tested *BAföG*, which is a combination of grants and loans. Greatly subsidized to the point of almost grants.
Kenya	Began tuition fees in 1991 and also reduced maintenance allowances. Kenya followed Uganda in the 1990s with dual- (or *parallel-*) track tuition fees: modest for state-supported, high for the private, or Model II, students, and provides a reasonably successful student loan program.
Korea	Aggressive but highly contested and politicized cost-sharing through (1) encouragement of large tuition-fee-dependent private sector, and (2) high tuition fees in public sector. Elections in 2012 promised 50 percent reduction in fees, but as of the end of 2017 this has not yet been realized.
Japan	Cost-sharing through an extensive, regulated private sector and financially strained by demographics. Japan attempts to fill places with foreign students, who pay more in fees. National universities corporatized in 2004, with limited authority to set moderately high tuition fees. Living costs high.
Russia	End of Soviet Union and ensuing austerity led to dual-track tuition fees that let in limited number of state-supported students, while others are admitted but pay high fees, allowing the pretense of legally mandated free education. Other transitional countries followed.

TABLE 2.1 International sample of tuition fee policies

Country	*Tuition Fee Policies*
South Africa	A history of tuition fees and an awareness that free higher education in a society with great inequality can exacerbate that inequality–clashes with the legacy of apartheid, redress, and increasing political pressure for free higher education access via the National Student Financial Aid Scheme.
Sweden	Like other Nordic countries, there are no tuition fees but also no officially expected parental contributions for high living costs, which fall mainly on students through student loans. Tuition fees for non-EU foreign students and high student debt levels are issues in 2017.

Sources: International Comparative Higher Education Finance and Accessibility Project (2017); European Commission, "Do Changes in Cost-Sharing Have an Impact on the Behaviour of Students and Higher Education Institutions? Evidence from Nine Case Studies," vol. 1: Comparative Report, 2014.

Note: As actual fees in most countries vary by institution, by sector, and year by year, this table presents no more than brief highlights of cost-sharing policies in a few selected countries.

State Delegation of Authority over Public Higher Education to Institutional and Multi-Campus Governing Boards

The states, in turn, have further delegated much of public college and university authority, including the setting of tuition fees, to institutional or multi-campus system governing boards. At the same time, public colleges and universities, even as public corporations, remain dependent on state appropriations for a critical share of their instructional budgets.[20] Thus, whatever formal authority may have been given may be compromised either by conditions attached to the appropriations legislation or by the indirect but considerable power of governors and state legislatures on the matter of tuition fees. Yet in comparison with most other countries where tuition fees are fiercely contested (and are even known to have brought down a government in Africa), these two features of higher education in America tend to buffer, at least slightly, the widespread anxiety over tuition fees from partisan politics.[21]

The Cultural Acceptance of an Expected Parental Contribution to the Higher Education Expenses of Their College-Age Children

In the Nordic countries, college students are considered to be financially independent from their parents. These countries feature no tuition fees, making them among the last bastions in the industrialized world of free higher education. But the very significant costs of living are, at least officially, considered to be the financial responsibility not of the parents but of the students and are most often paid for by government-provided loans. Similarly, in England, Australia, New

Zealand, and other countries featuring deferred tuition fees—to be repaid as student loans—parents are relieved of some of what might otherwise be their share of instructional costs. In the United States, as in Canada, Japan, China, most of Europe, and most of the rest of the world, traditional-age college students are considered to be dependent on their parents (to the degree to which their parents are financially able).

A Large and Significant Private Sector

Although private nonprofit colleges and universities claim a smaller percentage of institutions and enrolled students than in the past, they still number some 1,701 out of the nation's 3,221 degree-granting public and private nonprofit institutions of higher education.[22] More significantly, and unlike the private sectors in most countries that are decidedly less prestigious than the elite public universities, the US private sector includes 45 percent of the nation's 60 most prestigious research universities that make up the Association of American Universities as well as most of the elite liberal arts baccalaureate colleges.[23] The presence of such a large, significant, and highly tuition-dependent private sector in the United States, then, reinforces the acceptance of tuition fees in the public sector.

Extensive Philanthropic Support

As recounted in an earlier section, philanthropy supplements higher education revenues through both endowments and annual giving, in both public and private sectors, and for both operating and capital needs. On the one hand, the USD 40.3 billion of higher education philanthropy reported in the US for 2015, especially the portion going to public colleges and universities, clearly supplements governmental revenues. But the majority of this revenue goes to relatively few institutions; the top twenty recipients alone raised 28.7 percent of this philanthropic largesse.[24] Although public institutions have been increasingly successful in fund-raising, much of these funds go either for student financial assistance (mostly with a merit component). Other fund-raising revenue goes toward specialized projects, intercollegiate athletics, and new buildings. Funds raised for general operating costs tend to go disproportionately to those faculties that have the most affluent alumni, such as medicine, law, and management. This is not to disparage these recipients or activities or to diminish the great benefit that voluntary giving brings to public colleges and universities. But public sector philanthropy does little to replace the decline in state support to public sector instructional needs. Furthermore, the tax deductibility of this philanthropic largesse, however worthwhile, makes philanthropy also significantly subsidized by the government.

Abundant Financial Assistance

The United States features a high level of financial assistance for the high tuition fees and student living costs in both public and private sectors. Total financial assistance from all sources—federal, state, and private grants; institutional grants and discounts; subsidized and unsubsidized federal loans; federal work study; and federal tax credits and deductions—to all students (undergraduate and graduate) in 2015–2016 was estimated by the College Board at USD 240.9 billion. The board's estimate of financial assistance to undergraduates was more than USD 184 billion.[25] The extent of financial assistance in the United States is critical to cost-sharing in two ways. First, it undergirds the considerable revenue supplementation of high public sector tuition fees while allowing state and federal governments still to profess a priority on higher education access. And, second, it supports the cost-sharing made possible by a significant, tuition-dependent, but still relatively accessible, private sector.

Extensive and Workable Student Loans

The United States features several kinds of government-sponsored and guaranteed student loans, both subsidized and unsubsidized, available to all students attending public, private nonprofit, or degree-granting for-profit institutions who can demonstrate remaining financial need (after discounting expected parental contributions and other sources of financial assistance). Strictly private loans—with no governmental guarantee or subsidy and not subject to special governmental regulations—are also available, although declining in significance. Total student borrowing estimated by the College Board for 2015–2016 was USD 95.8 billion; total private borrowing was estimated at just short of USD 10 billion.[26] The point of including the provision of student loans as a distinction with relevance to cost-sharing in the United States is that, unlike many student loan schemes worldwide that are restricted to credit-worthy borrowers with parental cosignatories, student loans in America are both less subsidized (except for the in-school interest subsidy and the implicit subsidy of the governmental guarantee) and better collected. In contrast, many loan schemes, especially in low-income countries, are not truly instruments of cost-sharing but are mainly designed to put governmental money into the pockets of students (albeit with the hope that some of it may be returned someday). These loans often bear highly subsidized rates of interest due in part to political opposition to cost-sharing of any kind and a belief that if student loans are a necessity, they should be highly subsidized—and not collected too rigorously.[27] There are problems with student borrowing in the United States as of 2017, including interest rates that are arguably too high, the inability to discharge unmanageable debt through bankruptcy, and too many instances of simple overborrowing. But in spite of these problems and a default rate that reflects the high risk of such unsecured credit, government-sponsored student loans in the United States are part of a governmental policy not just to expand accessibility but also to shift a part of the costs of higher education to students.

Together, the above-mentioned features give the United States a distinctive balance in the proportionate shares of costs falling upon governments (both state and federal), parents, students, and philanthropists. These shares vary greatly by state, by level (that is, certificate, associate, baccalaureate, graduate, or advanced professional), and by sector (whether public or private). But on the whole, the proportion of instructional costs borne by parents, students, and philanthropists together is higher in the US than in most other countries. This is attributable in part to the comparatively high (although highly variable) tuition fees in both public and private sectors, in part to the substantial enrollments in the tuition-dependent private sector (both nonprofit and for-profit), and finally to the unmatched contributions of philanthropy to US colleges and universities, public as well as private.

THE FUTURE OF COST-SHARING

Cost-sharing nearly everywhere has meant a long-term shift away from governments toward greater shares borne by parents and students. However, the increasing resistance from parents, students, and taxpayers alike, exacerbated by the continuing rise of higher education costs in most countries, constitutes a worldwide struggle for the future of higher education finance—and thus for the future of cost-sharing. The struggle emerges from the fact that higher education institutions, governments, parents, and students have very different needs and constraints, and often fundamentally conflicting aims. For example, public colleges and universities will continue to seek more revenue from their governments to accommodate rising per-student costs and the desire for prestige and international recognition, even as they confront resistance from their governments and from students and parents pushing back from rising fees.

Governments everywhere will continue to lower or shift costs where they can, even while confronted by legal or constitutional prohibitions against tuition fees and the almost universal opposition from students and politicians on the ideological and political left. At the same time, governments in most countries will experience increasing political pressures from the need to accommodate rising higher education aspirations. There is also recognition that economies are becoming increasingly knowledge-based and that continuing prosperity needs the support of strong postsecondary education systems. Governments will also continue to be pressed by the tendencies of colleges and universities to spend ever more per student and by the political pressures from social advocates, most politicians, and university-educated elites to expand higher education participation.

Parents and students will continue to resist higher tuition fees. Students will continue to exhibit mixed reactions to loans. For many students, especially in low-income countries or countries without officially expected parental contributions, student loans may be the only way for low-income or older students to cover living costs. In the past, full-time university students in the United Kingdom and elsewhere in Europe sometimes opposed student loans, believing government-sponsored student loans to be a dangerous precursor to tuition fees. In Australia, New Zealand, and England, where tuition fees are mainly deferred, students seem not to construe the deferred fees as loans—or at least greatly prefer them to up-front tuition fees that parents may formerly have had to pay.

Amid these conflicting pressures and constraints, what are the futures of the major forms of cost-sharing? And what can countries learn from one another? For example:

- The Nordic countries, among the last bastions of free public higher education, will maintain policies of no tuition fees. However, some may try to relieve the pressure of increasing government-borne costs by allowing tuition fees to be charged to non–European Union foreign students. And in response to increasing student debt, some Nordic countries may increase student loan subsidies and improve provisions for debt forgiveness.
- Latin American and African countries that feature free or nearly free public universities will be hard-pressed to continue such policies, given the rapidly increasing demand for places, and will likely begin, however reluctantly, to charge modest tuition fees—although, as with the case in Chile, they may continue to vacillate with changing political parties in power.
- The East Asian and Latin American countries that have accommodated rising enrollments largely through private forms of higher education will most likely continue to limit the capacity of their public institutions but, as suggested above, may continue or begin charging modest tuition fees and expanding access in the private institutions through more financial assistance and loans.
- The so-called dual-track countries—mainly formerly communist or African socialist nations—will almost certainly see a narrowing of the distinctions between the state-sponsored and privately sponsored tracks. This may come about by continuing to limit enrollment in the state-sponsored tracks while at

the same time expanding enrollment, as well as lowering the fees, in the privately sponsored tracks. Or government could begin instituting a variety of special fees that can be construed as *other than* tuition fees in order to preserve a political fiction of free higher education.

- Australia, England, and other deferred-fee countries will likely maintain their major universities as *free at the time of entry*. If rising government-borne instructional costs make the continued deferral of all tuition fees unsustainable, these countries can move in the direction of greater cost-sharing by enhancing the recovery of the deferred tuitions in the ways employed by other countries with established student loan programs, such as raising the rates of interest, lowering the income levels at which repayments would begin, extending the repayment periods to lessen the volume of repayments forgiven, and adding guarantees in order to securitize the deferred loan assets. Or they can limit the institutions or the categories of students who will be granted the ability to have their tuition fees deferred.

The Future of Cost-Sharing in the United States

American colleges and universities, both public and private, already charge comparatively high published tuition fees. From the vantage point of 2017, the pressures to moderate or roll back these high tuition fees, while less intense than in most countries, are increasing, driven by both markets and politics.

For example, those private colleges and universities in America without deep and affluent applicant pools and substantial endowments will find tuition fees increasingly constrained by the flat or declining number of families who are both able and willing to pay the full tuition. Their ability to raise tuition fees will increasingly be limited by the less costly public institutions and by the unsustainable costs of tuition fee discounts. The very high tuitions in the private colleges and universities that are wealthy, elite, and selective—although much reduced for low- and middle-income students by discounts and scholarships, made possible by their endowments—will be increasingly constrained by political and civic pressures to moderate fee increases and provide more generous discounts.

Public colleges and universities will experience increasing political pressures at both the federal and state levels to slow down, freeze, or roll back public sector tuition fees, at least for undergraduates and especially at community colleges. Implementing significant changes in cost-sharing such as rollbacks, or taking policies from other countries—such as dual-track or deferred fees or free undergraduate education—will be difficult. The difficulty will be due in large part to the great financial cost of replacing hundreds of millions of dollars of tuition fees with additional state or federal expenditures. Beyond the cost to the taxpaying public, a significant rollback of public sector tuition fees in the United States would be confronted by the extreme decentralization of tuition-setting authority, which is disbursed among the legislative and executive branches of the fifty states as well as hundreds of public college and university governing boards.

The difficulty of a significant public tuition fee rollback will be magnified as states seek not simply to roll back fees but also to further limit expenditures for public higher education—at the same time seeking to expand access, improve completion rates, and elevate the scholarly prestige of their research universities—all of which seem to require more revenue (but certainly not less).

A more likely future for American higher education cost-sharing is a limited rollback in tuition fees by combined state and federal legislation and revenues that might include any combination of the following:

- free public community colleges (most of which are already effectively free to most low-income and many middle-income students via state and federal means-tested grants). This could be achieved not through a literal lowering or elimination of tuition fees but through an expansion of the amount of, and eligibility for, state and federal grants, including coverage for part-time and summer study;
- an expansion of the amount of, and eligibility for, state and federal means-tested grants, to make the first two years of all public colleges and universities effectively free (at least of tuition fees); and
- a less extensive and costly expansion in the amount of, and eligibility for, state and federal means-tested grants such that students could complete four years of public undergraduate education without the need to borrow.

In short, any future change in higher education finance and cost-sharing in the United States will require federal and state revenues, state-altered tuition fees, and both state and federal financial assistance, including grants and student loans. Adoption of European-style free higher education, deferred tuition fees, or dual-track models is unlikely. At the same time, a better understanding of these cost-sharing models and their country-specific political and structural constraints helps clarify the options and trade-offs confronting American higher education policies.

CHAPTER 3

Juxtaposing Global and US Private Higher Education: What Is to Be Learned?

Daniel C. Levy

Globally, one of higher education's fundamental transformations is from public systems to dual-sector systems. Whereas most countries previously had either no private sectors or only marginal ones, a staggering 98 percent of students are now in systems with both public and private sectors. Collectively the private sector holds a third of total global enrollment.[1] The size of private higher education is all the more remarkable considering the widespread dominance of public systems late into the twentieth century and the popular view that higher education is a public function—a social good that is properly nourished through national policies, structures, and financing. The United States is, of course, the towering historical exception (in both practice and norm) to public sector dominance.

While there is academic debate about how to define the terms *private* and *public*, this chapter adheres to mainstream definitions: *private* sectors encompass all institutions that are officially identified and counted as private by a governmental authority within a country; the same process defines *public*. By itself, however, this labeling tells us nothing about degrees of privateness and publicness. If privateness denotes nongovernmental resources, rules, and activities, and publicness denotes the opposite, then private institutions can still have a degree of publicness and public institutions can have a degree of privateness. The chapter consecutively analyzes the global panorama of private higher education with its regional configuration and astonishing US exceptionalism; the large diversity of private forms and roles and the policies that have shaped them; the increasing blurriness between publics and privates; and the dangers that US public sector reform poses to the exceptionalism of each US sector.

The chapter aims to convey both the striking privatization of global higher education—especially through the enormous growth of private sectors and through expanded privateness within public sectors—and the exceptionalism of the US case, especially in the stature of its private sector but also in the privateness of its public sector. Unmatched US success naturally exerts a magnetic attraction for observers globally, but analysis of the exceptionalism also suggests difficult challenges for countries interested in emulating particular successes. In turn, while there are some opportunities to learn from abroad for certain targeted purposes, analysis of the US system mostly suggests caution when it comes to looking abroad for roads to reform. Tempting reforms might involve trade-offs with crucial underpinnings of exceptionalism.

THE WORLD, THE REGIONS, AND THE US

Global Panorama

The first basic fact to appreciate about private higher education globally is its significant size: it is home to some 57 million students, or 33 percent of the global total. In absolute terms, private enrollment continues to soar even as the private share of total enrollment has stabilized. This significant size of the private sector may come as a surprise given the relative recency of major private growth and the still comparatively small presence of private higher education in most developed countries. Asia has the largest shares of the world's private enrollment, followed by Latin America. At the same time, Latin America has the highest proportion of its own total enrollment in the private sector—49 percent—followed by Asia at 42 percent, and then the US at 28 percent. US audiences should not think the size itself of their own private higher education system is an oddity not found in other countries.

Private enrollment is concentrated in countries with the largest higher education systems. The top ten countries in total enrollment (China, India, US, Russia, Brazil, Indonesia, Japan, Iran, Turkey, and South Korea), which hold 58 percent of the world's total enrollment, hold 69 percent of its private enrollment. Together the US, Europe, the developed British Commonwealth (Australia, Canada, and New Zealand), Japan, and South Korea hold 30 percent of global private higher education. With a striking four-fifths of their national enrollment, Japan's and South Korea's private sector shares are three times that of the United States.[2] These two cases are noteworthy because it was a conscious choice of Japan's and then South Korea's policy makers to funnel mass enrollment growth into the private sector, pushing access costs onto tuition-paying students rather than taxpayers, an Asian model that often has been praised and promoted by the World Bank and other international agencies.[3]

Just as noteworthy as the geographical concentration of private education, however, is its omnipresence. As recently as 1980, much of Asia and almost all of Africa and the Arab region had no private higher education. But in the early 1980s China began the wave of terminating communist public monopolies, and 1989 brought the fall of communist public monopolies in Europe and most in Central Asia as well. Only some ten countries still have zero private enrollment—and even a few of these have private sites, some internationally owned, though not leading to state-recognized degrees. These remaining countries are typically small, the exceptions being Algeria, Myanmar, Greece, and Cuba. Globally, debate over whether to allow private higher education has yielded to debate over trade-offs regarding its size and shape.[4]

The US Case

No policy field surpasses higher education when it comes to "American exceptionalism." This exceptionalism is especially spectacular in the private sector, but the subtler exceptionalism in the public sector also merits our attention. US higher education exceptionalism is most plain when it comes to academic quality and status, but it also involves relationships between the private and public sectors. This exceptionalism has implications for US policy makers who are looking to import higher education policy practices from abroad.

The high quality and status explain why the US private sector is almost never prominent on any agenda for basic reform. Nothing policy makers might happen to know about private higher education abroad, or glean from global rankings, makes them think about borrowing ideas or practices.[5] When it comes to private education, any question of international emulation concerns other countries' emulating the US, not the reverse. Nor is cross-sector emulation a major temptation, since the US is the only country where the private sector is generally regarded as superior to the public sector, and policy makers are more inclined to wonder what public institutions might learn from private institutions. Notwithstanding its composite high grade, however, private higher education in the US does have problems, both perceived and real. Leading the list is the fraud and low quality of for-profit institutions, long-standing concerns that have recently been major news and regulatory concerns. Another concern is ever increasing private tuition and persistent group inequalities in the student body. Moreover, private higher education is not immune from broad critiques of US higher education overall, even when the public sector is more vilified. One example is the worry that the US is falling behind in student learning outcomes and pathways to the labor market. Private higher education in the US could thus benefit from identifying some worthwhile and adaptable policies from abroad, even from countries whose private sectors are weaker overall than those of the United States.

However, this chapter mostly argues why US higher education reformers should be wary of attraction to broad foreign practice. Lifting policies from other countries' public sectors risks the quality and vibrancy of both US sectors.

ROOTS AND ROLES: DIVERSITY WITHIN THE PRIVATE SECTOR

Once we appreciate how large global private higher education is, we want to know what it does. What roles does it play and why? To understand the sprawling diversity of private higher education on a global scale, it has proven helpful to divide it into the following subsectors: "non-elite," "identity," and "elite."[6] As we understand their main roles and characteristics, we understand much about the "why" of private higher education and that the reasons for its emergence and continued functioning vary significantly by subsector.

Non-Elite Private Higher Education

The largest amount of private higher education is non-elite. In almost all countries, even the US, with its vaunted elite private institutions, most private enrollment is non-elite, packed in institutions whose names are unknown beyond their local turf.[7] Non-elite enrollment is always what accounts for majority private shares (Peru, Indonesia, Japan, South Korea, etc.).[8] Among the "BRICS," Brazil and India follow private majority suit, whereas China, Russia, and South Africa have emphatically favored the public sector as their main non-elite home.[9]

For policy makers, the "why" of non-elite private higher education is mostly cost-driven. This type of education is the chief vehicle to meet popular demand for access while not heavily burdening the public budget. For students and families, it is often the only path available. In developing countries, the most common non-elite type is "demand-absorbing," meaning that institutions do not have to offer much more than access itself to suck up the demand. These institutions generally resemble problematic US for-profit institutions more than those that are nonprofit, and they present serious regulatory challenges while pointing to a broad worldwide challenge for public policy: how to improve the ratio between demand absorbers and non-elite institutions with better student outcomes.[10] In fairness, this challenge could also be powerfully put to non-elite *public* higher education.

It is also fair to note that most of the developed world's non-elite private higher education is decent in quality, like most of its public higher education, and involves some consumer choice. Private non-elite institutions in Japan and the US often provide general higher education. Another type of non-elite education that might be of particular policy interest today is more specialized and "product-oriented." Private institutions that adopt such an orientation prepare students with specific technical skills that are needed in the labor force. Their focus is often in fields that public universities have ignored, at least until feeling market pressure. Given the sense of market-controlled quality in product-oriented education in much of the developed world, the product-oriented type seems a good target for more scholarly and policy attention in the United States.

Product orientation characterizes much Western European private higher education. Specialized institutions in Italy, France, and Spain benefit from close ties to businesses. In France, for example, both nonprofit and for-profit product-oriented institutions flourish across fields such as business administration, computer science, and fashion.[11] Product-oriented private providers are growing rapidly in the developed Commonwealth as well as in the UK itself. These countries have only recently come to envision a significant role for the private sector and have no major elite or religious private presence. In Australia the number of private providers grew from 6 to 150 between 2000 and 2007, which includes just three universities.[12] Ireland and South Africa have exhibited similar trends.

Product-oriented private institutions might also provide enrollment stability, considering how vulnerable demand absorbers are when demographic shifts lead to declining demand. Demographic changes are increasingly problematic in the developed world (and contributing now to the woes of the US for-profit institutions). As demand for higher education stagnates or falls while the public sector does not downsize much, it is no longer enough for private demand absorbers to offer easy access and the prospect of a credential. To date, the largest declines in private demand absorbers have been in European countries—Portugal in the west, Poland and Russia in the east. Such declines need not be regarded as bad for the public interest. They arguably show healthy market regulation. Institutions that might have been closed by more stringent public regulation die through their inability to attract students.[13]

Identity Private Higher Education

The distinctive function of identity institutions is to preserve or promote group affiliation. This private function has sometimes allowed a group representation that is disallowed in the public sector. It is the identity form of education that most neatly fits the notion of a public majoritarian sector not meeting the desires of discrete minorities who then turn to the private nonprofit sector.[14]

Religious schools are the most common type of private identity institution. Historically, Catholic institutions have often led the way for private sectors. Demand naturally suffers as developed societies later secularize; when religious institutions hold on, it is usually with considerable curbing of their religious mission. Whereas under nationalist liberalism or communism, it was the state that most restricted religious presence (and often all private presence), today (at least beyond the religious bans in China and Turkey) the main limitations on the religious presence come from society's own declining interest.[15] This is the main reason that religious private higher education is weak in most of the developed world; the major exception (notwithstanding their own decline) remains US Catholic institutions, flanked by an evangelical presence.

Both gender and ethnic group institutions have played much more important roles in the US than elsewhere, contributing to American private exceptionalism. Such factors were obviously more important in the past than today, once providing an access denied in the public sector, but even now they serve importantly as institutions of choice. Accordingly, once a creature of both sectors, US women's colleges survive only in the private sector. Historically black colleges have survived in the public as well as the private sector and, like women's colleges, have retained a diminished but not insignificant role. Enrollment remains single-group dominated in both the gender and ethnic institutions. Created for distinctive, planned purposes, private identity institutions often start to unravel and present students and their families—as well as donors and sometimes government—with trade-offs between hanging on to private distinctive missions and succumbing to a mainstream onslaught.

Identity institutions are good examples of where the US does not look abroad for fresh ideas while much of the world has looked to the US. The women's college is the leading long-standing example. Ironically, while they have struggled at home recently because US mainstream institutions have integrated, women's colleges have made increasing inroads abroad, particularly in Asia. On the religious side also, the US has been something of a model, including through proselytizing. Here, too, the identity subsector has a new vibrancy abroad even as it struggles at home.[16]

Elite Private Higher Education

Elite private higher education is where US exceptionalism is most spectacular. In the developed world, the United States stands alone in having its elite higher education institutions packed disproportionately in a private sector. And even that powerful generalization understates the reality: private world-class is nearly absent in the rest of the world. The two best-known rankings of the world's one hundred leading universities (2016) show just one non-US private university (Belgium's KU Leuven, a Catholic university). Of the seventy-four universities that make both rankings' top one hundred, twenty-one are private, and the US system accounts for twenty of those twenty-one. Only six non-US private universities make even the top two hundred on one list or the other.

South Korea is the only country outside the US that clearly has world-class private educational institutions and (among developed countries) that comes even close to private-public sector parity at the academic peak. That country alone accounts for the three Asian private universities in the top two hundred in the two cited global rankings. Korea University and Pohang University of Science and Technology each make one list, and Sungkyunkwan makes both. Yet the three private powerhouses also receive considerable government funding. Key actors setting out to build private elite universities should probably look at South Korea's huge yet unique success. Japan does not match it, probably in large part because of the extensive space occupied rather early by the country's elite public research universities.

However, Japan's private-public gap at the top is smaller than in most developed countries. Waseda and Keio Universities, both of which continue to have world-class aspirations, hover around the cutoff of making the top ten in national rankings, and International Christian and Sophia Universities also make the top twenty, but none makes the top three hundred in the two cited global rankings. Waseda's profile emphasizes business norms, innovation, and a critique of public sector bureaucracy. Like many leading private institutions globally, its curriculum, staff, and student body are internationally focused, with a US orientation. In research, top private institutions recognize that their competition does not extend to the public elite Tokyo University or Kyoto University, whereas in teaching they claim to be at the pinnacle. Thus they attract many top secondary school graduates, as they prioritize serious attention to students, while the top public institutions are more consumed in research.[17]

In all other developed countries outside of the United States, public institutions are overwhelmingly considered to be supreme. The major international rankings show three main groupings: non-US public universities in developed countries, US private universities, and US public universities. Among the handful of other countries' private institutions, several European ones are "government-dependent private"—a UNESCO (United Nations Educational, Scientific, and Cultural Organization) label for a private-public hybrid in which most of the ongoing funding and substantial management remains in public hands.

Another unique feature of private higher education in the US is its collection of elite liberal arts colleges, which are almost always private. The Amhersts and Swarthmores can be roughly as selective in their student body as can Brown and Yale. They, too, have no widespread parallel outside the US. But let us not exaggerate the extent of even their US presence. Most US "liberal arts" colleges have always been non-elite; moreover, even the true liberal arts character of these non-elite institutions has diminished through recent decades as concern with job credentials has driven a massive evolution into commercial or technical institutions. Trade-offs are often painful for institutions that are pressured to choose between retaining their liberal arts mission versus surrendering to the marketplace. Some colleges have even sold themselves to for-profit institutions.[18]

In some parallel with women's colleges, yet on a much broader scale, liberal arts interests and initiatives have developed abroad. Europe's Bologna Process, with its partial shift from professional to more general higher education, moves closer to liberal arts. While liberal arts is growing abroad, not all related international efforts are private, and how many are and will be academically elite is questionable. Yet even elite prospects are not to be underestimated, as the resources necessary to create elite liberal arts colleges are much more modest than those required for private research universities.[19]

Efforts to replicate elite private colleges and universities abroad have proven difficult. The most visible experiment to build a private world-class research university outside the US came in the 1980s with a financial empire backing Bond University, straddling Australia and New Zealand.[20] Businessman Alan Bond invested AUD 135 million for a 50 percent share and with a major Japanese investor built a AUD 146.3 million campus in 1986. Bond recruited from top universities at home and abroad, hoping to gain traction beyond its extant strength in business and economics training and from an associated neoliberal think tank. But the university failed to meet its early enrollment goals, had a deficit by 1990, and a few years later Bond himself declared bankruptcy. In hindsight, reasons for the failure seem predictable: lack of adequate philanthropy, Labor government opposition, and especially the fundamental reality of entrenched, well-functioning public universities offering quality education for low tuition. Although Bond University does extremely well on student satisfaction and employment measures, it lacks world-class standing (failing to make even the top five hundred of either of our two cited global rankings), because it is not a major research university.

Nor are any private universities in the UK in the world-class range. Alongside comparatively modest private non-university providers, the University of Buckingham was long the UK's sole private university. Buried in global rankings and small, it is only average in UK rankings, though, like Bond, it has a stellar record in job placement. The government's major higher education reforms of 2011 permitted for-profit and other private universities and promoted private prospects by imposing a sharp increase in public tuition coupled with loan availability for students attending private institutions. However, only a handful of universities have emerged (e.g., BPP, first a college, then a university college, and finally a university[21]), and none is on course to be a major research university. Almost all of the UK universities remain in the public sector, while the private sector overwhelmingly is one of non-elite providers. Emulating the American private universities abroad remains more cocktail conversation than serious experiment.

Turning to developing countries, observers may be surprised to learn that a notable elite presence exists. In these countries, leading private institutions may be viewed as elite at home though only "semi-elite" internationally. They make the private-public gap at the national academic pinnacle significantly smaller and more varied than in almost all developed countries. Sometimes elite private institutions stand toe to toe with public universities. In fact, their roots are often the result of public failure. Whether through student and faculty massification (not offset by comparable increases in resources), political disorder, or a medley of other problems, a country's top public institutions lose stature, and the best-off families, joined by business and even parts of government, place their bets on private alternatives. Thus these institutions play important elite roles in the broader society. Notably, they conspicuously draw ideas and inspiration from private institutions in the US and proudly proclaim goals of further emulation.

Latin America is home to arguably the most striking examples of elite private higher education in the developing world as with the long-standing Instituto Tecnológico Autónomo de México (ITAM) and Instituto Tecnológico y de Estudios Superiores de Monterrey (ITESM), two of Mexico's most prestigious higher education institutions.[22] The pattern is also particularly strong in South Asia, where even the public universities with the country's best talent, such as Quaid-i-Azam University in Pakistan, are profoundly troubled. This has allowed space for private elite institutions such as Aga Khan University, Lahore University of Management Sciences, and Hamdard University, many of which have full-time faculty and attract the country's top students.[23] A growing elite presence has also emerged in Africa (as in Kenya's US International University) and developing regions generally. More advanced in development, Turkey provides several vivid examples of an elite private presence. Bilkent, Koç, and Sabanci Universities, all with support from leading business conglomerates, have major international ties and offer English instruction, laboratories, library and cultural facilities, superior faculty, good salaries, and a claim to ample student-teacher interaction. Empirical evidence for the shared pinnacle characterization comes from the choices of Turkish students finishing with high scores on the national entrance exam.[24] With their characteristic professional management and entrepreneurialism, these Turkish private universities sometimes test the bounds of state rules.

Although the maintenance of strong public universities in developed countries precludes any pressing need for private elite alternatives, top private institutions find elite niche functions and structures in these countries as well, mostly in teaching, practical fields, and sometimes applied research. Japan's leading private universities fit this description. Moreover, the leaders among private product-oriented institutions and professional institutions approach elite standing.

Our analysis of the elite, identity, and non-elite subsectors has shown the private sector's vast internal diversity. Private higher education exists for varied reasons, serves varied groups, has varied strengths and weaknesses, and plays varied roles. This is the reality that private stakeholders operate in and that aspirational policy reformers should be at least reasonably aware of, surrendering any notions of a homogeneous private sector.

GLOBAL PRIVATE-PUBLIC DIFFERENCES AND REFORM

Because the private sector is not homogeneous, there is not a single private-public distinction. There are two salient realities about private-public differences. The first is how overwhelmingly distinctive the private and public sectors are from each other despite notable blurring.[25] The second is the existence of widespread policy efforts to infuse more privateness into public sectors.

Private Is Private, Public Is Public—Usually

The great majority of private colleges and universities around the world rank high in what studies have conventionally gauged as privateness in finance, governance or management, and missions, functions, or roles. Compared to their public counterparts, private institutions tend to draw a much higher share of their income from private sources (nongovernmental), have more institutional autonomy from government (however, much of their management is constrained by private external stakeholders), and have a large role in sustaining some of society's private institutions, from business to church. Direct government subsidization of private institutions on an annual basis remains rare. The relative autonomy of private institutions is a contributor to and reflection of privateness in governance.

Granted, the privateness of such institutions is obviously limited by growing government involvement. Starting a private institution and renewing its license generally requires government permission. Globally, concern with quality assurance has spawned accreditation agencies, and outside the US these are general public agencies. Some governments extend student loans to those attending private colleges and universities, policy choices then including whether to cover students at for-profit institutions. But we must be cautious in contemplating how governments "manage" (or should manage) their private institutions. Most private sectors emerge and quickly grow without central government planning and often even surprise government and the general public.[26] More broadly, a free market approach (in contrast to state control) allows for a degree of ongoing regulation as consistent with private institutions' relative autonomy to make their own decisions rather than just follow state-imposed policies.[27]

Just as the private sector is fundamentally private, the public sector is fundamentally public. This is especially clear in Europe, where higher education systems were created and function along the lines of a Continental model.[28] Here, responsibility for higher education is lodged centrally in the nation-state, the funder and the maker of policies that are standardized across the system. Granted, the UK and its developed Commonwealth have allowed more privateness at their public institutions than in most of Europe in terms of management, finance, and function. But even their public sectors remain much more public than private.

Some governments or other stakeholders restrict public and private distinctiveness from the outset through regulation. Meanwhile, private institutions themselves curb their private features when they seek to emulate existing public institutions. Keen to acquire legitimacy, private institutions often deny or at least downplay feared trade-offs: the Catholic university denies that its identity nature threatens academic freedom; the rather elite university denies that its business-orientation rides roughshod, through boards of trustees, over faculty voice; and the non-elite institution claims to emulate public standards and at times social goals.[29]

Whatever the private sector's original distinctiveness, blurring between sectors is a major tendency over time. Blurriness often develops through a mix of imposition and choice. Leading private universities may wish to relinquish some privateness if allowed to compete for public research funds. Non-elite institutions may likewise accept added regulations if their students become eligible for government loans. Blurring is often imposed by the environment, however, whether through new regulations, demographic changes, or shifts in the labor market. Anxious private leaders must weigh trade-offs between holding the fort and yielding some ground in order to save other ground.

Nonetheless, two analytical tendencies often exaggerate the degree of blurring. One is the temptation to use the United States as reference point. Here, the US configuration is exceptional because of its unusually extensive intersectoral blurring. The other misleading analytical tendency is to focus on institutional blurring while taking one's eye off the sector. Private colleges and universities do often lose distinctiveness over time, but as private sectors "should" do, higher education has spawned new forms, often quite private. Among salient recent examples are Evangelical institutions, cross-border institutions, private colleges affiliated with public (or private) universities, and distance education.

For-profit institutions in particular epitomize how new forms of higher education can make the private sector larger and higher in privateness. In Europe and the US, where private institutions have previously been overwhelmingly nonprofit, the growth of for-profit institutions has invigorated the privateness of private sectors and thus private-public distinctiveness.[30] Critics find too much privateness in the sense of too little regulation, applying a critique often made about developing countries' weak and abusive private higher education institutions.[31] Japan's contemporary experiment with for-profit private institutions has not worked out well, with obstacles including the country's huge institutional oversupply and the education ministry's opposition. France appears to offer a more accepted regulatory example: for-profits and nonprofits are treated similarly, and for-profits are not generally scorned. The regulatory regime in several developed countries (including Australia and the UK) may be worth exploring.[32]

Pushing Privateness into Public Sectors

The most widespread and significant contemporary manifestation of blurring is the infusion of private sector qualities into public sectors. The most obvious examples are financial: public institutions derive greater shares of their funding from nongovernment sources (mostly through tuition but also through contracts, sales, and even philanthropy). The partial privatization push also involves more market management. Though it is often bad domestic politics to acknowledge it, the US is at least the implicit inspirational model for pushing privateness into public sectors. Moreover, the world's historical leader for privateness within public sectors has hardly been immune from contemporary pressures to expand privateness in finance and management.[33]

One way to infuse privateness into the public sector is the creation of new public structures with some privateness from their outset.[34] The new structures may be full institutions, as with Latin American "public experimental" or "public alternative" universities in the 1960s and 1970s. Several African and Central European public universities offer "second module" programs that emulate private providers in finance and management. The modules are attractive on the market because they boast the public university name and degree while paying close attention to eventual employment and sometimes setting tuition a little lower than that at the top private universities.

Although alternative public structures also appear in developed countries, as with technical institutes or online delivery, the main push to increase privateness in the public sector comes from extant public universities. The chief motivations, while rarely responses to private challenges, are to make the public sector more productive and efficient, save government money, and contribute better to a knowledge society. In this there is a sense of public failure among those who see public universities as excessively averse to incorporating private sector characteristics and market dynamics. Some would say they are historically too averse; others, that a historically sensible publicness is unfit for modern times and the future.

Reforms to partly privatize the public sector have made inroads but have also suffered defeats and even retreats. The UK imposed significant fees at public institutions, while in Germany the move to introduce fees was thwarted. In Chile—Latin America's decades-long leader in tuition and other partial privatization of the public sector—political pressure to reverse charging fees has been strong. The debate about no (or low) tuition is often cast as a trade-off between fiscal discipline and access, but it is also a trade-off between fiscal discipline and political support. Tuition and other private income sources have been difficult to impose where society's historical norms heavily favor public funding. Although the establishment of private higher education was politically controversial in many countries, its presence today in almost every country comes with acceptance of substantial private financial burden from the outset. In this sense at least, private higher education is often the comparatively easy political route to substantial private funding.[35] For those who favor ample private contributions to "cost-sharing," the United States, Japan, and South Korea have had a tremendous advantage over the rest of the developed world resulting from both charging tuition in the public sector and having large private sectors.

THE UNITED STATES: UNIQUE PRIVATE-PUBLIC CONFIGURATIONS

US Public Higher Education: Uniquely Private—and Successful

Significant privateness within the public sector, so jolting for much of the world, has genetically deep roots in the United States. From the beginning, colonial higher education institutions were private-public blends, and these morphed into private institutions before the first public colleges appeared.[36] Even the public colleges, however, were open to business and church and fit the new country's affinity for limited and decentralized government. This is a stark contrast from Europe's long-dominating national public universities, with private institutions at the margins only.[37]

Since their origin, US public institutions have been set to compete with both private and public counterparts. Blessed with substantial autonomy (sometimes consecrated in state constitutions), public institutions are steered largely by their internal leadership. Within broad limits they have chartered their own waters, offered consumer choice, faced their own individual policy trade-offs, and forged multifaceted ties to outside forces—private and government alike. They have drawn support from and been accountable to their own constituencies.[38] From early on, the US public sector has spawned institutional differentiation and accepted stratification as natural. Public sectors in other countries are less comfortable with inter-institutional diversity and inequality and therefore are subject to stronger policies and tendencies toward "academic drift" and "equity." Arguably, the US did not "need" a private sector in the way many more state-run and standardized public systems did. Even without a private sector, higher education in the United States could be portrayed in contrast to "state control" or heavily "state-supervised" models.[39] Even as the US private sector remains unique in many respects, its public sector remains unique as well—significantly for its degree of privateness.[40]

The US public sector is also special for its high multifaceted performance. US public universities are the greatest collective success—other than its private universities—in world rankings.[41] Moreover, whatever its accompanying shortcomings, the much-praised general success of US public universities goes well beyond top world rankings to very widespread provision of higher education and research production, all with ample private-public cost-sharing.

In short, the US public sector has been—and remains—exceptional for its performance as well as its hardy privateness. What role private characteristics play in the public sector's performance is at best a matter of informed and considered speculation, but it would be reckless to ignore the question. Too much is at stake to make major policy reforms in the public sector without due consideration of possible harm to that sector. And the same can be said about the exceptionalism of the US private sector. How much of its exceptionalism rests on the unique privateness of the public sector? How might the private sector be imperiled by reforms in the public sector (while the US private sector is rarely itself a major target for reform)? We have seen how one set of public reforms would make the public sector more private, and we turn now to reforms that would make the public sector more public.

Dangers of Public-Sector Reform in the United States

Whereas the US remains exceptional for its degree of public sector privateness, and in certain ways moves still further in that direction, the distinct tradition of privateness has plainly been eroded by the increasing reach of both state and federal government, even when state governments decrease their share in public university budgets. Public university autonomy from government has diminished in important respects, and policy makers demand more direct accountability. State and federal governments increasingly ask universities to demonstrate their compliance, they expand regulations, and the courts become more involved. Even where government (especially federal) offers funds through market competition, its incentives and disincentives become so heavy that they are rising tools of control, more so than annually ongoing subsidization usually is. And threats of the withdrawal of all federal funds where a university fails to comply with one regulation or another is intimidating. So as government makes public universities more private in their income sources, it also makes them more public in other respects, and less freely market-driven, in a less decentralized system. Though to a lesser degree, the increased governmental reach has also come within the private sector, obviously reducing that sector's privateness.

Although we can legitimately make much of government regulation and how it diminishes the distinctiveness of the US from foreign public sectors, there is no serious claim that any significant borrowing of foreign ideas has been at play to date. In contrast, however, proposals to accelerate publicness sometimes have quite prominent foreign stamps on them. Consider one much publicized proposal to make the public sector more public: 2016 Democratic presidential candidate Senator Bernie Sanders advocated free tuition at public universities.[42] While the US may be a model for global reforms aimed at making public sectors more private, Europe emerges as a model for reforms to make the sector more public. Sanders pushed his higher education proposal like he pushed a public option in health care: as rights that government must finance—if *they* can provide such rights, why can't *we*? The argument assumes a shaming posture when it sees not virtue but vice at the very core of US exceptionalism: other (all or most) industrialized democracies publicly provide for natural rights while the US languishes on the political right.[43]

Free tuition for public higher education, whatever its debated merits, poses major dangers to the virtues of US exceptionalism in several respects. First, it risks deleterious effects on the viability of what has been the world's uniquely most vibrant private sector. Raising the tuition gap between public and private sectors generally threatens private enrollment, as many who prefer a private option will pay only so much extra for it. Even if US elite private colleges and universities could ride largely above the tide, non-elite and identity institutions could be imperiled. And along with risks to the private sector, a point only sometimes noted, there is also risk to the public sector itself, a point rarely noted. When debate on free public tuition considers impacts within the public sector, the discussion usually centers on whether free tuition would bring the progressive socioeconomic impacts its proponents anticipate. But free tuition should also be considered in terms of trade-offs it might bring regarding the unique privateness of the US public sector and its related internal differentiation and potent marketplace. Might further financial dependence on state government justify further regulation and demands for accountability to state government? Would free tuition jeopardize the political-economic base of autonomy, including plural funding sources and diverse accountabilities to civil society? How well would the US public sector's unique differentiation—its public peaks towering over other public universities as well as four-year colleges and two-year community colleges—fare in the face of demands for equity in access, treatment, and results? What might be the ramifications of relegating students and families from consumer status toward that of just taxpayer, as in public primary and secondary education?[44]

CONCLUSION

The United States is no longer alone in, or even unusual for, having a substantial private sector of higher education. Almost all countries, including all developed countries, have some private higher education; now usually it is significant. That the private sector is typically quite private in its finance, governance, and functioning makes it importantly distinctive from the public sector, where publicness still dominates. The new global importance of private higher education rests on both its greatly expanded size and its common distinctiveness from the public sector.

The striking contrast between private and public sectors does not deny the simultaneous reality of important blurring across sectors, the major contemporary manifestation of which is the partial privatization of public sectors. Nor does it deny the major diversity within the private sector. While almost all private institutions limit otherwise larger burdens on the public budget, some operate mostly for access purposes, some exist mostly to offer a choice, some link closely to the job market, and some serve elite functions.

The historic change from a world of mostly public systems to one where two sectors are usually consequential (and the private sector is itself diverse) makes global higher education vastly complex, and this complexity expands options for policy emulation. Indeed, much of the new complexity is the result of emulation of various sorts. But nothing suggests a single right—or even objectively superior—balance of private and public sectors; nothing suggests an objectively best balance between privateness and publicness, however configured within each sector. Certainly no magic private-public formula emerges to which countries should aspire. Neither do we suggest, however, that one country's mix of private and public is as good as any other, or even as good for any particular time period national setting or value set. It is not without some good reason that the world has shifted to systems with private as well as public sectors, and it is not without some good reason that it has looked much more to the US than to any other higher education system.[45] This chapter has noted much to herald about the unrivaled US private sector (with its publicness included) and also about its unique public sector (with its extraordinary privateness). At the same time, it has identified reasons and specifics of where even the vaunted US private sector might fruitfully look abroad selectively.

For US policy, however, our main conclusion from seeing the United States in global perspective lies not in the possibilities for emulation but rather in appreciating the exceptionalism of the United States. From a comparative perspective, the US private sector is staggeringly exceptional and successful. And we can characterize the US public sector in somewhat similar terms, though it is obviously not an equally extreme case. US exceptionalism should not lead to any blanket rule against adopting any particular practice for either its private or its public sector, or certainly against other countries continuing to look to either or both US sectors for possible guidance. The cautions do set a high bar, however, for those in the US considering reforms if one appreciates how higher education exceptionalism evolved over time in particular historical, political, cultural, and economic contexts to produce a uniquely strong private sector and a uniquely private public sector. Major reforms should not be considered without understanding the risks they may pose to unique private and public national treasures.

CHAPTER 4

The Practical and Ethical Underpinnings of Higher Education Access Policies

Anna Mountford-Zimdars

Access to higher education raises five fundamental questions no matter the country: (1) Who should have access to higher education? (2) What is access like? (3) What is this access to? (4) What explains access to higher education? And, finally, (5) how can access be influenced and changed?

These questions are, of course, interlinked, yet their study and answers are often found in different fields. Philosophers—and, indeed, politicians—consider what "should be" based on normative ideals and understandings of the meaning of fairness. Social theorists have developed various models for understanding participation and access in higher education. Empirical research by institutions, sector-wide organizations, social researchers, and the media investigates what patterns of access and participation are actually like.

But the question is not merely about access to higher education; access does not stop at the university gate. The question is about "access to what" in terms of the curriculum, knowledge, and other opportunities at a university as well as "outcomes" such as completing one's university studies and other employment and economic results. It also extends to social outcomes like marriage patterns, democratic participation, and cultural tastes. The question of "access to what" is particularly salient for potential, current, and past students. Lastly, a key policy question is how to enhance actual access and ensure that student experiences and opportunities more closely match philosophical and policy ideals of what they should be.

This chapter explores all five questions by first discussing different pipelines of access to the higher education systems in countries outside the United States. It then directly compares how the UK and Germany have structured their access policies and how each policy affects student outcomes. Overall, the chapter shows that designing optimal policies for higher education access is an elusive goal, not least because it entails complex trade-offs. Meanwhile, substantially different policies can often result in similar levels of access and student outcomes.

ACCESS IN THE CONTEXT OF SOCIAL AND ECONOMIC INEQUALITIES

> Colleges and universities depend on a pipeline that promotes opportunity and academic preparation for all students.
>
> —*William R. Fitzsimmons, dean of Admissions and Financial Aid at Harvard University*

As illustrated by this quotation from William R. Fitzsimmons, thinking about access to higher education naturally entails thinking about early opportunities in the home and in education.[1] Accessing higher education for young people is the next step after having participated in earlier forms of formal and informal education that do not preclude entering universities (which is not to say that higher education isn't or shouldn't be offered as a further opportunity later on in life). Indeed, the evidence from the literature suggests that the greatest impact on individuals and return to spending in education is equalizing opportunities in early-year interventions.[2]

Scholars of social stratification and social mobility think about education in the context of "origin and destination," which are linked through education.[3] While there is always a link between "social origin," such as social class or economic and social contexts, and "outcomes," such as employment outcomes, this link should be mediated by education: increasing equity in education is a route to providing upward social mobility for individuals and draws on the talents of many for the economic success of nations.

When the philosopher John Rawls asks us to imagine that we are born behind a veil of ignorance, in which we do not know our characteristics at birth, including wealth, gender, or race, most people would choose to live in a society where everyone can succeed in education and beyond regardless of the accident of birth that assigned them those characteristics.[4] This desire for equality of opportunity needs to be balanced, however, with the role of the family of social origin. One would be hard-pressed to find policy makers who advocate that all children need to be taken away from their parents and raised in institutions to provide complete equality of opportunity.[5]

It is not surprising that no industrialized country has succeeded in fully breaking the link between social origin, early schooling, and a person's final social and economic standing. Families differ in their social, cultural, and economic capital, all of which facilitate educational opportunity and achievement. Social capital provides access to information and networks; cultural capital helps navigate education, including the hidden curriculum of schooling and higher education; economic capital can be converted into experiences or directly buy admission into schools.[6] Developed in the 1970s, the powerful Featherman-Jones-Hauser hypothesis stated that regardless of government interventions, mobility patterns would be the same in industrialized countries based on the nuclear family.[7] As we shall see, some countries have succeeded in creating more equal opportunities in education than others.

Adrian E. Raftery and Michael Hout provided further insights into how resources of the family of origin would translate into educational achievement through introducing the *maximally maintained inequality* (MMI) hypothesis: the most advantaged strata of society will be able to reap the benefits of educational expansion and opportunity first, and only once their desire for education is saturated will less advantaged groups benefit.[8] Historically, for example, the growing educational opportunities for women first benefited girls from better-off families before opening opportunities for boys and girls from less advantaged families.[9] As educational opportunities have generally increased across industrialized countries, Samuel R. Lucas put forward the *effectively maintained inequality* (EMI) argument as a way of understanding the link between origin and education: at each level of education, he argues, the most advantaged groups in society will access the most advantaged forms of education.[10] In other words, Raftery and Hout are concerned with the length of education people pursue and how less advantaged groups will leave education earlier. Lucas, on the other hand, highlights that even when individuals pursue the same length of education, more advantaged social groups participate in the most prestigious forms. In terms of university access, this means we expect fewer disadvantaged students to reach higher education (MMI), and those who do will be less likely to be in the most selective courses and institutions (EMI). From this theoretical perspective, we can expect different access modes to higher education even in countries that have broadly similar outcomes, with benefits of higher education disproportionately reaped by already privileged strata in society.

ACCESS IN THE CONTEXT OF STRUCTURAL INEQUALITIES

Inequalities by social origin exist across the world. Furthermore, structural inequalities between, for example, different ethnic and racial groups and geographic inequalities influence access to higher education—although wealthier groups will be able to overcome additional disadvantages more easily than poorer groups.

An example of structural inequalities between ethnic groups is the case of Arab Israelis in Israeli higher education. While this group constitutes 26 percent of young adults in Israel, they earn only 9.7 percent of undergraduate degrees and are far more likely to drop out of postgraduate study than their non-Arab peers.[11] The root of this disparity lies in the structure of the secondary schooling system, which is divided into Hebrew and Arab language tracks. This puts Arab speakers at a disadvantage after high school, because the language of instruction in higher education is Hebrew. In terms of exam schedules, there is no consideration for non-Jewish holidays, and little Arab representation exists among staff and students.[12]

Ambitious current policy initiatives seek to enhance access, completion rates, and postgraduation outcomes for Arab Israelis. Some initiatives focus on raising attainment and preparedness before attending university. Others aim to raise consciousness of language barriers and create initiatives to overcoming them—for example, by introducing bilingual Arab/Hebrew signs, more inclusive scheduling, and promoting Arab role models.[13] It is common for some wealthier Arab Israelis to study abroad in Jordan or for the Palestinian Authority to overcome the structural disadvantages those students currently face within Israeli higher education, thus showing how individuals' economic position influences their ability to overcome disadvantages.[14]

There are also examples of how traditionally disadvantaged groups can use their social and cultural capital to overcome their less advantaged position. Chinese immigrants in New York City, for example, have been able to educate their community about opportunities in the education system, leading this group to be disproportionately successful in achieving admission to academically ambitious schools.[15]

ACCESS IN THE CONTEXT OF GEOGRAPHIC INEQUALITIES

Another dimension in access to higher education is the geographic distance to colleges and universities. This is a prominent factor in countries such as Australia, Georgia, Turkey, China, and Iran, where there are often many more opportunities in cities and urban centers than in less populated areas. In Australia 30 percent of the population lives away from the heavily populated coast, and young people living in those communities have lower transition rates into universities. [16] This is also true for Georgia, among other countries.[17] When policy makers recognize this as a key challenge, they can target geographically underrepresented groups through outreach and by offering more flexible or distance learning degrees.

Even in quite densely populated countries like the UK, there is concern regarding access to and completion of higher education for children from rural and coastal regions. However, professional parents with rural residency are again much more able than their less affluent peers to financially and socially support their children in living away from home. Policy makers in some countries see geography as a salient target area for outreach activities. National and historic circumstances tend to influence whether policy makers and the public see the "accident of birth" as something to address when it comes to access to higher education.

POLICIES TO INCREASE FAIRNESS

At the macro level, countries make decisions about the structure, finance, and general rules of higher education, and each of these can have direct or indirect effects on access. This includes choices as to whether all higher education providers should have equal status, state funding, equal degree-awarding powers, the ability to select their own students, their educational mission, or whether there should be differentiation among providers. For professional degrees such as medicine, pharmacy, or law, there are often macro-level decisions about using a shared curriculum and sometimes shared admission systems across institutions. At the institutional level, universities may be able to decide whether they want selection and screening at university entry or a system where everyone who wishes to do so can enroll. They might choose to place professionals in charge of university access or academic staff, and there might also be some discretion over the allocation of student funding. The institutional level also includes teaching and learning strategies, mission statements, and the ethos of teaching, learning, and student support at the institution.

Regardless of the range of policies countries can adopt that affect access, no country has completely broken the link between social advantage and advantageous schooling. Even so, the link between social origins, education, and outcomes is malleable by policy. One strategy for moderating the effects of social origin on education is the adoption of generalized social welfare policies that increase general equality and can filter down to equalize educational opportunities and outcomes. Some countries have smaller gaps between students who complete secondary school, go on to access higher education, and ultimately complete their degree programs. Notably, Scandinavian countries are better at providing opportunities to most students regardless of social origin.[18] In these countries there is comparatively low structural inequality and thus differences in the economic condition at social origin. Indeed, the gap between the richest and the poorest in Scandinavia is smaller than in other countries, with the Gini index, which measures disposable income inequality (0 being the most equal and 1 the most unequal), being around 0.25 for Scandinavian countries compared with 0.42 for the United States.[19] The educational system into the Scandinavian countries is based on state comprehensive schooling where children with different abilities learn together for longer than children in other systems. This model is widely considered to explain Finland's outstanding performance in the PISA test.[20]

Inequality in higher education completion can also be addressed through pricing and financial aid policies. In some Scandinavian countries, the government pays students' tuition and living costs while they are enrolled at a university, meaning there is a much smaller economic barrier to access higher education. For example, students in Denmark receive a monthly government grant of DKK 5,903 (approximately USD 900), plus the possibility of a loan for the duration of their study.[21] Additionally, students are eligible to receive the grant if they attend recognized universities abroad, thus supporting geographic mobility regardless of an individual's economic situation.

Aside from national policies regarding social welfare and financial aid, universities themselves can also develop policies to increase fairness in access to higher education. Although it is worth bearing in mind that even when fairness is a stated aim of admission processes, institutions usually have other interests they pursue through admissions. Universities across the globe are similar in how they use examinations as a filtering mechanism for admission. European nations (with the exception of Sweden) have high-stakes curriculum-based examinations they use for university admissions. The high school exit examinations often double as university admission tests. The US approach is different, where school examinations are generally insufficient for admission to many universities. Instead, they require applicants to also take a psychometric and general ability test, typically the SAT.

Therefore, university admissions might be a straightforward and open process that is conditional on passing a high school exit examination, but sometimes additional screening processes are needed if courses are oversubscribed. One example of such a process is the introduction of lotteries. The Dutch medical lotteries, which were phased out in 2016, are a famous case study among scholars interested in admissions. To allocate places for medical degrees, a simple lottery, and later a "weighted lottery" (with guaranteed places for top achievers and sliding chances of admission based on prior attainment), had been instituted.[22] Lotteries are also increasingly used in French higher education for oversubscribed courses such as kinesiology or psychology. The appeal of lotteries is that they eliminate any kind of reasoning—good or bad—from decision-making. Weighted lotteries allow mixing the luck of the draw with criteria such as attainment.[23]

There is strong theoretical appeal to the idea of lotteries, and they have been practiced in primary and secondary education.[24] However, in practice, not only did the Dutch lotteries prove to be unpopular or polarizing with the general public, but busing students to schools outside their neighborhood, a technique used in the United States in an attempt to make access more equal and less ethnically and economically segregated, was also unpopular, especially for those traveling long distances and circumvented by movement patterns.[25] Only one local government authority in the UK (equivalent to county-level governance in the US)—the only one led by a Green Party member of Parliament—uses a lottery for school admissions.[26] Although lotteries have the theoretical appeal of removing human biases that lead to occupational reproduction and social mobility, this concept does not resonate favorably with those who potentially stand to lose individually from such policies. Moreover, the removal of agency—whether it is real or perceived—from an individual's university admissions journey is unpopular.

The Dutch medical schools are now going down the inverse route of lotteries, introducing more holistic decision-making processes. However, while there is precedent for this practice, especially with regard to oversubscribed courses or at oversubscribed higher education institutions, the introduction of more reason can be equally controversial. Examples are the use of holistic admissions criteria at Ivy League and other highly selective institutions in the US and the use of contextual data—again often in the most selective universities—in admissions in the UK. Such procedures allow considerations such as athletic abilities, legacy status, contribution to the diversity of the learning environment, civic contributions, and other factors to enter admission decisions along with a detailed consideration of schooling and the relative performance of disadvantaged students.[27] Using holistic considerations in crafting a class in the US has been critiqued by the political left for giving preferential admission to legacy or donor students, and by the political right for its considerations of race in admissions. Contextual admission in the UK has been controversial for parents with children in private school who fear their children would miss out on being admitted but has become a mainstream practice at the group of twenty-four leading research and graduate education institutions collectively known as the Russell Group.

TWO CASE STUDIES OF ACCESS: OPPOSITES CONVERGING IN BRITAIN AND GERMANY

The previous section included examples of how some countries and individual institutions of higher education can employ various strategies for providing fairness within their university admission systems. This section focuses on two detailed case studies of access in order to further illustrate the differences and similarities in strategies. The first is the hierarchical and stratified university system in Britain, which is built on a comprehensive secondary schooling system. The second is the nonhierarchical binary university system in Germany, which is built on a highly stratified secondary schooling system.

Britain

The US, UK, France, and Japan are examples of countries with "stratified" national higher education systems.[28] At the macro level these countries have a range of higher education institutions with different missions. Many scholars, observers, and young people considering higher education would point to the implicit hierarchy of such systems with "top" universities in terms of research leadership, prestige, endowment, and impact on positions of national importance. Names like Harvard, Stanford, Oxford, Sciences Po, and the University of Tokyo are examples of such internationally recognized top universities. Admission to one of these institutions is exceptionally competitive but can provide lifelong advantages in terms of graduate outcomes such as salaries and access to professional employment. These universities also pride themselves in being national and international institutions by recruiting from all parts of their nations and overseas.

In 2015 there were 164 higher education providers in the UK. A quarter of higher education courses—usually more vocational courses and apprenticeships—are offered in "further education" colleges.[29] Since 1992 the university sector includes formerly technical and vocational colleges. Private universities are fewer in number but are a growing part of higher education since the Higher Education Act 2004 opened up opportunities for obtaining degree-awarding powers. Higher education providers vary in their course profiles, perceived prestige, endowment sizes, and the composition of their student bodies. The twenty-four universities that make up the Russell Group focus on undergraduate and postgraduate education and research, award the majority of doctorates, and receive the largest endowments.[30] Conversely, there are smaller endowments, fewer research students, and lower research grant income at most of the newer (post-1992) universities.

Overall, the UK has high participation in higher education, with 44.7 percent of the twenty-five-to-fifty-four-year-old population having participated in tertiary education, compared with a European average of around 33 percent. The pipeline to university is relatively open because Britain has a comprehensive schooling system where all children take a national examination, the General Certificate of Secondary Education (GCSE), at age sixteen. Admission to university is based on high school qualifications and scores on this examination. Many UK applicants take A-level courses, which are the most advanced classes taught in British high schools, or a range of vocational qualifications (BTECs, NVQs) at the age of eighteen, and admission to college is usually conditional on achieving certain grades in these classes.[31] As a rule of thumb, the higher the status of an institution, the higher the admission requirements. So for institutions like Oxford and Cambridge, applicants are usually expected to have completed three or four A-level courses with the highest grades and to have received stellar GCSE scores in subjects related to the course they wish to study at university. Other "recruiting" universities can accept lower grades, vocational or alternative qualifications, and may not have required GCSE subject scores for entry. The UK's Open University, which has no formal entry requirements for undergraduate study, literally opens opportunities for higher education for anyone with a minimum competency in English.

In terms of the openness of the pipeline to university, it is noteworthy that more than nine in ten British children participate in the public primary and secondary education system. However, just as in the United States, there is a link between the quality of public schools and home prices, thus creating some segregation. In addition, Britain has a vibrant private primary and secondary school sector, and a relatively small number of those schools account disproportionately for enrollment at selective universities. At Oxford and Cambridge, half of the new students are recruited from the 7 percent of children who attended private schools, although private schools account for 18 percent of secondary school education for sixteen-to-eighteen-year-olds just prior to potential university entry.[32] There are also academically selective public schools (grammar schools) in operation across the UK, and, again, their students are disproportionately concentrated at Russell Group universities. Generally, white, middle-class, and privately educated children are likely to go to the more prestigious universities while poorer students more often rely on whatever happens to be their local university. Thus, a closer look at the link between schooling and higher education in England shows perhaps more stratification than one would expect at first glance from a largely comprehensive schooling system.[33]

Policy makers in the UK introduced tuition fees as a cost-sharing mechanism between the government and students in 1998. Since then, tuition has increased rapidly from GBP 1,000 per year to GBP 9,250 (roughly USD 13,000) in 2017. Since the 2006–2007 academic year, students have been able to take out government-issued loans to cover the full cost of tuition and repay the loans through income-contingent repayment plans.[34] Fee waivers and some limited assistance with living costs are available based on financial need. Generally students with a family income below GBP 42,000 (about USD 58,000) can qualify to have some of their tuition fees waived and can also receive some support for their living costs.

Because universities are required to reinvest 25 percent of tuition fee income into increasing and supporting the participation of nontraditional students in higher education, a perhaps unintended side effect is that the most prestigious and richest universities also have the most generous funding for their comparatively small intake of disadvantaged students.[35] Universities that serve a greater number of nontraditional students as their core student body have less funding for each nontraditional student available.[36] For example, a UK student with a household income below GBP 16,000 studying at the University of Oxford in 2018 could expect to receive a grant of GBP 3,700 (about USD 5,100), a reduction of GBP 3,000 (USD 4,200) in their fees per annum, and additional career supports. In contrast, the same student would only receive GBP 1,000 (about USD 1,400) to be used on fee reduction or as a grant per year at London Southbank University.

The UK has high completion rates at colleges and universities. In 2015, 90.2 percent of students who registered at an institute of higher education continued or qualified at the same institution the next year, 2.4 percent of students transferred institutions, and 7.4 percent were no longer in higher education.[37] Continuation rates of more than 98 percent are found at Oxford and Cambridge as well as specialist art and music institutions (the Royal Academy and the Royal College of Music). Completion rates are generally higher for young entrants to higher education and those at Russell Group universities, with higher dropout rates occurring at further education colleges and newer universities, where dropout rates can surpass 20 percent.[38]

These impressive continuation rates mark some differences in experiences and achievement at university. In terms of the structure of higher education, there is a relationship between social background and the type of higher education students participate in with "nontraditional" students (those from poorer backgrounds, ethnic minorities, or older students), who are less likely to be at the most prestigious universities—although nonwhite students are overrepresented in higher education overall.[39] This latter observation might surprise international readers; indeed, the UK is an unusual country in that the educational attainment of some immigrant groups (especially in early education) surpasses attainment of British-born students.[40] A benign interpretation of this finding is that England succeeds in providing opportunities for all, while others have critically noted that ethnic minorities need to perform better to achieve the same labor market outcomes as their white counterparts due to disadvantages in the labor market.[41] That said, students from poorer backgrounds, those entering higher education over the age of twenty-five, and ethnic minorities are less likely to achieve as highly at university than their white or more affluent counterparts. Nonwhite students also report slightly lower satisfaction with their student experience.[42]

Progression into employment and further study is high in the UK. Ninety percent of graduates were employed or enrolled in further education six months after graduation.[43] There is still an influence of social origin, however. Russell Group graduates and students who are more affluent are most likely to continue into graduate study.[44] While the content of curricula and the opportunity for critical learning and engagement may be available across the range of colleges and universities, there are differentials in returns to higher education after graduation that are associated with the status of the institution attended, existing social networks, and a lifelong earning premium of those who participated in private secondary education regardless of their higher education institution.[45]

General research on returns to education shows that higher education correlates with a range of favorable outcomes, including economic success, better health, and family stability.[46] In terms of monetary returns, research in England shows that degrees from Oxford and Cambridge (colloquially referred to as "Oxbridge") and other Russell Group universities are the surest way to earn higher wages: the earnings across a person's lifetime are estimated at GBP 1.78 million for Oxbridge graduates and GBP 1.59 million for other Russell Group graduates (USD 2.5 million and USD 2.23 million, respectively). However, those going down the vocational training route of level 5 apprenticeship (equivalent to a higher education certificate, higher education diploma, or foundation degree usually available in the fields of business and administration, health and social care, information technology, and management and leadership) earn more than non–Russell Group graduates. Average lifetime earnings for students who complete a level 5 apprenticeship are GBP 1.43 million compared with GBP 1.38 million for non–Russell Group graduates (USD 2 million and USD 1.93 million, respectively).[47]

There are similarities between the UK system and other countries with hierarchical higher education systems. For example, in the US admission to the most selective universities can be fiercely competitive. Only five in one hundred applicants gain admission to Harvard.[48] Again, akin to the UK, it is the wealthiest private universities that are able to offer the most generous support for poor students, including financial assistance for living costs and fees, and support may take the form of a scholarship rather than a loan. However, the majority of poor students, if they do enter higher education, would enter community colleges or local universities and often combine study with part-time work for an extra income source. While historically a college education has led to measurable enhancement of a range of outcomes, including earnings, concerns exist that the content of some higher education is only for credential signaling and part of social reproduction with no learning gains.[49] A positive finding from a social mobility perspective is that individuals and groups who are less likely to pursue a college education benefit more than traditional college students from their experience.[50]

Germany

In contrast to the hierarchical higher education system in the US and the UK, countries such as Germany, the Netherlands, and Switzerland have historically had a "binary" system of higher education with *Fachhochschulen* and universities. There is more vocational-oriented higher education in the *Fachhochschulen* (e.g., health-related courses like physiotherapy). Universities, on the other hand, combine teaching and research and have historically offered more academically oriented degrees (social sciences, humanities) as well as professional qualifications such as law and medicine. However, cross-over between institution types and offerings is increasing, so it is possible to study some subjects at either a *Fachhochschule* or a university (for example, engineering).

Germany continues to offer early selection in its schooling system, where children are streamed into one of three types of schools, usually around age ten (or twelve in some parts of Berlin). Only those going to the academic track school, the gymnasium, are predestined for higher education, although it is theoretically possible for those at the lower vocational school (*Hauptschule*) and the higher vocational school (*Realschule*) to eventually enter higher education after completing some vocational training; or, with sufficiently good grades, they can undertake two further years of academic study before going to university. There is, however, de facto relatively low track mobility. Most students will complete their schooling in the school type assigned to them at age ten.

Although tracking is supposed to be based purely on ability, there is overlap in ability for students in different tracks. Social origin is thus a key factor in determining which educational track young people will attend over and above their ability, with the most privileged strata of society disproportionately represented in the gymnasium.[51] In a comparison with the tracking system in Italy, which occurs later on in a child's life, family background has slightly less of an impact than it does in Germany.[52] *Gesamtschulen* (comprehensive schools), which educate just under 10 percent of students, allow pupils to complete either *Hauptschule*, *Realschule*, or gymnasium, but their prevalence varies across states, and the gymnasium has remained a firm favorite for the middle-classes.[53]

Some have argued that the existence of early educational selection eliminates the need for further screening in university admission. Most university courses are open access conditional on passing the German high school exit examination, the *Abitur*. Only some courses have local institutional access restrictions (usually law, business studies, psychology), and only medicine and pharmacy have nationally coordinated access restrictions. The access restrictions, or *numerus clausus*, relate to attainment in the Abitur and can vary from year to year depending on the number of applicants to desirable courses. Numerus clausus cutoffs are based on grades that students have already achieved. This is different from the US system, where admission decisions are based on predicted grades. The calculation of the numerus clausus gives bonus points for taking time out after school and preferential local admission to local students and those with disabilities. Overall, the majority of prospective higher education students do not undergo an admission process per se but simply a matriculation system of enrolling at the universities of their choice.

Germany participates in the European Higher Education Area and the Bologna Process, which has changed most degree formats to the Anglo-Saxon model of an undergraduate (stipulated to be three years) and then a postgraduate degree (two years), although a system of "state examinations" exists alongside this model for law and teacher training.[54]

Despite the prescreening of higher education hopefuls through the early selection system in schooling, there is further differentiation among those who enroll for higher education after taking the Abitur and in their selection of institution within German higher education. Both processes further skew the profile of graduates toward students from more educated families.

Navigating universities in Germany is notoriously challenging. After the low barrier for entry, there are high dropout rates, and those who do complete their studies often take significantly longer than the stipulated times. Many times this is for reasons beyond students' control, such as being unable to enroll in compulsory, oversubscribed courses. Findings for the 1964 birth cohort showed that half of the children of higher educated parents enrolled in higher education after secondary school, compared with 34 percent of children from low educated parents. Dropout rates were also higher for students with less educated parents.[55] For this same cohort, only 70 percent of students of higher educated parents eventually graduated from university compared to 58 percent of those with lower educated parents. Overall, detailed studies currently put dropout rates in Germany at around 28 percent, with 33 percent at universities and 23 percent at *Fachhochschulen*, meaning one in three students on academic courses does not complete their studies.[56] Reasons for dropping out include feeling "overwhelmed by the amount of material," the level of specialist requirements, and the level of autonomy that is necessary for the organization of their studies.[57] Predictors of dropout are lower academic attainment at matriculation, working during term times, not having German citizenship, and lower educational attainment of parents, as well as not being fully informed about the content and curriculum.

Germany has lower participation rates in higher education compared with other countries in Europe, with 29 percent of the twenty-five-to-fifty-four-year-old population having participated in tertiary education, compared with a European average of around 33.4 percent and the above quoted UK figure of 44.7 percent.[58] Part of the lower participation statistics stem from issues involving comparability—for example, nursing is a degree course in the UK but an apprenticeship course in Germany—but also because there is a strong vocational training sector with a tradition of offering a genuine alternative to a degree.

Higher education is largely free since the reversal of a short-lived initiative to introduce tuition fees, which occurred across certain German states in the late 2000s.[59] In addition, need-based support is available along with some limited merit-based scholarships. In 2015, 15.1 percent of students received need-based aid (*BAföG*), and just under half of the recipients received the maximum amount of EUR 735 per month (about USD 900).[60] The way this financial aid package works is that half of the *BAföG* aid is a grant, meaning that portion does not have to be paid back, and the other half is a loan. Maximum debt is capped at EUR 10,000 (USD 12,300), and a minimum-income repayment threshold exists to protect borrowers with lower earnings. It is estimated that 4 percent of higher education students receive other aid, usually achievement-based scholarships. These can vary in value, with typical scholarships worth between EUR 300 and EUR 735 per month (about USD 370–900.)[61] A small but growing private higher education sector in Germany charges relatively high tuition fees.

Large returns in the labor market can be expected for those who manage to graduate from German universities: 93 percent of graduates are employed one year after completing university, and the earnings premium for a degree is higher than in many other Organisation for Economic Cooperation and Development

(OECD) member countries.[62] Given the high thresholds to completing degrees, it might be that those who graduate are particularly resilient and entrepreneurial and that these skills are rewarded not only at universities but also in the labor market. Graduates' lifetime earnings are on average EUR 1 million above the earnings of nongraduates.[63]

Table 4.1 compares some of the key statistics and characteristics of the German and English education systems at both the secondary and postsecondary levels.

DISCUSSION: POLICY TRADE-OFFS IN ACCESS

On the surface England and Germany appear to have very different access systems for higher education with different policy trade-offs. The UK has a largely comprehensive secondary schooling system and a hierarchical structure in higher education with highly selective elite universities and high fees. Initial admission decisions are based on predicted grades in the last year of school, and continuation rates are high, especially at the most selective institutions. Germany has a stratified primary and secondary school system with a binary structure in higher education access. It also differs in that it has free tuition, an admission system that makes decisions after all high school exit examinations have been taken, and lower continuation and degree-completion rates, particularly at universities compared with the *Fachhochschulen*.

In both England and Germany, middle-class children are more likely to demonstrate high academic achievement in early schooling. In both systems this means that they, like their upper-income peers, are more likely to go on to selective universities and graduate. For example, the small percentage of middle- and upper-class British children educated in private schools (less than 10 percent) and the grammar schools that what would be equivalent to gymnasium-type selective schools in Germany (5 percent) are disproportionately represented in elite higher education in England. It is also the middle classes who are more likely to be enrolled in gymnasiums in Germany and thus on track for higher education. They are also more likely to stay and graduate than their lower-income peers. In other words, despite the differences in access systems, there are strong similarities between middle- and upper-income students attending institutions that are considered to be more elite.

When one drills down to the level of subject choice at university, one could argue that opportunities in Britain are actually decided earlier than in the German system, as most schoolchildren take only three or four subjects in their two

TABLE 4.1 Key statistics and characteristics of the English and German education systems

	Germany	*England*
Secondary Education		
Type of secondary system	Stratified, early selection	Comprehensive, late selection
Percent of year group leaving secondary education without any qualifications[1]	6%	8%
Percent of 19-year-olds with higher education eligibility[2]	53%	60%
Percent of school-aged children in private schools[3]	9%	7%
Postsecondary Education		
Alternatives to higher education	Large vocational and apprenticeship system	Small vocational system
Tuition fees	None, other than small administrative fees	High, currently capped at £9,250 annually
Percent of 25–54-year-olds with a higher education qualification, 2016[4]	29.0%	44.7%
Average university dropout rates[5]	28.0%	9.8%
Lifetime earning premium of degree holders versus those without tertiary education[6]	€1,000,000 (approximately USD 1.2 million)	£748,230 (approximately USD 1.03 million)

[1] Not completing high school could be either through dropping out or not reaching the minimum passing grades for qualification. Figures for Germany from Sabine Menkens, "41 Prozent der Jugendlichen machen inzwischen Abitur," Veröffentlicht am 17.06.2016, www.welt.de/print/die_welt/politik/article156291438/41-Prozent-der-Jugendlichen-machen-inzwischen-Abitur.html.

[2] Figures are for 2015. In the UK "higher education eligibility" includes all individuals who have attained their level 3 through A-level courses and individuals who have completed an advanced apprenticeship program. In the UK 38 percent have attained level 3 through A-levels and a further 18 percent through advanced apprenticeships. Additionally, a small share of students obtain higher education eligibility through international baccalaureate and AS-levels. In Germany the figures include all individuals with *Abitur* (41 percent) and *Fachhochschulreife* (12 percent).

Source: United Kingdom Department for Education (DfE) administrative data. DfE reports level 2 and 3 attainment in England; Attainment by age 19 in 2016, www.gov.uk/government/collections/statistics-attainment-at-19-years; and German Statisches Bundesamt, Schulen auf einen Blick 2016, www.destatis.de/DE/Publikationen/Thematisch/BildungForschungKultur/Schulen/BroschuereSchulenBlick0110018169004.pdf?__blob=publicationFile.

[3] Figures for the UK are the most recent ones available (no year) from the Independent Schools Council available at https://www.isc.co.uk/research. Figures for Germany are from 2015, Statisches Bundesamt, Schulen auf einen Blick 2016, https://www.destatis.de/DE/Publikationen/Thematisch/BildungForschungKultur/Schulen/BroschuereSchulenBlick0110018169004.pdf?__blob=publicationFile.

[4] Eurostat "Educational Attainment Statistics," 2017, http://ec.europa.eu/eurostat/statistics-explained/index.php/Educational_attainment_statistics.

[5] Authors' calculation based on data from *Spiegel Online*, "Studenten: Wer das Studium abbricht - und warum," *Spiegel Online*, July 29, 2015, www.spiegel.de/lebenundlernen/uni/welche-studenten-ihr-studium-abbrechen-und-warum-a-1045486.html; Higher Education Statistical Agency (UK), "Non-continuation rates (including projected outcomes) introduction," HESA, March 9, 2017, www.hesa.ac.uk/data-and-analysis/performance-indicators/non-continuation.

[6] Available data in the UK and Germany do not separate earnings by degree program or level, thus the earnings premiums include both undergraduate and graduate degree program completers. Authors' calculations based on data from P. Kirby, "Levels of Success: The potential of UK apprenticeships," Sutton Trust, 2014, www.suttontrust.com/wp-content/uploads/2015/10/Levels-of-Success3.pdf, p. 14-15; Achim Schmillen and Heiko Stüber, "Lebensverdienst nach Qualifikation–Bildung lohnt sich ein Leben lang," IAB-Kurzbericht, 2014, http://doku.iab.de/kurzber/2014/kb0114.pdf.

final years of schooling, and this usually sets their path for the subjects they can study at university. With the general Abitur test in Germany, it is still possible for eighteen-year-olds to study virtually any subject.

Comparisons become even more complex when one is trying to holistically compare not only the process of higher education but also its role within wider society. In both countries there are substantial returns to higher education, but returns to skilled vocational training are high as well. One key difference is that vocational training is much more widespread in Germany than in the UK. Germany enjoys a strong tradition of vocational training as an attractive alternative, even for high school graduates who have taken the Abitur, which might discourage some working-class graduates from pursuing further studies at a university.[64] Overall, university education is arguably less necessary in Germany for achieving a middle-class position than in the UK, where there is a continued struggle to increase the number of apprenticeships and the status of vocational training.

Germany and the UK could not be more different on the issue of tuition. Fees in the UK are framed as a progressive policy that abolishes a middle-class subsidy and enables poorer children to participate in higher education with the revenue for universities that those fees generate. In Germany a middle-class outcry arose against tuition fees that were introduced in the mid-2000s and then recently repealed. "Free" certainly has a surface appeal of suggesting openness of education regardless of ability to pay fees, but the reality is that middle-class adolescents disproportionately reap the individual returns to higher education. However, some argue that these students also disproportionately contribute to the common good in terms of providing the professions that benefit everyone.[65] The different tuition policies of the two countries is also noteworthy because it does not seem to have resulted in substantially different degrees of access to higher education, although the fees might at least partially explain the higher completion rate in the UK.

In Britain research has also found that middle-class parents are aware of the advantages provided by higher education and are happy to pay for their children to participate in higher education, especially if this means limiting access for others. They are "pulling up the ladder behind them."[66] Targeting and inclusion of select individuals from historically disadvantaged groups for upward mobility through education is viewed by some as a policy trade-off that legitimizes a hierarchical and elite system of higher education that partly functions as a smokescreen for reproducing middle-class advantage or a "surface meritocracy."[67] It does not fundamentally break the link between the accident of birth and opportunities early on in life, where a poor child with exceptional ability benefits from

FIGURE 4.1 Comparing the UK and German systems for three hypothetical students

A very high achieving poor student who has applied to university. This student would do very well if admitted to a Russell Group university in the UK, as they might not only have their fees waived but also obtain a living cost bursary. The student would also do well in Germany in terms of gaining some government support and would not have to pay fees. However, on average, this type of student would be more likely to complete their studies in the UK (especially at a Russell Group) compared with Germany, where this student would be at increased risk of dropping out. On balance the UK system would be more beneficial to this student.

A middle-attaining middle-class student who has applied to university. This student is likely to gain admission and matriculate at university and to complete their study and transition into professional employment in both countries. This student would be financially better off in Germany, as they would not have to repay their tuition fees. However, they may take a little longer in Germany to complete their degree, in which case they may forgo earnings for longer. On balance this student might be ever so slightly better off in the German system.

A lower-attaining student considering university. This student is unlikely to enroll at a Russell Group university in the UK and more likely to enroll at a more local university. If this student were from a poor background, they would receive some limited support for university in both the UK and Germany. They are still likely to have to repay their tuition fees in the UK, but because their earnings might not reach the loan repayment threshold for some time, they might be eligible for loan forgiveness. In Germany this student would be likely to consider vocational training instead of a university degree, in which case their lifetime earnings might be higher than graduating from a less prestigious university in the UK or risking dropping out of university in Germany. On balance this student is likely to go down the vocational route in Germany and a low-prestige university route in the UK, which may ultimately mean they are better off in the German system.

the system alongside his or her affluent peers is very much the exception rather than the norm.[68]

As this discussion shows, it is difficult to make clear-cut policy inferences as to whether either the UK or the German system is inherently fairer in terms of access or outcomes. That is mainly because each design involves trade-offs, and neither is clearly the optimal one. Figure 4.1 illustrates these points by examining which university system would be "better" for particular types of hypothetical students.

CONCLUSION

This chapter has argued that there may be no single best access policy and that systems that use different approaches to admissions, outreach, or even finance can end up with similar results—good or bad. That said, there are clearly differences in who benefits the most from a particular system.

For policy makers a key question is whether the structural difference in university access and their pipeline actually lead to differences in social mobility. Here, the unanimous verdict is that the greatest challenge to fair access to university is not with admissions and other access policies but with the structure of prior inequality and early educational opportunities. That is an important lesson, because policy makers in many countries, particularly the US, look to their higher education systems as a primary mechanism to increase social mobility and reduce economic inequality.

University programs and higher education policies have limited influence to change wider inequities in society. Although higher education can raise wages, career trajectories postgraduation are defined by more than academic accomplishments. Moreover, it can be difficult for even university graduates to break into social elite circles that are defined by more than income and wealth. However, universities and policy makers are not powerless. At a minimum, procedural fairness of having clear, transparent, and accountable admission criteria is helpful. Outcome fairness in terms of who is admitted is more controversial and usually depends on the normative consensus of the outcome, whether it is high enrollment numbers, high completion numbers, student diversity, or even preparation for civic society. Nevertheless, processes without consideration for outcomes are unlikely to achieve deep fairness.

Of course, universities and countries may wish to achieve things other than fairness in university entry. In other words, fairness in access is only one of many competing goals in higher education policy. Private universities might wish to maximize financial returns—international students can be part of such a strategy—and public universities might wish to academically screen students during their degree study as a way of managing the large numbers enrolling in the first place. Or universities might seek to increase their national or international ranking through their admissions policy—for example, by enticing particular students to enroll, regardless of whether or not doing so might reproduce existing social advantages.

While this chapter has focused on access to higher education in international systems, policy leaders in many countries have begun to recognize the limitations of access alone. The global movement to enhance access to universities and postsecondary education generally has rightly shifted the focus away from considering only what goes "into" and comes "out of" universities to a focus on progression, experiences, and opportunities at universities and beyond. In the US this is also true, with policy makers taking a greater interest in degree completion rates, job placement, and graduate earnings. Globally, innovative institutions of higher education are becoming more welcoming and supporting diverse learners. They are funding and supporting study abroad for students who could not afford it otherwise and are requiring companies recruiting on their campuses to have transparent and accountable recruitment procedures. Paid internships are becoming more accessible for students who can't afford unpaid summer opportunities, and some institutions are integrating employability and job placement into their curricula. The collective realization is that the equity and social mobility that higher education is supposed to bring about cannot be achieved with access alone.

CHAPTER 5

The Architecture of Student Loan Systems

Alex Usher

In most developed countries, it is politically impossible to impose tuition fees without the government providing aid to at least some set of students. The most cost-effective and practical form of such student aid is loans. Loans transform student aid by providing a more stable path of consumption. Ultimately, loans allow the cash-poor young people of today to take money from their future, educationally credentialed selves and use it to pay fees that might otherwise deter them from participating in higher education.

But student loan programs are not simple. They are among the most complicated area in most national social policy systems, because they require policy makers to focus simultaneously on distribution of assistance and the collection of repayments. In most countries, only pensions—which face the same issue in reverse—are of comparable complexity.

Precisely because of their complexity, and the sheer number of policy decisions that go into designing them, loans can vary significantly from one country to another. At the front end, they can vary by—among other factors—how many students they cover, what costs they cover, and the length of time students may use them. At the back end, repayment can vary significantly based on the period of repayment, whether repayment is based on income or an amortization schedule, the collection mechanisms used, and the degree and timing of loan forgiveness. No two loan programs are alike, and policy comparisons across countries can be somewhat fraught because of national differences in the design of a country's education system.

The aim of this chapter is to catalog the main policy dimensions of student loans and to chart how the systems operate in various countries. In doing so, it reveals several common patterns in why countries have opted for different designs and eligibility rules in their loan programs. First we look at the history of student loan programs, and then we examine the main features of student loan programs both at the front end (eligibility and loan limits) and the back end (interest rates, repayment options, and collection mechanisms). Income-contingent loans are discussed in the section on repayment. This design is often seen as an "ideal type" of collection system, though its success is predicated upon certain features of a nation's tax system, which are not necessarily exportable.

A BRIEF HISTORY OF STUDENT LOAN PROGRAMS

The tradition of providing aid to worthy but needy students as a gift (i.e., bursaries) has a history almost as old as universities themselves, and the concept of lending money to students—both commercially and at below-market interest rates—is nearly as old. In thirteenth-century Oxford, lending to students by local loan sharks was considered sufficiently predatory that King Henry III issued a decree limiting interest on loans to two pennies per week per every twenty shillings one pound lent (which works out to a rate of 43 percent).[1] To keep students away from such predatory lending, Oxford encouraged the creation of endowments whose funds could be used to provide students with interest-free loans.[2] These loans were securitized against a scholar's possessions—books, fine cutlery, or other valuables—which would be forfeited if the student did not repay the loan within a year.[3]

The first set of national government student loans appeared in Sweden in 1918.[4] In the Americas the first government loan program was founded in Colombia in 1950 by Education Minister Gabriel Betancourt.[5] That program, ICETEX, originally operated by the International Bank for Reconstruction and Development, offered flexible lending terms to Colombian students to pursue higher education.[6] In Germany the "Honnef Scheme" was implemented in 1957 as a forerunner to their current student aid system, the *Bundesausbildungsförderungsgesetz* (*BAföG*), which offers students a combination of grants and loans to finance living expenses during college.[7] The United States and Canada created national government-guaranteed loan programs in the 1960s. For the next twenty years, loans mostly spread through Latin America in the form of nonprofit nongovernmental associations, the largest and most successful of which was FUNDAPEC in the Dominican Republic.[8] From the 1980s to the early 2000s, as an increasing number of countries introduced cost-sharing policies between families and higher education institutions as a means to help finance the cost of expanding postsecondary education to more students, these same countries also turned to student loans. Loans ensured that the introduction of fees for students would not compromise access. Among English-speaking countries, these loan systems developed in Australia, the United Kingdom, and New Zealand. Elsewhere, countries such as South Korea, China, Vietnam, Tanzania, and Nigeria followed suit.

As the first country to achieve truly mass higher education, the United States has more often than not been a global model for education with respect to expanding access. However, when it comes to student loans, that has not been the case. It was neither the first country to provide loans to students, nor was it especially innovative in their delivery. In practice the US was exceptional for relying on private lenders to make the loans, which were backed by a government guarantee, rather than making the loans directly with the government's own funds. While this strategy made the growth of student loans easier in the short term, in the long term it meant that the administration of loans was in private hands, which added complexity, reduced reliability, and increased costs. As a result, the US converted its loan program to a federal program (known as the direct loans) in 2010.[9]

DIMENSIONS OF STUDENT ASSISTANCE: THE FRONT END

One of the key considerations in designing a loan system is deciding how generous it should be. Generosity has several dimensions; most obviously it can refer to how much money a student can borrow, but it can also refer to such factors as the breadth of eligibility criteria and the consideration and strictness of need assessment. A generous loan system has advantages: more people get access to financing, and those who receive it have more money and hence will either have more institutional choice, will live more comfortably, or both. Equally, there are downsides. Offering loans to more students usually means a greater portion will go to students who are academically marginal or more likely to drop out, thus increasing defaults and losses; offering larger loans means more student debt in the future. There is no correct level of generosity for loan systems; each country makes different decisions about the trade-offs between generosity and default/debt that make sense given policy makers' and students' preferences. In this section we briefly examine the range of policy options used in developed higher education systems and what motivates policy makers to choose one option over another.

Eligibility Criteria

Student loan programs vary with regard to which students are eligible to receive loans. Some countries strictly limit loan eligibility while others have almost no restrictions, as is the case in the US. Loan eligibility requirements typically vary in the following five dimensions.

Institutional eligibility. In some countries, students at private institutions are ineligible for publicly financed loans or (as in Chile) only have access to a separate and less generous student loan program.[10] In other jurisdictions (Norway, Quebec), loans cover not only higher education but certain types of upper secondary school as well. As of 2015, Canada also has a special loan system to cover registered apprentices.

Academic standing. Some countries have minimum academic standing requirements to access loans. In Italy, loans are to some extent merit-based. Japan has two types of "scholarship loans"—one with interest and one without; high academic standing is required to access the latter. In Sweden, where college is free but living expenses are high, students must pass 75 percent of their courses each year to continue receiving aid.

Credential limits. Though tuition fees for graduate programs in the UK date from the 1990s, loans for domestic students to attend master's programs were only introduced in 2016. Unlike the US, loans are not necessary in most countries for doctoral students, because they are considered university employees.

Full-/part-time studies. Part-time study is rare outside of Anglophone countries and so tends not to be supported by student loans. In Canada students taking 60 percent of a full course load or more are eligible for full-time loans; a less generous part-time program exists but has very low participation rates.

Age limits. In some countries—notably Germany—aid through the *BAföG* system is restricted to those who are below a certain age when they start their program. For example, German undergraduates must be under thirty years of age to qualify for *BAföG.* For postgraduate students, age is restricted to individuals under thirty-five years.[11]

In some countries, literally all students qualify for aid. In Sweden, for instance, all students have the right to both a grant and a loan for living expenses in addition to free tuition. The amount of both is fixed: SEK 712 (roughly USD 85) per week in grant aid and SEK 1,792 (USD 213) per week in loans. In global terms the US has relatively open eligibility requirements in terms of the types of institutions it admits into its program. It is also broader than some programs in that students in all tertiary programs—undergraduate and graduate—are allowed in the program. Some of its rules regarding satisfactory academic standing are more rigorous than equivalent programs in, for instance, Australia, but they are similar to Canada's rules and much less demanding than those of Italy and Japan. Its minimum requirement of half-time study in order to receive full-time aid is possibly the most generous of any country.

Availability of Aid

The availability of aid (that is, some combination of loans and grants) and what it is meant to cover varies as well. Developed countries fall into one of three categories:

- Free tuition systems in which student aid exists solely to meet living expenses (e.g., Sweden, Finland).
- Tuition-charging countries with integrated student aid to cover both fees and living costs (e.g., United States, Canada).
- Tuition-charging countries with separate programs to cover tuition and living allowance, with the former usually covered by loan and the latter usually covered by grant (e.g., Australia, New Zealand). In Australia's case the grant program is not just for students but for all young people. The program, known as Youth Allowance, functions as income support for students and unemployed youth alike, although different age criteria apply to students and nonstudents.

Many countries with student assistance—Sweden and the Netherlands, for instance—operate on an allowance system: all students who qualify for loans qualify for the same amount. They are not necessarily obliged to negotiate the full loan, but the size of the aid package reflects tuition expenses plus some fixed amount of money per week or month.[12] Similarly, among countries with tuition fees, three of them—Australia, New Zealand, and the UK—automatically provide students with loans to cover tuition fees with no needs test.[13] All of these systems are thus relatively simple to administer.

The main alternative approach eschews allowances in order to make aid variable and individualize it for borrowers based on their costs and resources. Canada and Germany are the main countries that use this approach, and the United States also uses it for its subsidized loan program. In all three cases the amount of aid awarded is a function of both assessed costs and assessed resources, based at least in part on parental income. However, in the case of the two North American systems, the amount awarded may not fully cover fees, because students might be deemed to have enough resources to cover part of the fees on their own, or because the loan limit is below the level of fees for a given program or institution. (The United States in a sense follows both approaches, because in addition to its subsidized loan program, it also has an unsubsidized one, where students may borrow up to a given limit without reference to income. This is similar to places like Sweden; however, the amount loaned may still not cover all of a student's tuition.) This more targeted approach allows loan and grant providers to make very minute distinctions between students and their ability to pay; the drawback is that such systems are more complicated to administer and to communicate to clients.

Perhaps the most interesting variation on need-based assessment comes from Chile, which is the only country that takes the so-called Bennett Hypothesis seriously when it comes to student aid.[14] Historically, Chile has had a mostly private higher education system, and there was concern about providing government aid for tuition expenses, because policy makers worried that it would fuel price inflation at private universities.[15] Therefore, Chile's student loan system was designed not to fund tuition but rather to cover the "reference tuition," which is a somewhat arbitrary figure set by the Chilean government based on what it deems to be the actual cost of a given program. The relationship between actual and reference tuition can vary considerably, but the latter is always smaller than the former.

The extent to which aid is divided between loans and grants varies considerably as well. In some countries the division between loans and grants is fixed. For instance, in Germany every dollar of loans is accompanied by a dollar in grants; in Sweden the allowance for loans is always 2.5 times greater than the grant allowance. In other countries—Canada and the United States, for instance—the amounts of grants and loans are (for the most part) unrelated to each other: loans are based on a maximum that a particular type of student may borrow and the price of the institution he attends, while government grants are based on need (i.e., costs minus resources).

Borrowing limits are highest in the UK, where annual loans can rise to GBP 19,702 (roughly USD 25,600) per year for a student studying away from home in London. In Canada, depending on the province of residence and the student's type (e.g., if they have children), maximum annual available aid can approach USD 15,000, though for most students the maximum is below USD 10,000. Elsewhere, annual loan limits tend to be capped at USD 10,000 or less, but this cap can sometimes apply just to living expenses, since tuition may already be "free," as in Sweden.

Loan Origination and Administration

A final major dimension on which student aid varies across countries stems from how loans are originated and administered. It is most common for governments to handle these tasks, but there are exceptions. Canada and the United States were long outliers for using government guarantees to mobilize private capital to make the loans, though both have now abandoned this practice and moved to direct lending. There have also been experiments with risk-shared loans as an alternative to guaranteed loans: both China and Canada (1995–2000) paid financial institutions on a per-dollar-lent basis to assume the risks in government-issued student loans. For this policy to work, the risk premium per dollar lent has to be lower than that of the losses incurred through either a guaranteed or a direct lending system. This state of affairs can be difficult to achieve: the Canadian experiment in risk sharing ended when the financial institutions decided they were losing too much money on the program and demanded a higher per-dollar fee than the government was prepared to pay.

DIMENSIONS OF STUDENT ASSISTANCE: THE BACK END

Just as student loan systems differ in generosity on the front end, they also differ in generosity on the back end when students must begin repayment. Though much of the policy focus on student loans is on differences in collection mechanisms (specifically, whether the tax system is used as the primary means of loan recovery), perhaps more important are the many ways loan repayment is subsidized through various forms of interest rate relief or loan forgiveness. The burden of loan repayment—which can be quite acute for some students, particularly in the years immediately following their education—can be alleviated in a variety of ways, but the degree of alleviation is mostly related to the size of the subsidy. A system that makes life easy for borrowers tends to be expensive to taxpayers and vice versa.

This section first outlines various collection techniques on traditional loans—including the capping of overall loan debt, grace periods on loan repayment, and loan interest subsidies—and then turns to "income-contingent" loan programs and how they operate.

A number of jurisdictions try to limit debt by forgiving debt on an annual basis or at time of graduation. In Canada, from the 1990s to the 2010s, most provinces provided some form of loan "remission" or "forgiveness" to students, usually at the end of the year, conditional on completion. In Ontario, until 2016, students could receive up to about USD 10,000 in loans (or USD 14,000 if the student was married or had children) and have this amount reduced to roughly USD 6,000 at the end of each year. In general, Canadian governments adopted the lend-then-forgive approach to replace a more generous system of grants that they eliminated during a period of austerity in the 1990s. Alberta has since eliminated this program to save money; Ontario has eliminated it to return to a more generous system of up-front grants. The system is still in use in some Atlantic provinces. The other country where this occurs is Germany, where total debt for undergraduate students is limited to EUR 10,000 (about USD 12,300). In addition, German students who graduate in the top 30 percent of their class are forgiven 25 percent of their debt.

Another area where policies vary is with respect to the length of the period after the end of studies during which a student is not required to make payments on that loan. In most countries a first repayment is required either six months or one year after the end of studies; in Germany it is five years.

With respect to interest rates on student loans, countries generally use one of four major policy approaches: zero nominal interest rates, zero real interest rates, interest rates equal to the government rate of borrowing, and interest rates mirroring those on unsecured commercial loans.

Zero Nominal Interest Rates

Under this policy there is simply no interest charged on the loans. However, because inflation erodes the value of money over time, this policy amounts to paying students to borrow, since the dollars with which students repay their loans are worth less than those they borrowed several years earlier. The cost of this subsidy can be very high, especially in high-inflation environments. Germany and New Zealand are notable countries that use this option.

Zero Real Interest Rates

Here the value of the loans increases each year by the rate of inflation, which is an amount equivalent to the Consumer Price Index. Aside from the year-to-year inflation, no other "real" interest is charged. Students are not being paid to borrow in the way they are under a zero nominal rate, but there remains a significant government subsidy, because the government's cost of funds (the price at which the government can borrow money plus the risk premium associated with making loans) is almost always higher than inflation. Australia is perhaps the most prominent country using this policy.

Interest Rates Equal to the Government Rate of Borrowing

With this option, interest on outstanding loans rises by a rate equal to the rate at which the central government is able to raise funds on the open market through the sale of short-term treasury bills. Students may pay more than in the other approaches, but they are still getting a better deal than they would on the private market, because the rate of interest on these government loans is substantially lower than the rate of any commercial loan. The Dutch student aid program uses this policy, as did the UK until 2012, when it changed its policy in order to encourage students to pay back their loans more quickly.

Interest Rates Mirror Rates of Interest on Unsecured Commercial Loans

Under this policy, the interest rate on the student loan is similar to those available to low-risk bank customers seeking an unsecured loan. This can be somewhat difficult to measure definitively, as different banks may have different lending policies, so a proxy linked to the prime lending rate may be used instead (e.g., prime plus 2.5 percent, which is the default rate in the Canada Student Loans Program). Under this system, students are not receiving any subsidy vis-à-vis commercial rates, though the loan program still provides a benefit in that without a government-sponsored program, students who lack collateral would likely be unable to obtain any loans at all. A loan repaid in full under this final option creates a net return for government but does not necessarily imply a "profit." Loan programs around the world suffer huge losses from defaults, and, without exception, programs that charge these higher rates of interest use the surplus to offset losses from defaults.

Some twists can be added to these four core interest options. For example, Malaysia previously had a policy of charging interest not equal to inflation but to "inflation minus one percent"; similarly, Sweden offers a policy of "government rate of borrowing plus one percent." The US sets fixed interest rates at ten-year government bond rates plus a predetermined sum. Thus, the actual rates are linked to one of each of the four options without following it exactly.

Another twist is to apply different policies depending on whether the borrower is in school or in repayment. For instance, the US and Canada charge nominal zero rates while students are in school and higher rates afterward (in the US the rate may differ among loan programs but is typically pegged to the government rate of borrowing; in Canada the rate is linked to the prime lending rate). A third variation is to offer different types of loans for different types of students. Japan provides zero nominal interest loans to students with very good scores from secondary school—generally speaking, available only to students in the top third of their class—but offers loans at prime to students with weaker results (the former type of loans are also income-contingent while the latter are not). In the same vein, the US offers more expensive ("unsubsidized") loans to wealthier students while providing subsidized loans to students from less affluent backgrounds.

For the most part, loan subsidies increase the purchasing power of borrowers once they are in repayment rather than while they are students. That is to say, the money in practice goes to well-educated and relatively well-paid graduates (assuming they completed their studies) rather than to students who are struggling financially. It is a matter of some debate among advocates for students whether this allocation of scarce subsidy money is a good idea.

LOAN REPAYMENT: INCOME-CONTINGENT LOAN SYSTEMS

On the issue of repayment itself, there is a variety of different ways that loan repayment can be structured. Terms such as "mortgage-style" loan, "income-contingent repayment" (ICR) loans, and even "graduate tax" are used, but these distinctions are not as hard and fast as is commonly assumed. For instance, German and Dutch student loan programs require students to pay their loans on a "mortgage-style" amortization basis, but no payments at all are required if the borrower's income falls below a certain level. The American and Canadian systems also have similar means of sparing low-income borrowers from monthly repayments and also have what are known as "income-based repayment" features, which to some degree mimic classic income-contingency in that minimum payments are tied to income; however, these programs are not mandatory, and neither country uses the income tax system for loan collection.

Though income contingency is sometimes thought of as a "foreign" idea because its first use at a national level occurred in Australia, the idea has thoroughly American roots. The origin of income-contingent student loans is usually attributed to a 1955 article by Milton Friedman titled "The Role of Government in Education."[16] This is, however, only partially correct. While the article did focus on the issue of the difficulty of borrowing for human capital because of a lack of collateral, Friedman did not suggest a lending-based solution but an equity-based one, which, notably, no country has adopted. Specifically, he proposed:

> A governmental body could offer to finance or help finance the training of any individual . . . by making available not more than a limited sum per year for not more than a specified number of years, provided it was spent on securing training at a recognized institution. The individual would agree in return to pay to the government in each future year x per cent of his earnings in excess of y dollars for each $1,000 that he gets in this way. This payment could easily be combined with payment of income tax and so involve a minimum of additional administrative expense.[17]

There are a number of elements to the Friedman proposal that would later appear in student loan programs, but the key point to recognize is that under this model the student was not expected to repay a specific debt or obligation. Rather, students were simply expected to repay a percentage of income (which varied based on the amount borrowed) for a set period of time, no matter how much was paid relative to the amount borrowed.

A version of this idea was taken up by a reformist Labor Party government in Australia in the late 1980s. Australia had eliminated university fees in 1973 but reintroduced a nominal AUD 250 charge for higher education in 1986. The then minister of education, John Dawkins, was interested in bringing in much higher fees, mostly on redistributional grounds (free education primarily benefits families from richer families, while taxes are paid by all), and he asked the economist Bruce Chapman to work out how to extract money for fees without impairing students' ability in the short term to afford higher education.

The system Chapman developed became known as the Higher Education Contribution Scheme, or HECS. It had several revolutionary elements: universal availability, loan collection through the tax system, escalating payments based on income, and a threshold beneath which no payment was required (based, more or less as Friedman had suggested, on average industrial wages). Within a few years it had become evident that the HECS system was a success. It brought in more money for universities, which was invested back into Australia's higher education system in order to expand the number of students admitted. Student enrollment increased, and the enrollment of vulnerable populations (low-income students, aboriginal students) did not seem to decline.

Chapman demonstrated that it was possible to introduce tuition fees without affecting access and to do so in a financially stable way. Prior to the introduction in the mid- to late 1980s, enrollments were growing between 1 and 5 percent per year, and afterward, in the early 1990s, growth climbed to between 5 and 10 percent per year (fig. 5.1). In terms of distributional impact, research has tended to show that lower-income students fared about as well as everyone else under the new system—that is, the new students who came into the system both after 1988 and 1996 were drawn from more or less the same backgrounds as those who came before them.[18] As far as equality of opportunity was concerned, there was no negative effect of fees but no positive effect of increased enrollment either. The enrollment rates of both women and indigenous Australians increased faster than the population as a whole. This showed the potential for a system that combined tuition fees and income-contingent loans as a way to increase access—at least if the proceeds were reinvested directly into expansion.

FIGURE 5.1 Enrollments in tertiary education, Australia, 1985–1992

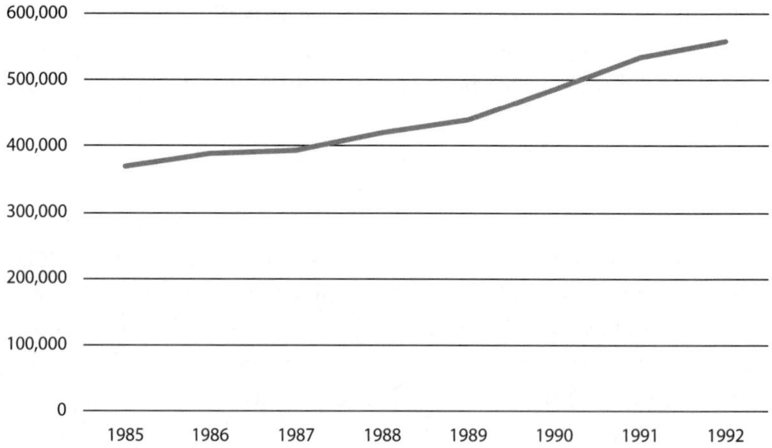

600,000
500,000
400,000
300,000
200,000
100,000
0
1985 1986 1987 1988 1989 1990 1991 1992

Source: National Report on Australia's Higher Education Sector, Department of Employment, Education, and Training, Commonwealth of Australia, 1993, http://www.voced.edu.au/content/ngv%3A6862.

In quick succession, other countries began to copy the Australian model. Sweden introduced income-contingent loans in 1989 as a method of repaying loans taken for living expenses (the introduction of income-contingent loans in Sweden had no relation to fee policy, and fees remain free to this day, though Sweden abandoned ICRs for a form of "graduated loan repayment" in the mid-2000s).[19] New Zealand introduced an income-contingent loan system with repayment through the tax system in 1992. In that same year, Bill Clinton was elected president partly on the strength of a promise to make income-contingent loans widely available. An ICR option for Stafford Loans was introduced in a limited way in the mid-1990s, but the number of students who chose to take advantage of these loans was low, and it would not be until the Obama era that major strides in the direction of income-based repayment were taken. South Africa and the UK also instituted ICRs in the 1990s.

The appeal of income-contingent loans was not restricted to the developed world. Rwanda tried to make an income-contingent system work in the 1990s, though it was found to be effectively impossible because of the lack of technology and the difficulty in implementing individual tax numbers by which individuals could be tracked over time (this remains an issue in much of the continent). In 2006 Thailand actually redesigned its entire tax system in order to enable the launch of an income-contingent loan system; then prime minister Thaksin Shinawatra, who had won power by offering cheap loans to farmers, reckoned he could win over troublesome urban voters by repeating the trick with students (the reform was abandoned after the military coup later that year).

In short, by the early 2010s income-contingent loans were a generally globalized phenomenon, though far from a uniform one. As they spread internationally, they mutated from country to country with no two programs quite alike. Some of the obvious areas where the programs differ are the minimum threshold to qualify for repayment, the percentage of income collected, and how the government collects the loan.

The Level of the Repayment Threshold

In Australia this level has tended to be set fairly high at or near the average wage. In the 2017–2018 school year, the threshold was about AUD 55,000 (roughly USD 47,500). For the 2018–2019 school year, policy makers lowered the repayment threshold to about AUD 52,000, and at the time of this writing serious consideration is being given to further lowering this figure in order to increase repayment rates. New Zealand is at the other extreme, with a threshold of slightly over NZD 19,000 (USD 13,000). In the UK the threshold has risen over time, mainly for political reasons. In effect, every time the UK government has raised tuition fees, it has also raised thresholds, presumably on the theory that one measure seen as being anti-student (higher fees) can be offset with one seen as pro-student (lower repayments after graduation). Currently the threshold in the UK sits at GBP 21,000 (roughly USD 28,000).

The Repayment Rate above the Threshold

In New Zealand student borrowers pay 12 percent of income above the repayment threshold, while in the UK the repayment rate is 9 percent of income above the threshold. Australia's system is somewhat more complicated for two reasons. First, it has multiple repayment rates, depending on a borrower's income (see table 7.1); and, second, these rates apply to all income, not just on marginal income above the threshold as in the UK and New Zealand. This creates some significant cliff effects in repayment, particularly at the point where repayments first kick in. For example, in 2017, a graduate earning AUD 55,873 (one dollar below the minimum threshold for that year) in Australia would not be obliged to make any contribution, while one earning AUD 55,874 would incur an obligation of AUD 2,234 annually (about USD 1,700), which is equivalent to 4 percent of his entire income.[20]

The combination of differing thresholds and repayment rates means that different income-contingent systems require varying levels of repayment effort from

FIGURE 5.2 Monthly student loan payment, by income level, assuming USD 20,000 debt

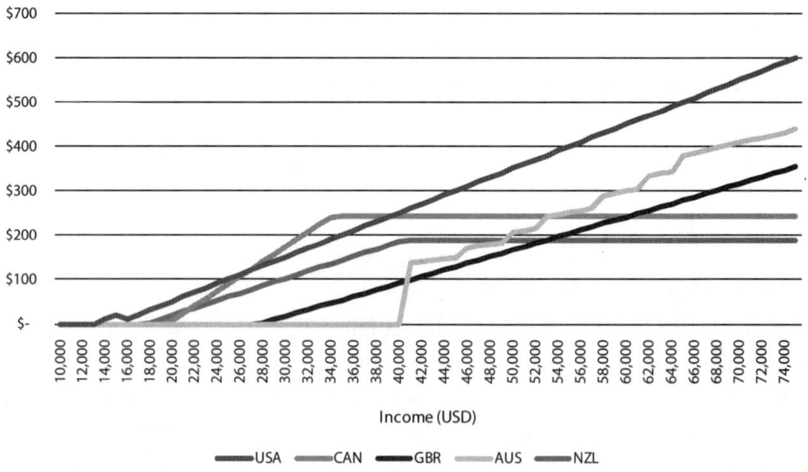

Source: Authors' calculations.

Note: Conversion rates were calculated using the May 2017 Federal Reserve exchange rates. Australia values are for the 2017-18 school year, prior to a reduction in the repayment thresholds.

different types of graduates. Figure 5.2 shows how thresholds and rates combine to create student loan repayment "curves" across the five Anglophone countries (the US, Canada, the UK, Australia, and New Zealand), all of which have either income-contingent or income-based loan programs. In effect, income-based repayment programs look very much like income-contingent ones until the point where the required payments reach the level that they would under a regular amortization schedule, at which point payments cease to be linked to income.

Figure 5.2 shows how large the difference is between the US, Canada, and New Zealand (where thresholds are relatively low), and the UK and Australia (where thresholds are relatively high). But the shape of the curve also tells a story. The UK and New Zealand have diagonal curves, reflecting the fact that their repayment is a simple percentage of income. Canada and the US look identical to the UK and New Zealand *until one reaches the point where mortgage-style amortization payments exceed the percentage of income.* This acts as a cap on monthly payments, which explains the straight lines. Australia represents a third type of curve, leaping upward from zero at the point of the threshold and then moving more or less diagonally thereafter.

Of potential interest here is the fact that income-contingent systems are considerably *more* onerous than non-income-contingent systems at higher rates of income. Figure 5.2 assumes a debt of USD 20,000 in both Canada and the US in order to draw a curve (no assumptions about debt size are necessary in the other three countries, because repayment is based exclusively on income). At that level of indebtedness, the United States actually has the least onerous repayment system once income rises above USD 55,000. At higher levels of debt, the point at which the US becomes the cheapest repayment system increases (if debt were USD 30,000, this phenomenon does not occur until income is in the low USD 60,000s).

Forgiveness Provisions

The third major area of variation is forgiveness provisions. Many loan systems have provisions to forgive loans after a certain number of years, meaning the government incurs the remaining balance of the loan. In Canada loan forgiveness occurs after fifteen years of payments, while in the US loan forgiveness occurs after twenty years, and only after thirty years in the UK.[21] In New Zealand and Australia loans are not forgiven and persist until the borrower's death.

Collection Mechanism

Finally, there is the issue of collection mechanisms. Australia, New Zealand, and the UK all use the tax system to collect their loans. This facet of their loan system is the one that seems to excite the most interest in the United States because of the undeniable efficiencies in loan recovery such a system provides, so it is worth delving into the administration in some detail. In all cases the ability of government to collect loans in this fashion is due to specific elements of tax system design that may not be available in other countries. For instance, in New Zealand individuals need not file annual income taxes provided all of their income has been taxed at source by an employer; as a result, the income-contingent loan system there is significantly more hassle-free than one that, for instance, was tied to the current US tax system. The final parts of this chapter take an in-depth look at how three specific countries—Australia, New Zealand, and the UK—operate their student loan programs.

LOAN COLLECTION IN AUSTRALIA

In the Australian system a fair bit of responsibility is placed on the individual taxpayer (as opposed to the employer) to ensure that he or she has the correct deductions for expenses such as student loans, child support, and superannuation. At the time a borrower begins a new job, she must declare to her employer that she has a student loan obligation. Because the employer already knows this person's salary, they can correctly code the size of the payroll deduction to make. But, importantly, the employer does not know automatically that the borrower has a loan; again, the onus is on the borrower to opt into loan repayment. Similarly, if a borrower has two jobs, neither of which on their own totals more than the minimum income threshold for loan repayments but when taken together exceed the earnings threshold, it is up to the individual to work out with one or the other employer to deduct an amount that is sufficient to pay the joint liability under both jobs. If a borrower fails to do this correctly, the government will notify the employee when it is time to file annual income taxes, at which time that borrower will owe the missed payments and possibly a penalty. It is also a borrower's responsibility to tell the employer to stop payroll deductions once her HECS obligation is finally paid off.

The Australian system is also facilitated by the country's relatively comprehensive tax tracking system. The Australian Taxation Office (ATO) can keep track of individual HECS accounts because employers must provide a detailed accounting either monthly or quarterly (depending on the size of the corporation) to ATO regarding every individual on their payroll. For each individual, the amount paid, the amount of tax withheld, and the amount of student loan withheld are all itemized. This means that changes to a student's loan balance can be reflected on a monthly or quarterly basis. Note that this process is separate from the process of remitting payroll taxes, which occurs every two weeks. The US tax collection system does not track nearly that level of detail, and most information is collected only once per year, during the tax filing season, many months after the calendar year closes.

Until 2001, HECS payments were managed by borrowers themselves without employer involvement. Payments were withheld as a surcharge that individuals calculated and paid upon filing an annual tax return. The annual return is still used to verify that regular source deductions have been made in the correct amount and to collect data on and receive payment for nonwage sources of income, such as self-employment or rental income. Self-employed borrowers have the option to make quarterly payments, but most prefer to pay annually, as this gives them more flexibility in managing their income across the fiscal year.

LOAN COLLECTION IN NEW ZEALAND

In New Zealand student loans are disbursed by Studylink, which is an arm's-length government agency that manages student financial aid. However, collection is done by New Zealand Inland Revenue.

All New Zealand taxpayers have an individual online account with Inland Revenue known as MyIR. The government manages a number of programs and services for individuals through these accounts—not only individual income taxes and student loans but also child support and the Working for Families tax benefit. This is the portal through which all of the student loan management takes place.

The repayment threshold in New Zealand is currently NZD 19,084 a year, or NZD 367 per week (roughly USD 13,328, or USD 256 per week). New Zealand does not make a distinction between "in-study" and post-study periods. The basic assumption is that everyone who has a loan, regardless of study status, is repaying a loan. At the time a borrower begins a new job, they must declare to the employer that they have a student loan on special form. If they expect to earn more than the repayment threshold, then they must tick the "SL" tax code, the consequence of which is that the employer will withhold 12 percent of all income over NZD 367 per week. Individuals who earn more than NZD 367 per week for a period of time but do not expect to earn more than NZD19,084 that year need to file for a deduction exemption; individuals not earning NZD 367 per week are not obliged to tick the SL tax code.

Complications arise for borrowers who have more than one source of income. To deal with this, individuals file different forms for their primary and secondary jobs (the primary job is the one that provides the greater income; all other jobs are considered secondary). For the primary job, the borrower pays 12 percent on the fraction (if any) that is above the weekly repayment threshold (NZD 367); for the second job, the 12 percent threshold is applied from the first dollar. In some cases this will result in borrowers paying more than their "correct" amount (for example, if one job pays NZD 11,000 and the other NZD 9,000, the "correct" repayment would be around NZD 100, but the actual deduction would be just over NZD 1,000). In such cases there is no "squaring up" at the end of the year, as the administration of dealing with this type of complication is simply too burdensome. Overpayments are credited to the loan as early repayments.

Inland Revenue can keep track of individual accounts because employers must provide a monthly accounting about every individual on their payroll. For each individual, the amount paid, the amount of tax withheld, and the amount of student loan withheld are all itemized for each individual. This means that changes to a student's loan balance can be reflected on a monthly basis, and borrowers can track this on a real-time basis in their MyIR account. Again, this is far more comprehensive and timely tracking of information than what the US tax system is currently set up to provide the government.

In fact, the New Zealand reporting system is so advanced that the government has a nearly real-time record of everyone's income and payroll deductions, and annual income tax returns are not necessary in New Zealand unless a taxpayer earns nonwage income. Roughly 20 percent of borrowers have some other source of income, be it rent, self-employment income, inheritance, or other sources. These borrowers must use the annual income tax return to report such income and pay the 12 percent of that income toward their student loans as well.

LOAN COLLECTION IN THE UNITED KINGDOM

The UK system shares a great deal in common with the New Zealand and Australian systems. As in the New Zealand loan system, money is disbursed partly to the institution and partly to the individual. Repayment begins only in the tax year following the year the borrower ended their studies.

Loan repayment calculation and administration in the UK is fairly similar to that in New Zealand, with the complication that management of the account is split between Her Majesty's Revenue and Customs (HMRC) and the Student Loan Company (SLC). The repayment rate of loans issued since 2012 is 9 percent of income over GBP 21,000 (for pre-2012 loans the threshold is GBP 17,450). Provided a borrower has only one loan (either a pre-2012 or a post-2012 loan), the calculation for employers is simple: they simply withhold anything over GBP 404 per week, or GBP 1,750 per month depending on payroll frequency (about USD 550 and USD 2,400, respectively). It gets more complicated for borrowers with loans from both time periods because of the different repayment thresholds, as the resulting blended rate depends on the mix of debt from the two time periods. This situation requires a fair amount of manual intervention. HMRC will actually contact each employer to give them the proper deduction code for that individual.

Borrowers must inform their employers about their loan status and request deductions. However, HMRC also receives regular data transfers from the SLC on the identity of borrowers and matches this with individuals' National Insurance numbers from payroll reporting and will contact employers to make sure they are correctly deducting pay. As in Australia and New Zealand, the end-of-year self-assessment tax return is used to capture income from no-wage employment and assess liability for extra payments. Borrowers may also make extra payments voluntarily by setting up an online account with the Student Loan Company, which can then direct-debit the individual's bank account.

Through this method, HMRC and SLC estimate that they have contact with 88.7 percent of the eligible borrowing population (75.4 percent in repayment,

13.3 percent awaiting a first tax return). Of the remainder, 2 percent are considered to be not paying or in arrears (these are nearly entirely borrowers who have moved abroad), and 9.3 percent are considered "unverified." Some of these "unverified" borrowers may be unemployed, some may simply not be filing tax returns, and a few are suspected of being outside the UK.[22] A key point to underline here is that repayment under an income-contingent loan system is only as good as the reach of the tax system on which it is based. To the extent borrowers leave the country or avoid filing taxes, there will be "defaults" in ICR systems just as there are in "mortgage-style" systems.

CONCLUSION

The foregoing discussion allows us to look at the United States' system of student assistance in global perspective. In terms of differences at the front end—such as caps on borrowing limits, eligibility criteria, and need-based assessment policies—the US system is overall more generous than most systems abroad, having among the fewest restrictions on borrowing and among the highest borrowing limits (which in turn leads to higher levels of average debt). At the back end the US uses a loan repayment system that is less technically efficient than the tax-based systems used in Australia, New Zealand, and the UK, but this does not necessarily mean the system is more financially burdensome for students. In fact, the average level of graduate student debt in the US requires one of the lowest repayment rates of any major student loan system.

Looking at loan systems globally, it is difficult to come up with a single one that captures all the various policies influencing the front end and back end of loan programs. The much vaunted ICR loan programs of Australia, the UK, and New Zealand differ from one another in important areas (for instance, whether the loan covers living expenses) and at the same time share significant program features with other systems that are not considered ICR. In large part this reflects the fact that few loan programs are ever redesigned from the ground up but rather represent an accretion of program tweaks concocted over various points in time in response to different policy pressures. New Zealand, for instance, has a system that is quite generous by many measures at the front end but among the least generous on the back end. The German loan system arguably is the reverse. Possibly, these examples are the result of deliberate trade-offs, but for other countries the case is not quite so clear.

One final note is perhaps worth underlining: specific elements of national student aid systems may seem intriguing and beneficial, but they are often difficult to transpose from one country to another. Policies tend to be embedded in larger and more complex systems and may not translate well from one system to another. It is worthwhile to examine other systems to learn about their strengths and weaknesses and, in doing so, learn about one's own system as well. But the larger goal, correctly, is to learn about the implicit trade-offs involved in policy making rather than to engage in cherry-picking policies from potentially incompatible systems.

PART 2

Case Studies: Lessons from Individual Countries

CHAPTER 6

Chile: The Challenges of Free College

Andrés Bernasconi

In the wake of the massive student protests of 2011 against market-based education policies, Chilean presidential candidate Michelle Bachelet proposed in 2013 to make higher education tuition-free (*gratuidad* in Spanish) for all students from families in the bottom 70 percent of the country's income distribution. President Bachelet won the election based partly on that proposal, which she made great strides in achieving during her 2014–2018 term, reaching students up to the bottom 60 percent of income. There are also plans to expand free tuition to all students regardless of family income, contingent upon expected increases in tax revenue over the next decades.

Through government-issued scholarships and subsidized loans, some 50 percent of all Chilean higher education students, overwhelmingly from the lower half of the family income distribution, received total or partial financial aid before gratuidad was first introduced in 2016. About half received scholarships and half obtained subsidized loans. Therefore, the free tuition policy mostly replaced other forms of government aid rather than provide a completely new benefit for previously unaided segments of the population.

The government promoted the free tuition policy not as a measure to increase access or foster equality but as an expression of higher education as a right for the people. In the view of the policy's supporters, if higher education is a right, no economic barriers should impede access to it.

The sheer magnitude of the cost of the free tuition policy initially offered by candidate Bachelet, combined with a downturn in the Chilean economy, made the campaign pledge financially unviable. In response, the government reduced the scope of the program in a number of ways but still claimed to have achieved the free tuition policy.

In 2016, its first year of application, the policy reached 139,885 students, or just 12 percent of overall enrollment. It was limited to students from the bottom 50 percent of the income distribution among those enrolled in higher education. Since free tuition is seen as a right among its supporters, and not a government handout, all students who meet the income criterion receive the benefit. Free college was afforded to those students from thirty eligible universities, defined by accord between the executive branch and Congress, through an amendment to the 2016 budget bill. The set of eligible institutions was expanded in 2017 to include twelve vocational and technical schools, which reached an additional 143,637 new beneficiaries as of June 14, 2017, bringing the number of students covered by gratuidad to 22 percent of total undergraduate enrollments.[1] The cost of free tuition for these students now represents 47 percent of the budget for all financial aid benefits provided by the government to higher education students. The remaining amounts pay for scholarships and loans to students in institutions not participating in gratuidad and those who are above the income cutoff for the program.

The cost of gratuidad for 2017 was USD 1.17 billion (CLP 750 billion) and was projected to increase by an estimated USD 300 million (about CLP 200 billion) in 2018 as the benefit extended upward to those in the sixth decile of family incomes.[2] These costs are partially offset by cuts in other scholarship and loan programs that free tuition replaces. With these offsets, the Ministry of Finance estimates the net increase in spending on higher education to be some USD 300 million in 2017 and USD 485 million in 2018, or 0.2 percent of Chile's gross domestic product (GDP).[3] If free tuition were available to Chilean students from all income levels, the net additional cost would be USD 3.1 billion (CLP 2 trillion), the equivalent of 1.4 percent of Chile's GDP.

This chapter describes how tuition-free higher education emerged as a popular proposal in Chile and how it evolved into its current form. It concludes with a discussion of the trade-offs involved in implementing and sustaining the tuition-free policy.

OVERVIEW OF HIGHER EDUCATION IN CHILE

Chilean higher education took its current shape during the dictatorship of General Augusto Pinochet (1973–1990). The military regime opted for expanding access to higher education through private institutions and introduced tuition fees at public universities.[4] It also introduced two new categories of technical and vocational institutions of higher education in addition to universities: professional institutes and technical training centers.[5] These would offer two-year technical programs, similar to an associate's degree in the US, and four-year degrees in professional applied fields not requiring a grounding in basic science or general education.

Private universities in Chile are required to be nonprofit charitable organizations, while professional institutes and technical training centers can be either for-profit or nonprofit. The rationale behind the difference between universities, professional institutes, and technical training centers with regard to their profit-seeking status was that new private universities would be few and far between and would most likely be established by philanthropists, churches, scientific societies, and other organizations not interested in the business possibilities of education. That had been the case with the only six private universities created since 1888, three of which were established by the Catholic Church. The vocational and technical sector, on the other hand, needed the opportunity to earn profits, which would entice entrepreneurs, allow them to raise capital in the markets, and help finance the desired expansion of enrollments.

Reality thwarted expectations, though. By 1993, 44 new private universities had opened in addition to 218 professional institutes and technical training centers.[6] Most new universities were founded by entrepreneurs, who devised numerous ways to circumvent the prohibition on profits by setting up shell companies that provided services to the universities. This high rate of expansion in the number of institutions was aided by very low regulatory barriers to entry. A university could start with one degree program, in rented space, and with only part-time teachers in the faculty.

Chile now has sixty-two universities (eighteen public, forty-four private), forty-three professional institutes (all private and most of them for-profit), and fifty-four technical training centers (all private and almost all for-profit).[7] Fifteen new public technical training centers were established by an act of Congress in 2016 but are not operating yet.[8]

Tuition for postsecondary education in Chile is among the highest in the world, currently around USD 7,600 on average at public universities (see fig. 6.1).[9] If one looks at the average tuition alone—the sticker price that universities advertise—the price of higher education is equivalent to approximately half of median family income in Chile.[10] Only American private universities and British universities have higher sticker prices relative to per capita gross national product.[11] However, this sticker price does not consider the large amount of government grants and available scholarship aid, which can significantly reduce the net price that students pay.

Tuition discounts are offered at the university level in the form of scholarships, and together with grants from the government, this aid can cover most or

FIGURE 6.1 Average annual tuition for full-time bachelor's degree students at public and private universities

	Public	Private
Chile	$7,654	$7,156
U.S.	$8,202	$21,189

US dollars (converted using PPP)

Source: OECD, Education at a Glance 2017: OECD Indicators, Table B5.1, www.oecd-ilibrary.org/docserver/download/9617041e.pdf?expires=1520434273&id=id&accname=guest&checksum=F822EC2FC38E8C397141DDB258EA9BDE.

all fees for students with low and middle incomes. The average scholarship for low-income students covers between 63 and 70 percent of actual tuition costs.[12] In addition to grants, government-backed student loans are also available, which allow students to borrow for almost the entire cost of tuition and feature below-market interest rates, income-based repayment terms, and loan forgiveness after a certain number of payments. However, student loans in Chile cannot be used for cost-of-living expenses. The scholarships are generally available to students from the four lowest income quintiles, with most scholarships limited to students from the lowest two quintiles (see fig. 6.2). Overall, about half of all undergraduate students received financial aid in the form of scholarships or loans before gratuidad was introduced in 2016.[13]

Given the sharp rise in the number of operating universities, the government introduced an accreditation system in 2006. It is voluntary for institutions of higher education, but only students attending accredited institutions are eligible for government financial aid, including gratuidad. Institutions need to seek accreditation every two to seven years, depending on the degree of fulfillment of the evaluation criteria. The different accreditation periods serve as a proxy for a

FIGURE 6.2 Distribution of Chilean government-issued scholarships by income group in 2015 for 4- and 5-year programs

	Quintile				
	20% Poorest	*2nd*	*3rd*	*4th*	*20% Wealthiest*
Percentage of Total Scholarships	22%	35%	30%	12%	0%

Source: Alonso Bucarey, "Who Pays for Free College? Crowding Out on Campus," Table 14 (Job market paper, Massachusetts Institute of Technology, Cambridge, Massachusetts, 2018), http://economics.mit.edu/files/14234.

Note: Percentages do not sum to 100% due to rounding.

ranking of quality, often used by public policy to target programs to institutions with longer periods of accreditation, which are seen as being of higher quality.

Today, together with South Korea and Japan, Chile is one of the few countries worldwide with a greater proportion of students enrolled in private institutions than public ones (85 percent). Among Organisation for Economic Cooperation and Development (OECD) member countries, governments typically cover about two-thirds of higher education costs, with students and private entities funding the rest. The funding structure in Chile is inverted, meaning the government covers 37.5 percent of the overall cost of higher education, and tuition payments cover most of the remainder.[14]

THE COUNCIL OF RECTORS

An idiosyncratic feature of Chile's higher education system is the Council of Rectors, which plays a role in the free tuition policy. The Council of Rectors of Chilean Universities (CRUCh, by its acronym in Spanish) is an advisory board to the country's minister of education. It is also supposed to facilitate coordination among members, a role that is mostly moot given the free-for-all competition among institutions that escalated as a result of the reforms of the 1980s.

The Council of Rectors was established in 1954 at a time when only seven universities existed, two of which were public and five private. Another private university joined the council in 1956, the year of its foundation. From then on, no new universities were established until the reforms of 1980 and the ensuing outburst of new private institutions, but these were left out of membership in the council. An exception to the closed membership of the council was made to include former branch campuses from council member universities acquiring autonomy between 1981 and 1992 and for two new state universities created in

2016. Today eighteen state universities and nine private ones make up the council. Chile's other thirty-five private universities are not members. Only CRUCh members can receive direct subsidies and funding for operational expenses from the government.

THE 2011 STUDENT MOVEMENT AND ITS AFTERMATH

President Sebastián Piñera was elected in 2010 becoming the first right-of-center president in Chile since the dictatorship of General Pinochet. A year after Piñera's election, Chilean students demonstrated massively against what they called the "marketization" of the higher education system. In their view, this "commodified" education consisted of expensive tuition and high student debt, profiteering, concentration of enrollments in the private sector, and abandonment by the government of public education generally.[15]

This was not the first organized expression of student dissatisfaction. Equally massive street demonstrations had occurred in 2006, with a similar agenda but more modest results, while other small demonstrations focusing on human rights dotted the final part of the Pinochet years.[16] Student unrest remained and shifted focus to denouncing insufficient financial aid throughout the two decades following the return to democracy in 1990. There were yearly or biennial outbursts of coordinated student mobilization across the country, but free tuition had never been part of their agenda before.

The student movement made four main demands throughout 2011. First, they called for greater equality of access to higher education, especially for lower-income families. This, they argued, would be achieved by abolishing tuition, first for students in the lower 70 percent of family income, in order to eventually reach universal gratuidad. In the meantime, they demanded that the government increase subsidies on loans, curb tuition increases, and allocate financial aid based on need, not merit. Second, they demanded an expansion of enrollment of the public sector in education at all levels and the creation of more state colleges and universities. Third, they wanted increased government regulation to limit profiteering and poor quality private institutions. Finally, students demanded participation in governance structures within universities themselves.[17]

The students' demand for gratuidad, which until then had remained a rather utopian idea, was grounded on a corpus of philosophical and social policy ideas that were widely disseminated among student leaders, left-of-center politicians, and some engaged academics. This doctrine, elaborated in a series of works by Fernando Atria, a legal scholar, required abolition of payments as a condition of a new citizenship—one that was expunged of market-based rationales and based, instead, on the notion that education is a social right and should not require payment.[18] The model he pointed to was England's National Health Service, which is free at the point of use and funded through taxation. These ideas served to contest the very concrete problem of student indebtedness with lofty categories of social justice and common good.

Thus, gratuidad became part of an intellectual movement linking it to fundamental values of social justice and equality. It took on an air of necessity to overcome what critics claimed were "neoliberal" structures in education—educational institutions operating in markets, privately funded, and regulated mostly through competition. Free tuition was justified not primarily as a policy to increase access to higher education but as a moral obligation that would bring about a more just society. It therefore had to be universal, not means-tested: there could not be market education for some and a social-right education for others. Free higher education for all became a sort of symbol and standard of the transformations required to undo the educational legacy of the Pinochet regime.

President Piñera did not agree to abolish tuition fees, but in a nod to the student protests, he greatly expanded scholarships and increased benefits in the loan program by adopting an "income-contingent" design. Under these 2011 reforms, payments on student loans are capped at 10 percent of a borrower's income, and any outstanding balance is forgiven after twenty years of payments. Piñera also reduced the interest rate on the loans to 2 percent.

The idea of free tuition had gained political momentum among those committed to challenging market-based policies. In the 2013 presidential campaign, free higher education became a central pledge of then candidate Michelle Bachelet (Socialist Party), together with a tax reform intended to raise the funds necessary to finance the program. It was both a symbol and a concrete expression for the overarching theme of ending the market-based structure of Chilean education. Ms. Bachelet's government plan described the proposal in the following terms:

> To make progress towards universal and effective gratuidad in higher education, in a six-year process, reaching during the coming presidential term all students belonging to the 70 percent most vulnerable among the population.[19] This elimination of tuition will be available in institutions of higher education meeting, among others, the following requisites: to be accredited, abide strictly by the norms forbidding profit-making, and observe the tuition caps determined by the Ministry of Education.[20]
>
> Gratuidad shall be effective, for all state universities and those private ones adhering by contract to public funding (committing to end profits, mandatory

> accreditation, tuition caps, remedial and support programs for students) won't be able to charge fees different from those determined by the Ministry. To set tuition fees, a new organization will be created, which will include a group of experts in charge of determining and periodically reviewing those fees.[21]

In other words, the first stage of the proposal would reach all students in the lowest 70 percent of family income. That target was to be achieved during the 2014–2018 presidential term. Universal free tuition for students of all families, regardless of income, was to be reached in 2020. The extent to which this plan was vetted by public finance specialists in the campaign team is unknown, but some calculations must have been done, since Ms. Bachelet's government included an estimate of the overall costs of all her proposed measures. Michelle Bachelet was elected with 62 percent of the vote in 2013 and won comfortable majorities for her coalition in both houses of Congress, which was understood by the political establishment as a firm endorsement of her policy agenda, including gratuidad. However, the schedule for universal free higher education that was ultimately presented to Congress, as explained below, greatly exceeded the goal set in the proposal and made the path toward universal abolition of tuition dependent on increases in tax revenues that were contingent on growth in Chile's GDP.

ECONOMIC CONDITIONS AND GRATUIDAD

The Bachelet administration spent its first year enacting tax reform. The aim was to increase tax revenue by 3 percent of Chile's GDP (a total of USD 2.4 billion) in order to fund the administration's policy initiatives, gratuidad among them.[22] The tax plan was expected to bring in USD 8.2 billion more in revenue in 2013 (about CLP 5.24 trillion). By 2016, however, a downturn in the economy cut the actual figure in half. The president, however, was keen on delivering her campaign promise. She used her state of the nation address in May 2015 to pledge that gratuidad would begin in 2016. President Bachelet said:

> Oftentimes scholarships do not cover tuition entirely, and our most vulnerable and middle-class youth end up deep in debt to cover the difference. . . . Beginning in 2016 we shall guarantee that the 60 percent most vulnerable attending accredited and nonprofit technical training centers and professional institutes, or university members of the Council of Rectors, will have complete and effective exemption of fees, without loans or scholarships.[23] This will benefit almost 264 thousand youths. [24]

However, the government had not finished drafting its higher education reform bill in time to meet that pledge and instead added a rider to the 2016 budget that would create an initial form of tuition-free status for some students at some institutions. These riders (*glosas* in Spanish, which are literally footnotes to the regular budget lines) had been used before to introduce small new spending programs within a larger budget category of expenditures. Opponents of gratuidad, however, claimed that introducing such a significant new funding system via footnote and valid for only one budget year was irresponsible and possibly unconstitutional.

But the Bachelet government would have to come up with more workarounds than this legislative trick to enact gratuidad. The Ministry of Finance calculated that free tuition for all would cost CLP 2.1 (USD 3.3 billion) per year, an amount deemed unattainable given the level of economic growth and tax revenue at the time. Moreover, the price of copper, a significant source of investment and tax revenues for Chile, had fallen by 50 percent between 2012 and late 2015. At the same time, economic growth slowed to its lowest level in five years. The ministry also argued that most countries with free tuition policies had higher fiscal revenues as a proportion of GDP, compared to Chile's 23.5 percent, making it easier for them to finance such policies.[25]

In the end, the ideal of universal free tuition was no match for fiscal realities. Means-testing the benefit seemed the only way to enact the policy with the available revenue, so the Bachelet government reshaped the plan to apply only to students in the lower 50 percent of the family income distribution for the first two years.

The government had the congressional majority to approve the gratuidad rider, and it passed together with the broader budget bill in late 2015. The limitations the government agreed to place on the policy clearly reduced the size of the program. The final cost came in at a fraction of the original proposal, just CLP 536 billion for 2016 (roughly USD 840 million), and that cost was partially offset by cuts to the scholarship and loan programs that gratuidad was meant to replace.[26]

THE DEBATE OVER WHICH INSTITUTIONS SHOULD QUALIFY

As approved by Congress, students eligible for gratuidad included freshmen and higher division students who matriculated into eligible institutions. These institutions were all of the sixteen public universities then in operation plus the nine private universities that belong to CRUCh. Private universities not in the Council of Rectors had to have an accreditation of four or more years to qualify for gratuidad. Additionally, they had to meet a governance requirement that student or administrative staff participate in their governing bodies. In order to exclude universities suspected of exacting earnings through a loophole in the law governing charitable organizations, eligible universities could not have any for-profit entities as members or associates.

Lastly, eligible technical training centers and professional institutes, all of which are private, had to be organized as nonprofit charitable foundations or associations and have an accreditation of no less than four years. Bear in mind that, unlike universities, professional institutes and technical training centers can be legally organized as for-profit companies. Excluding some of them from gratuidad because their legal for-profit status seemed to be discriminatory and was challenged in the legal dispute soon to follow. Excluding them, however, was in line with a principle that government officials and President Bachelet herself had often voiced: no entity should earn profits with public money.[27] In a July 2014 statement to the press, confirming the intention of the government to advance toward gratuidad, she put it this way: "Another principle in the reform is to end profit making with public money. There aren't two opinions on this: a good education is not achieved by turning a profit with public moneys intended to improve the education of all boys and girls. Public resources have to be targeted to the learning of boys and girls."[28]

This statement was directed toward several parties: for-profit elementary and secondary schools funded through government vouchers for their students, for-profit professional institutes and technical training centers, and universities that were effectively violating their nonprofit status by using questionable contracts with companies owned by the universities' proprietors. All were accused of sustaining poor-quality businesses through the state-provided financial aid that their students received, akin to the charge often made against for-profit universities in US higher education.

Universities in the Council of Rectors were spared the requirements imposed on other institutions, which included the four-year accreditation standard (three of them would not have met this requirement at the time), the participatory governance requirement, and the exclusion-of-profits clause. All for-profit professional institutions and technical training centers were excluded from gratuidad despite being organized in a form that Chilean law permits. Why did the Bachelet government carve out the shape of its free tuition policy in such an irregular manner? It is likely that this was another convenient way to trim the cost of the program—the number of beneficiaries would be matched to the available money by limiting the number of institutions that could participate. Limiting institutions rather than students was important to this end, because participating institutions could not themselves limit enrollment. On the contrary, they were required to enroll as many students as available resources could support.

Different eligibility conditions for certain types of institutions raised constitutional objections from the opposition in Congress. They challenged its constitutionality before the Constitutional Court on procedural grounds (the use of the *glosa* mechanism instead of a permanent law) and on substantive grounds: discrimination. The charge of arbitrary discrimination was sustained by the court in a late 2015 ruling, which declared that requiring an accreditation threshold for private universities who were not members of the Council of Rectors, as well as for technical training centers and professional institutes, but not requiring it for private and state universities who *were* council members violated standards of justification of differential treatment. If a certain number of years of accreditation was a safeguard for quality, it had to be applied evenly.[29] The court also found the student governance provision to be unwarranted, for it bore no relationship to the quality of the institution or the needs of the students—likewise for the requirements regarding nonprofit status or composition of the members of the institution. The court did not object, however, to the *glosa* mechanism to legislate gratuidad.

The ruling wrecked gratuidad as it was designed and budgeted for 2016. It undid all of the fiddling to limit the number of institutions that could participate. Dropping the four-year accreditation threshold as the court required would mean that all for-profit institutions could participate, increasing eligible institutions from about 30 to all 157 higher education institutions. These institutions could thus receive government funding for all students in the bottom half of the income distribution enrolled in their institutions (which account for 47 percent of overall higher education enrollment) so long as they waived their tuition.[30]

In response to this setback for the president's signature proposal, the Ministries of Finance and Education rushed an amendment to the 2016 budget through Congress to correct some of the discriminatory provisions and reduce the cost of the program. This "Short Tuition Free Act" was enacted by late 2015.[31] Had this new legislation been challenged in court, it too would likely have been struck down, but it wasn't challenged. The government reached an agreement with the opposition, and since the court can act only if called upon by members of Congress, the Short Tuition Free Act was unopposed. The law was good news for everyone's constituencies.

The compromise legislation maintained the different accreditation requirements for state universities and private ones, kept the exclusion of for-profit providers, and eliminated the governance provision. Professional institutes and technical training centers were excluded from free tuition for 2016 but offered assurances that they would be included in 2017, which the government eventually followed through on.[32] Professional institutes and technical training centers largely enroll the neediest students in Chile: 55 percent of their students are in the 50th percentile of family income or below. It is therefore an ironic effect of the compromise plan that they were omitted from gratuidad. This was facilitated by the lack of political clout of the technical and vocational sector vis-á-vis universities. Additionally, the issue of profits divided the sector between the nonprofits and the for-profits: the government was troubled by the prospect of directing funding to the latter, not to the former. Finally, professional institutes and technical training centers were compensated in the budget for 2016 with greater funding for scholarships, regardless of their juridical status, but would have to wait until 2017 to be included in gratuidad.

Gratuidad had an immediate political payoff for President Bachelet's government. A national poll conducted in January 2016 shows that for the first time since mid-2014 a majority of Chileans (54 percent) support the educational reforms in the government's agenda. Bachelet's approval rating, in turn, rose four points, and the minister of education's rating rose nine points. Poll numbers also indicate that support is higher among lower-income respondents.[33] However, the rationale for universal free tuition seems to have been a tougher sell: by mid-2016, 68 percent of respondents in a national poll were against *universal* free tuition, preferring coverage only for students from families in the bottom 70 percent of the income distribution.[34]

To sum up, the final version of gratuidad enacted in 2016 provided USD 810 million (about CLP 518 billion) in funding to enable free higher education for incoming freshmen and already enrolled students whose families belong to the bottom half of the income distribution among higher education students. On average, these families earn less than USD 250 per person per month. Eligible students must be enrolled in state universities or in private universities that have chosen to take part in the program. All public universities are required to adhere to gratuidad. With respect to private universities and gratuidad, only those operating as nonprofits, with at least four years of accreditation, can participate. Students enrolled at nonparticipating institutions, or those enrolled in participating institutions who are above the income threshold for gratuidad, can still apply for government scholarships and receive a government-backed subsidized loan. There is one final caveat to the program. Free tuition is provided only for the stated duration of an educational program—that is, for the number of years of study outlined in the curriculum of each program. In practice, however, time to degree for Chilean students in associate's degree programs is 50 percent longer than the study plans indicate. In professional programs, which officially last four to five years, students typically take between 10 and 30 percent longer than expected, depending on the complexity of the program.[35] The current regulation for gratuidad has made no arrangements for funding this excess of study time. This is obviously a political and financial time bomb.

GRATUIDAD'S LIMITED REACH

In 2016, its initial year, thirty universities out of the sixty operating in Chile participated in the gratuidad program, and only students in the lower 50 percent of the income distribution were eligible for gratuidad. As a result, about 140,000 students benefited from the program.[36] This was below the target of 160,000 expected by the Ministry of Education.

At least three eligible private universities opted not to participate.[37] These universities charge high tuition and enroll students from wealthier families, making few of their students eligible for gratuidad. Moreover, these institutions have the largest gap between the tuition they charge and the limit they would have to adhere to under gratuidad. Therefore, gratuidad's prohibition on charging students more than the tuition cap would have had a significant financial impact on their budgets.

Because of gratuidad's limiting provisions, the first year of the program reached just 12 percent of undergraduate students. Its impact in terms of increasing educational opportunity also appears minor. According to ministry data, 87 percent of students in upper courses already had financial aid in 2015 (some of it only partial if tuition was higher than the loan or scholarship cap) and exchanged it for free tuition in 2016. The remaining 13 percent had no prior assistance. In the case of freshmen, analyses by the Ministry of Education show that 15 percent of entrants in 2016 would not have enrolled under the prior financial aid scheme, meaning gratuidad made a decisive difference for this group.

This, of course, underscores the substitution effect among students. Those in the lower 50 percent of the income distribution were already entitled to financial aid. Those who were not already receiving aid had been excluded by the academic standing requirements for government scholarships and loans, such as minimum scores on the university entrance selection test or a minimum high school GPA. Gratuidad, however, is unconditionally offered to students at qualifying institutions. There are no academic performance standards beyond the criteria set by the university itself for admission. Given that some participating universities have admission standards below those required by the loan and scholarship programs, the students who matriculated into those institutions gained the most from gratuidad. This argument is borne out by the data on the distribution of beneficiaries across participating universities. The three institutions that enrolled the most gratuidad students are the least selective of the thirty participating universities, and most of their students would not have had access to other forms of financial aid, because they would not meet the academic standards.[38] From the perspective of the government, substitution is not problematic. Nor is the size of the program's effect on increasing access. Instead, gratuidad is a matter of principle: if education is a right of citizenship, it should be free of charge for the student "at the point of use."

A new round of funding for gratuidad came during the budget debate in 2017.[39] This time the government had learned the lessons of the previous year and preemptively reached an agreement with the opposition that left the bill out of reach of the Constitutional Court. There were no changes to student eligibility rules, accreditation requirements, or the exclusion of institutions with for-profit structures. A new provision allowed professional institutes and technical training centers that had been accredited for four or more years to participate. These institutions had to be organized as nonprofits or formally commit to transform into a nonprofit entity during 2017.

By May 2017 free tuition had grown to cover 22 percent of total undergraduate enrollment. Professional institutes and technical training centers, participating in the program for the first time in 2017, accounted for 35.6 percent of the beneficiaries, while universities accounted for the rest. Still, the enrollment figures fell nine thousand students short of the expectation in the ministry that some one hundred thousand of the newly eligible students in professional institutes and technical training centers would be using gratuidad.[40] In its third year, 2018, the program intends to expand to include students in the lower 60 percent of the family income distribution.

The last act in the implementation of free tuition was the approval by Congress, in January 2018, of the higher education reform bill, which includes a schedule toward universal gratuidad that would add to the program students in the seventh to tenth income decile stepwise depending on predefined thresholds ("triggers") of tax revenue as a proportion of Chile's GDP. Whether these expansions will materialize depends on future increases in fiscal revenue.

DILEMMAS AND TRADE-OFFS

While participating in gratuidad is obligatory for state universities, it is optional for private universities, professional institutes, and technical training centers. If they opt in, they receive funding from the government but must abide by all of gratuidad's rules. While all sixteen state universities participated in 2016, and two new ones joined in 2017, only fourteen of the forty-four private universities in Chile chose to do so as of the end of 2017. The rest of the private universities either decided not to join or were ineligible because they had not been accredited for at least four years or had for-profit controllers. There are also six professional institutes and six technical training centers participating.[41]

Crowding Out Low-Income Students

Advocates for gratuidad usually argue that free tuition would allow more low-income students to enroll in college. While the Ministry of Education purports that access has increased, an independent study suggests that the policy risks producing the opposite effect for low-income students.[42]

The research suggests that expanding scholarship eligibility to students from families with middle-class incomes in 2012 (four years prior to gratuidad) prompted universities to become more selective and admit students with higher test scores. Lower-income students tend to have lower scores and were thus crowded out of more selective universities that they would have been admitted to before the expansion in scholarship aid. Those slots went to middle-income students who were newly eligible for aid and also tended to have higher scores.

If the program is fully phased in to cover all students regardless of income, Chile should expect a 20 percent decline in the number of low-income students who enroll in universities relative to the number enrolled before gratuidad as upper-income students crowd them out of the admission process.

Gratuidad Supplants Existing Student Aid

According to the Chilean Ministry of Education, 87 percent of non-first-year students who received gratuidad in 2016 already received some form of government-issued financial aid in 2015, meaning just 13 percent had no prior assistance. Before gratuidad, students from families in the lower half of the income distribution qualified for scholarships and loans. Some of those students received subsidized loans that they may have needed to fully repay or grants and scholarships that only partially covered their tuition expenses. In that regard, gratuidad increased aid for those students. However, the OECD and the World Bank estimate that the average scholarship award for low-income students covered between 63 and 70 percent of the actual cost of tuition fees in the years before gratuidad.[43] This underscores that gratuidad has mostly supplanted existing forms of student aid.

Nevertheless, students who had been ineligible for scholarships prior to gratuidad because they did not meet the academic requirements gained significant amounts of aid. Gratuidad does not include any merit requirements. There are no academic performance standards beyond the criteria set by the university itself for admission.

Given that some participating universities have admission standards below those required by the loan and scholarship programs, the students opting to attend those institutions benefited most from gratuidad. There is some support for this argument in the data. As noted above, the three institutions that enrolled the most gratuidad students in 2016 are the least selective of the thirty participating universities, and most of their students would not have had access to other forms of financial aid, because they would not have met the academic standards.[44] This suggests that the government might have increased enrollment among lower-income students by a similar number if it had simply removed the academic requirements on its existing scholarship programs instead of adopting gratuidad.

Gratuidad's Effect on University Revenues

Under gratuidad the government pays tuition on behalf of each student an institution enrolls. Therefore, the amount per student that the government pays to each participating institution is crucial for the sustainability of the program. And here there are already signs of trouble. The government is not paying what could be described as full tuition for every "free" student. Skeptical that institutions will arbitrarily raise prices with access to such large amounts of federal subsidies, Chilean policy makers created a formula to determine the amount they believe a program *should* cost, called "regulated tuition." This formula sets a per capita funding allocation to higher education institutions depending on the length of their accreditation term (which ranges from two to seven years and is seen as a proxy for quality). It then sets a regulated tuition amount for each program, which is equal to the average of the tuition fees a school charged before gratuidad, plus a maximum 20 percent bonus for those with actual tuition fees that are higher than this regulated value. For institutions with the highest tuitions fees, this formula results in a net loss in revenue compared with what they could earn previously, when students had to pay for the difference between tuition charges and government-issued student aid.

This problem will hit the most expensive universities—usually the most selective and prestigious—the hardest. Under gratuidad they will not receive full funding from the government for their students on the free track and will have to either self-generate the missing revenue or cut spending. Meanwhile, caps on enrollment growth will limit yet another source of revenue. The rectors of the more elite universities have been calling attention to the funding squeeze they are being made to bear and its consequences.[45]

This problem is not easily solved by lifting the cap the government imposes on tuition fees. Government scholarships and loans are also capped. But at least with those sources of aid, unlike with gratuidad, the institutions are still free to charge students more than the regulated tuition level, and students pay the difference out of pocket. Complying with gratuidad and its ban on cost-sharing with students puts institutions in a tighter straitjacket.

Rectors argue that the system would work better if the government increased funding for research and other investments at universities to make up for the lost tuition revenue. However, the funding for science provides an additional example of trade-offs. Bringing Chile's scientific capacities to a level closer to the OECD average would require adding USD 2.1 billion (CLP 1.34 trillion) to the science budget over a period of fifteen years, a demand for funding that competes with free tuition within the budget of the Ministry of Education.[46] Not surprisingly, the budget for Chile's funding agency for research, the Comisión Nacional de Investigación Científica y Tecnológica (CONICYT), has remained flat since 2016.

Facing these constraints, the Bachelet government proposed in its higher education reform bill that future expansions to gratuidad be contingent on tax revenue growth, a proposal ultimately accepted with broad political support in Congress. Under the Higher Education Reform Act passed in January 2018, gratuidad would reach only 60 percent of the student population in eligible institutions by 2018 and 2019. Extending the program to the promised 70 percent would be subject to a trigger: if the government's tax revenue reached a threshold of 23.5 percent of the county's GDP for two years in a row, then the additional students would become eligible. A further expansion to 80 percent of students would require revenue of 24.5 percent of GDP, an expansion to 90 percent of students is pegged to 26.5 percent, and universal coverage would be triggered when revenues reached 29.5 percent of GDP. The triggers are ingenious. They link the expansion of free tuition to growth in government revenues, but the exact timing of each expansion is left open-ended. Meanwhile, the budget for 2018 is extending gratuidad to the sixth decile, adding 120,000 students to the program, to reach 32 percent of enrollments.

WHAT IS THE PURPOSE OF FREE TUITION?

There is a tension between using free tuition to increase access to higher education among underserved populations and using it to realize a principle. In the first view, gratuidad is a pragmatic means to an end and can be adjusted as circumstances dictate. In the second, free higher education is an end in itself and cannot be compromised, because it is seen as a right. The difference has bearing on two questions: (1) whether co-payments or partial loans are admissible to help bear the financial burden of a higher education, and (2) whether gratuidad should be universal, available even to those who can afford to pay tuition.

To put the tension in simple terms, consider a design for a higher education system where free tuition were available to students from families in the lowest 30 percent of income, government scholarships that covered most of the tuition were accessible for the next 40 percent of students, and loans and out-of-pocket payments were required for the rest of the population. Perhaps this approach would result in greater access to the lower-income group, without the high costs of a free tuition or the budget constraints it imposes on universities. This potentially more optimal approach is impossible under gratuidad and was never considered by the Bachelet government.

The philosophical underpinnings of the abolition of tuition may also explain a surprising feature of the policy: gratuidad was not offered solely through public universities. In higher education systems where public and private institutions coexist, free tuition policies are usually exclusive to public universities, while private universities rely on tuition. The reason why policy makers made gratuidad available at both types of institutions (with limits) is that they saw it as a right of the students. Therefore students should be able to exercise that right regardless of the public or private status of the institution of their choice.

Another element in the evaluation of gratuidad is its effect on access to higher education. One piece of information from Chile's major household socioeconomic survey (CASEN) for 2011 suggests that the problem of access among the poorest is more complex than availability of financial aid: only 17 percent of young people among the 10 percent of poorest households say they do not participate in higher education for financial reasons. Not finishing high school, being a parent, not having passed the qualifying examinations for higher education, being needed at home, or even lack of interest, are also important factors.[47] Free tuition, however, puts all the weight of government resources onto the phase after a student has decided to attend. This is not to say that gratuidad has no influence on that decision. Free tuition is more convenient to the student than scholarships and loans, but there may be many students who do not understand the difference or have priorities other than studying. These youths need to be brought in by means other than financial aid, whatever its form.

CONCLUSION

In December 2017 Chile elected a new government that is right of center, headed by former president Sebastián Piñera. The president elect said during the campaign and after the election that free tuition will not be rolled back and that the present level of gratuidad for 60 percent of students will be maintained. Moreover, in April 2018 President Piñera sent to Congress a bill that would provide free higher education to students in the seventh decile of income enrolled at institutions in the vocational and technical sector beginning in 2019 and will seek to reach all students up to the ninth decile in four years. This proposal attests to the political allure of free tuition.

Ideally, then, from the point of view of rational allocation of scarce resources, free tuition will target the neediest students, while the other financial benefits will help students with the capacity to shoulder some of the cost of higher education, presently or deferred to the future. The effects of this three-pronged approach to financial aid (gratuidad, loans, and scholarships) are difficult to gauge now, but there are some early signs that can be analyzed. For instance, data on the persistence of 2016 freshmen indicate that students with free tuition were more likely to remain in school in 2017 than the other freshmen in their institutions: 86.7 percent of gratuidad students persisted, compared to 82.6 percent of students not in this program. It is too early to know if this will be a sustained trend, whether it is a causal relationship, and whether it is due to free tuition or some other factor.

There are also some early signs that gratuidad has increased access and has not increased attrition. Specifically, 15 percent of gratuidad beneficiaries likely would not have enrolled if required to pay tuition, even though they would have had access to a scholarship.[48] Students see gratuidad, rather than other forms of aid, as a greater incentive to enroll, as they know ahead of time that money would not be an issue if they enrolled. Alternatively, this 15 percent of students may just be students with GPAs and test scores below the cutoff point for eligibility for scholarships.

There are other latent problems with gratuidad. One sure to emerge in a few years is that free tuition runs out at the moment the student completes the official duration of his program, even if he has not yet fulfilled graduation requirements. Policy makers will likely address that issue either by extending gratuidad or by supporting the student with a new scholarship. Or they may leave it to the institutions of higher education to foot the bill, as those institutions fear. Recall that in an effort to save money, the government opted not to design the program in a way that accounts for when students take longer to complete a program than its specified duration. Legislating through budgetary footnotes resulted in this not inconsequential loose end.

Another problem relates to funding for universities. The per capita allocation for students covered by the program is insufficient to pay for the cost of education in the high-quality institutions, which may lead to downward leveling of expenses and quality. Similarly, the cost of this program to the national budget may displace other worthy policies for the support of higher education development, such as spending for science and for establishing much needed new academic posts for newly trained PhDs or development funds for institutions with aging infrastructure and no capacity to accommodate more students.

Policy driven by moral principle, such as gratuidad in Chile, understood as an absolute, unqualified right of the people, is inevitably checked by fiscal reality. As a result, it has to be recast as yet another form of financial aid in a high-tuition, high–financial aid, market-driven higher education system, as is Chile's. Moreover, while free tuition seems to be popular, people in Chile seem to judge universal free tuition as unfair, inasmuch as "rich" people receive a benefit they don't need.

Lack of popular support for extending gratuidad to more affluent families, together with the fiscal realities of a stagnant economy and the inevitable changes in priorities in the policy agenda, is unlikely to allow for an expansion of free tuition beyond the sixth decile of family income. As a form of student financial aid, the effects of gratuidad, compared to scholarships, loans, and no aid, will have to be judged on the basis of the impact of each on access, persistence, graduation, institutional admission strategies, and other variables typically used to measure effectiveness of student aid. Such work lies ahead as gratuidad consolidates and its effects continue to be measurable.

CHAPTER 7

Australia: The Price of Greater Access to Higher Education

Vicki Thomson

Australia has an enviable reputation for the quality of its universities, both in terms of teaching and research and the domestic and international graduates it produces. In 2016 six Australian institutions appeared in the Top 100 of the Academic Ranking of World Universities, placing it third behind only the United States (fifty institutions) and the United Kingdom (eight institutions).[1] International students flock to Australia's universities, and the revenues from these students are worth AUD 22 billion (about USD 17 billion at today's exchange rate), making it the nation's third-largest export sector behind iron ore and coal.[2] And until 2018, domestically all Australian students were able to access bachelor-level programs, regardless of background or socioeconomic status, with universities empowered to make their own decisions regarding enrollment numbers and admission standards.

Australia's financing structure helped make this high degree of student choice and access possible by funding public universities directly for each domestic student they enrolled, through what was known as the demand-driven system. Though still required to pay for a component of their study, domestic students at public and private institutions can defer repayment through what is arguably the most generous student loan system in the Western world. Students take on government-issued, low-interest loans and repay them as a share of their incomes through tax withholding. As of July 2018, borrowers repay only when their earnings are over AUD 51,957 (USD 44,946).[3] For students who do not earn above that level, tuition is effectively free, as the loans never need to be repaid. This has allowed Australia to achieve one of the highest shares of tertiary-educated adults relative to the Organisation for Economic Cooperation and Development

(OECD) average at 43 percent; however, it also has probably contributed to Australia having the fifth-highest proportion of private funding for tertiary education relative to the rest of the OECD.[4]

Australia's enviable higher education system today is the result of cumulative public policy decisions stretching back to the late 1980s. Many of these have involved important trade-offs that are not often discussed when policy audiences in the US praise the Australian higher education system and argue that the US should borrow from that model. There are unintended consequences that may not be as visible from the outside, and as a result, many would argue that the system is now badly in need of reforms.

The introduction of the demand-driven system in 2012 resulted in a surge of graduates with bachelor's degrees hitting the market within a relatively short time frame. At the same time, short-term graduate employment rates and starting salaries declined. Indeed, full-time employment rates for new bachelor's graduates fell to 68.8 percent in 2015, a level last seen during the Australian recession of the early 1990s.[5] As a result, the student loan program experienced a significant cost blowout from rising losses. In 2016 this prompted policy makers to lower the income threshold that students must begin repaying their loans, which took effect in July 2018.[6] In early 2018, lawmakers in the Australian Parliament introduced legislation that, if passed, would further reduce the threshold to AUD 45,881 (USD 39,689).[7]

The other factor that needs to be considered is how the current Australian funding model hampers an institution's ability to generate revenue for nonteaching purposes. While all Australian universities are legislatively required to conduct research as well as teaching, publicly accessible data sets make it clear that the level of research intensity varies significantly at the institutional level.[8] Funding for research is scarce, forcing universities to cross-subsidize those activities with teaching revenue. The amount that universities are permitted to charge domestic undergraduate students remains federally regulated, despite the removal of enrollment caps. Although universities can enroll as many Australian bachelor's students as they like, the price they can charge remains the same regardless of whether institutions are intensively active in research or pursuing other missions. In response, many universities have recruited ever larger numbers of international students whose tuition fees are not subject to federal regulation. However, many of these students are clustered around particular cities and disciplines, bringing into question the universities' capacity to offer them a truly international experience.

While the higher education system provides greater access to more students than ever before, these successes have come at the expense of more cost-sharing from students, greater numbers of international students, and a reduction in government support for universities. It is likely these trends will continue, as policy makers have favored other spending priorities over higher education in recent political negotiations.

THE DAWKINS REFORMS: AUSTRALIA ABANDONS FREE HIGHER EDUCATION TO INCREASE ACCESS

Any contemporary discussion of the Australian higher education system must start with the 1980s Dawkins reforms. These crucial reforms moved the Australian system away from a tuition-free model as a necessary step in providing access to more students.

In the 1970s the Labor (Whitlam) government put Australia's university sector under a model of "free" education fully funded by the government. This had been intended as an equity hallmark by removing financial barriers believed to be limiting access for people of less advantaged backgrounds. However, by 1987 John Dawkins, then federal minister for employment, education, and training, was forced to admit that despite years of Australia's free tuition policy, the benefits of higher education were still being "enjoyed disproportionately by the more privileged members of our community."[9]

The reason for this was simple: admitting more students is expensive, and in promising to cover the full costs of study, the government had to limit the number of places offered. Entry was determined by academic performance, and those able to meet the entry criteria were mostly from middle-class and wealthier families. This created the perverse, if unintentional, outcome whereby poorer taxpaying Australian families were likely subsidizing free education for the children of wealthier ones. Acknowledging this policy failure gave Dawkins the courage to make large-scale changes.

Dawkins recognized that industry would increasingly demand graduates with the kind of "broad educational foundation" and "well-developed conceptual, analytical and communication skills" that higher education offers but also with skills more traditionally associated with vocational education and training.[10] Under his reforms, known colloquially as the Dawkins model, Australia would achieve this via a "Unified National System," in which the existing binary system that included both universities funded to perform teaching and research and colleges of advanced education (CAEs) funded only to teach would merge.[11] In 1989 Australia had nineteen public universities and seventy non-university providers. By 2017, nearly thirty years after these reforms were introduced, there are forty-one universities and no CAE equivalents.

To fund the expansion that followed, Dawkins also introduced the Higher Education Contribution Scheme (HECS). An Australian invention, HECS was designed to allow the government to recoup some of the costs of a student's education while maintaining access that was free at the point of entry. Students were therefore able to pursue tertiary education without the burden of up-front fees, financing the costs with income-contingent loans repaid as a surcharge on their income taxes after they left school and only if they earned above a certain threshold, currently set at AUD 51,957 for the 2018–2019 school year. The loans charge an interest rate equal only to inflation as measured by the Consumer Price Index.

The legacy of the Unified National System—that all higher education institutions should be modeled on the comprehensive research university—became enshrined in legislation in 2000.[12] Non-university higher education providers still exist in Australia, but most fit within the private sector and tend to be specialist providers.[13] All universities are required to fit into a comprehensive research-intensive university mold and devote substantial resources to research. This coupling of research along with teaching as a core requirement of being a university, which remains a key feature of the Australian system, is unusual by international standards.[14] As discussed below, it poses a number of operational and financial challenges.

THE MOVE TO A DEMAND-DRIVEN SYSTEM

While the Dawkins reforms established the foundation of the Australian higher education system that remains today, major reforms introduced in 2009 have also done much to shape current policies. In 2008 then Labor education minister (later prime minister) Julia Gillard commissioned a sweeping review of the sector, led by Emeritus Professor Denise Bradley. The Bradley Review, as it became known, made forty-six recommendations, spanning areas as diverse as governance, education targets, employment needs, and funding. Perhaps the most consequential outcome was the introduction of the demand-driven system (DDS), which ultimately restructured how the government funded universities and removed enrollment caps. The DDS was devised to achieve two enrollment and access targets recommended by Bradley. The first was to have at least 40 percent of twenty-five-to-thirty-four-year-old Australians with bachelor's degrees or above by 2025. The second was that students of low socioeconomic status should make up 20 percent of undergraduate domestic enrollments by 2020.[15]

The former goal was motivated by the view that the Australian economy needed a more highly skilled labor force and that Australia was falling behind other countries in the share of its population with advanced degrees. The latter reflected a concern that the share of students in higher education who came from low socioeconomic status was flat or declining. Providing equitable access has rightly been a concern of the Australian higher education system since at least the early 1970s, and the move to DDS was meant to further increase access to higher education by freeing institutions to pursue the enrollment of disadvantaged cohorts without regard to enrollment caps imposed by the government.

Prior to the implementation of the DDS, the number of domestic student places at each institution had been determined by the federal government via negotiations with the education department. Under the new arrangements universities could enroll as many bachelor's students as they could accommodate into whatever courses they pleased. With a guarantee that the government would subsidize every domestic bachelor's student a university enrolled, universities could raise revenue simply by taking in more students, and enrollment statistics demonstrate that a number of institutions did exactly that. However, a greater number of students requires greater resources, and the government's decisions to maintain control of domestic fees and reject the Bradley Review's recommendation to increase per-student funding for universities by 10 percent put increasing strain on university finances. The eruption of the global financial crisis just as the Bradley Review was delivered may well have put constraints on a serious funding injection at the time, but subsequent governments have also continued to ignore this recommendation. By 2012 the phasing in of the DDS enrollment policy was complete.

SURGE IN ENROLLMENT FOLLOWING DDS

There is little doubt that the DDS achieved its goal of increasing the flow of people into university. Between 2009 and 2013, domestic undergraduate places in public universities increased by 22 percent (from 444,000 to 541,000).[16] Publicly accessible enrollment data show some institutions more than doubling their intake between 2008 and 2015.[17] However, the market-driven nature of the DDS meant that this growth did not occur evenly across the sector. Between 2008 and 2015, enrollment growth across institutional groupings varied from an increase of 19 percent at Australia's eight most research-intensive universities, known under the collective moniker of the Group of Eight, to 58 percent across regional institutions and 67 percent for those not associated with any group. While such numbers would be expected under a policy intended to increase access, this rapid expansion has led to concerns about the preparedness for university study of some nontraditional cohorts of students. The most disadvantaged cohorts also tend to be those with the greatest need for learning support, with more intensive assistance required to help them bridge the transition to higher education. This may mean that many of the institutions with the largest increases in enrollment are also those that took the largest financial risks. Their students may be more likely to drop out or fail to find a job after graduation that pays enough to fully repay their student loans. As noted in *The Australian* in November 2017, "The overall university dropout rate has been rising steadily since 2010."[18]

This surge in enrollments means that the Bradley target for twenty-five-to-thirty-four-year-old Australians is likely to be met well ahead of time. In fact, for women this goal has already been achieved.[19] However, progress toward the second Bradley target, focused on increasing enrollment of students from low socioeconomic status backgrounds, has been weak. Though no one would argue with the well-intentioned nature of the goal, achieving it has proven elusive, despite repeated policy interventions. This may suggest that the barriers to higher education for people from disadvantaged backgrounds are more complex than is currently understood. Nevertheless, parliamentary budget papers for 2017–2018 show that by financial year 2020–2021 the proportion of domestic undergraduates from a low socioeconomic status background is projected to reach anywhere between 16.4 percent and 18.2 percent, depending on how it is measured, falling short of the original goal of 20 percent when the DDS was adopted.[20]

TOO MANY BACHELOR'S DEGREES AND FALLING WAGES

Achieving the enrollment and access targets under the DDS is only part of the story. Employment rates and earnings of graduates in the wake of the DDS have been problematic. Graduate Careers Australia (GCA) data shows that by 2015 graduate employment rates had plummeted to levels last seen during the early 1990s recession, with median graduate salaries at 75.8 percent of the annual rate of male average weekly earnings (MAWE), down from 83 percent in 2009.[21] Both of these measures show the continuation of longer-term trends: full-time employment of graduates with bachelor's degrees has been falling since 2008, and salaries as a percent of MAWE have been dropping overall since the late 1970s, though the latter stabilized at around 80 percent for much of the early 2000s (see figs. 7.1 and 7.2).[22] Overall, as noted by one commentator, this could mean there "is now a real risk that, in attempting to expand access to higher education, gov-

FIGURE 7.1 Full-time employment rate of bachelor's degree graduates

Source: Author's calculation based on data from Graduate Careers Australia, www.graduatecareers.com.au/research/researchreports/gradstats.

FIGURE 7.2 Median graduate starting salary (GSS) for bachelor's degree graduates, as a percent of male average weekly earnings (MAWE)

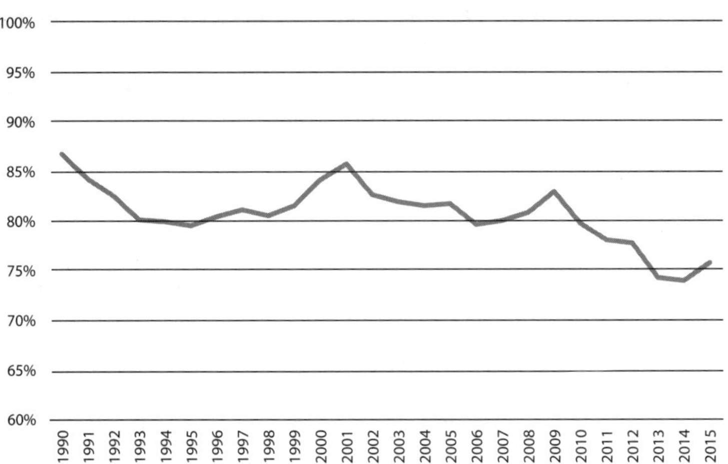

Source: Authors' calculation based on data from Graduate Careers Australia, www.graduatecareers.com.au/research/researchreports/gradstats.

Note: Data includes only individuals who completed a bachelor's degree program in Australia, are less than twenty-five years old, and are in their first full-time employment.

ernments and universities have effectively flooded the job market with new graduates, at a time when employer demand for them was slipping."[23]

Part of the rationale for the DDS was that universities acting in a market would more accurately follow employment needs than federal allocation of places, since students and universities would have more flexibility to respond to the economic needs of Australia.[24] Yet falling graduate employment rates, rising rates of graduates going on to further study (a common response to a sluggish employment market), and an oversupply of graduates in key professions casts doubt on this assumption.[25] By 2015, only three years after full implementation of the DDS, concerns were already circulating within the higher education community and the media that Australia might be producing too many graduates in certain professions for the market to absorb, including teaching and law.[26] At the same time, enrollment rates in the vocational education and training sector have fallen since 2012, despite the fact that these graduates are experiencing better employment rates and starting salaries than those with bachelor's degrees.[27]

The DDS has also had economic implications for non-college-goers. Where high school graduates not seeking to further their education could previously have entered the workforce directly, they now find themselves up against the twin problems of increased automation, which has been decreasing the number of unskilled jobs available, and applicants with bachelor's degrees spilling over into these roles while they pursue other employment.[28] Community attitudes have also shifted. There are higher parental expectations that university is now the sole post-school pathway, and the DDS has made that an easier option for more students. This pressure has contributed to the declining interest in apprenticeships and a higher than optimal rate of university attrition, now sitting at 15 percent across the sector.[29] This does not automatically mean that students who drop out are not capable of university-level achievement, but it does signal that some institutions may be enrolling applicants who are unprepared or unsuitable at the time of commencement.

In designing the DDS, neither the government nor the Bradley Review contemplated how the policy might look if the labor market changed following the reform. Having a much higher proportion of its population with an undergraduate degree will inevitably alter the relationship between graduate and employer. While it can be argued that education bestows certain intrinsic values, it is not clear that the rapid rises in enrollment that flowed from the DDS were driven by a desire for self-improvement rather than increased employment prospects. The truth is that the DDS has flooded the marketplace with graduates holding bachelor's degrees when it is not at all clear that the marketplace was in immediate need of them.[30] Today, Australian graduates are taking longer to find employment. When they do, it can be at a lower entry level than might have previously occurred. Some are therefore being placed in the unenviable position of gaining employment (albeit temporarily) in a role they could previously have secured without a degree while incurring a significant student debt, plus the foregone earnings from time spent out of the workforce while pursuing further study. There has also been an increase in the number of graduates who work part time, which depresses the earnings statistics for graduates.[31]

The programs and majors experiencing weaker than expected employment outcomes are not necessarily the ones observers might expect. Despite ongoing rhetoric about the need for Australia to invest in more STEM (science, technology, engineering, and mathematics) skills, graduates from some of the sciences have been found to have among the worst graduate employment rates.[32] As Glyn Davis, professor and vice chancellor of the University of Melbourne, noted in 2016:

> There are 111,000 more people under 24 now in higher education programs than in 2008. . . .
>
> This would be fine if most university graduates could look forward to meaningful employment. Yet there are areas of significant oversupply. There are more than 400 courses offered in aspects of teacher training across [Australia], attracting some 80,000 students. In any given year however, only 7,000 full time teaching positions are available.
>
> At a minimum, we need a way to ensure potential students are aware of the risks of undertaking a degree, since they and the taxpayer will together cover the cost of their training. We may even question the wisdom of funding further expansion in fields of known oversupply.[33]

In 2008, prior to the Bradley Review and the implementation of the DDS, 85 percent of graduates had secured full-time employment four months after graduation, and the median annual starting salary for graduates with bachelor's degrees under twenty-five years of age and in their first full-time job was around 81 percent of MAWE.[34] By 2015 the proportion working full time within the same period had fallen to 69 percent, and salaries had fallen to around 76 percent of MAWE.[35]

Australia's graduates are still expected to earn a premium over the course of their careers compared to those without a tertiary education.[36] However, the combination of more graduates, increasing automation, and the impact of globalization on individual economies means it is becoming more difficult to predict the point at which a degree will switch from conferring a premium to becoming merely the price of entry to—but no guarantee of a place within—a shrinking workforce. It is possible that this point has already passed.

This is not to say that having more graduates in the economy is necessarily bad. However, it is vital that community expectations are commensurate with the likely outcomes of investing in further and higher education and the differences between the two. Universities are institutions of higher learning that exist to prepare young adults to make an economic and social contribution to society. Unlike vocational education and training institutions, they are not designed for the sole purpose of job training. Yet media headlines in 2017 such as "Students' False Hope on Jobs" and "Vocational Education Is a Better Pathway to a Job Than a University Degree" suggest that the purpose of government-subsidized higher education is not as well understood as it should be in a society investing in mass higher education.[37] Fortunately, some graduates are responding to changing economic conditions and a lagging demand for bachelor graduates by embracing entrepreneurship and start-ups rather than seeking more traditional employment routes. Still, many graduates are unable to find a position in the career they have chosen and studied toward.

FINANCING TRENDS AND STRUCTURAL PROBLEMS

It is now clear that full implementation of the DDS created significant budget pressures for the government. The cost of the Commonwealth Grant Scheme, the program that provides direct subsidies to universities for each domestic bachelor's student they enroll, escalated from AUD 4.1 billion in 2009 to AUD 6.1 billion in 2013 (at today's exchange rate, USD 3.2 billion to USD 4.7 billion).[38] This growth has alarmed many policy makers and the higher education sector alike.

In addition, the popularity of the HECS student loan repayment scheme (later renamed the Higher Education Loan Programme, or HELP) led policy makers to extend it to cover the vocational education sector as well as universities. Together this led to a significant cost blowout. By April 2016 the Australian Broadcasting Corporation (ABC) was reporting that the government was "forecasting losses of $13.5 billion [Australian dollars] on just four years' worth of loans," and a report issued by the Parliamentary Budget Office (PBO) found that the cost on an underlying cash basis was projected to increase from AUD 1.7 billion annually in the 2015–2016 school year to AUD 11.1 billion in 2025–2026, or an annual increase from roughly USD 1.3 billion to USD 8.7 billion.[39] Weaker employment outcomes were also taking their toll. According to the PBO, "doubtful debt," or the amount not expected to be recouped through the taxation system, was projected to rise from its present level of AUD 1.9 billion to AUD 4 billion (the equivalent of USD 1.5 billion to USD 3.1 billion) over the same period.[40] The report also found the following:

> HELP loans also increase the size of net debt because the borrowing used to fund these loans exceeds the value of loans on the balance sheet, which is reduced to account for the concessional [below-market] interest rate and the provision for doubtful debt. Net [government] debt attributable to the HELP portfolio is projected to rise from $13.4 billion in 2015–16 to $48.1 billion in 2025–26. This will see the proportion of net debt attributable to HELP increase from 4.8 percent in 2015–16 to 18.3 percent in 2025–26.[41]

The 2017 federal budget proposed a number of measures designed to address these issues. These included a dramatic drop in the salary threshold at which graduates would be required to commence loan repayments, which would be a further reduction from the changes that took effect for the 2018–2019 school year, as shown in table 7.1.[42]

However, these efforts by the government to shift more of the cost burden back onto students did not occur in isolation. Rather, it is part of a long-term trend in which the government cuts back on direct support, forcing universities to seek outside sources of revenue, often by enrolling international students.

Ever since the introduction of HECS, the share of costs financed by the government has steadily declined. In the late 1980s, 84 percent of all university funding came from the government. Today, on average, this has dropped to 42 percent, though it varies at the institutional level.[43] Professor Glyn Davis described the evolution in the following manner:

> The term ["public university"] suggests commitment to merit-based and equitable entry. A public university means a curriculum that emphasises intellectual inquiry regardless of the course chosen. It indicates staff, facilities and services to support student learning, and campus life to encourage exploration and growth. A public university is home to academic freedom in thought, teaching and research, with governance that ensures academic oversight of academic matters. . . .
>
> A generation ago, public universities received almost all their income from Canberra. This changed from 1989. Within a decade, public universities were raising most of their income. Today, direct Commonwealth recurrent funds cover just 23% of the running costs of the University of Melbourne.[44]

TABLE 7.1 Income thresholds for Australian student loan repayments

Repayment rates	*2017–18 thresholds*[1]	*2018–19 thresholds*[2]	*Proposal for new 2019–20 thresholds*[3]
1.0%	—	—	$45,881
2.0%	—	$51,957	$52,974
2.5%	—	—	$56,152
3.0%	—	—	$59,522
3.5%	—	—	$63,093
4.0%	$55,874	$57,730	$66,878
4.5%	$62,239	$64,307	$70,891
5.0%	$68,603	$70,882	$75,145
5.5%	$72,208	$74,608	$79,653
6.0%	$77,619	$80,198	$84,433
6.5%	$84,063	$86,856	$89,499
7.0%	$88,487	$91,426	$94,869
7.5%	$97,378	$100,614	$100,561
8.0%	$103,766	$107,214	$106,594
8.5%	—	—	$112,990
9.0%	—	—	$119,770
9.5%	—	—	$126,956
10.0%	—	—	$134,573

Source: Parliament of Australia, Department of Parliamentary Services, "Higher Education Support Legislation Amendment (Student Loan Sustainability) Bill 2018," Parliamentary Library, March 26, 2018, http://parlinfo.aph.gov.au/parlInfo/download/legislation/billsdgs/5869097/upload_binary/5869097.pdf.

[1] All values are in Australian dollars. In 2017–18, borrowers earning less than $55,874 annually pay nothing (0 percent of their income). Borrowers earning over $103,766 Australian dollars pay back 8 percent of their income.

[2] These are the current repayment thresholds that took effect on July 1, 2018, and apply to all borrowers. The repayment rate applies to all income; unlike the US, there is no deduction.

[3] In 2018, the Higher Education Support Legislation Amendment Bill was enacted into law. It lowers the minimum repayment threshold to 45,881 Australian dollars. The new thresholds are set to take effect on July 1, 2019.

In fact, as policy makers have become more reliant on student fees to finance higher education, and as universities have shown themselves adept at recruiting increasingly more international students, it has made it politically easier—and almost reflexive—for the government to cut direct funding when seeking extra dollars. Universities Australia, one of the sector's representative bodies, estimates that universities and their students have suffered cuts of around AUD 4 billion since 2011.[45] In 2013 the same Labor government that had introduced the DDS announced plans to cut some AUD 2.3 billion from universities to fund elementary and secondary schools instead. In 2017 the government has sought to abolish the Education Investment Fund, a AUD 3.8 billion government fund established to address the need for research infrastructure, to fund the National Disability Insurance Scheme instead.[46] These moves ignored the findings of an independent panel commissioned by the minister for tertiary education, which found that "the average level of base funding per place should be increased to improve the quality of higher education teaching and to maximize the sector's potential to contribute to national productivity and economic growth."[47]

The Dawkins reforms of the late 1980s are now around thirty years old. Like many structures of that age, they are struggling to cope with the dramatic shifts in social, economic, and industrial practice that have occurred since then. The DDS has added to the strain, but cracks were already showing even before those reforms in the early 2010s. In September 2016 Dawkins himself made public statements to the effect that the reforms he ushered in are now "completely out of date" and no longer appropriate in a twenty-first-century context.[48]

Successive Australian governments have attempted to alter this policy and give institutions of higher education some freedom to set their own tuition prices and thereby increase revenue. So far they have been unsuccessful. The last time an Australian education minister directly increased the tuition caps to increase revenue to the nation's universities was in 2005. An attempt by the conservative Abbott government to let universities set their own tuition fees in 2014 was so politically unpopular that it is unlikely to be tried again anytime soon.

THE ROLE OF INTERNATIONAL STUDENTS

Because Australian universities are required to finance a growing share of their budgets with tuition, but at levels capped by the government, they are relying more heavily on fee-paying international students for their revenues. This has proven to be somewhat of a double-edged sword. Since first opening its doors to international students in the mid-1980s, the Australian higher education industry has attracted many students from outside Australia who successfully return to other regions of the world upon graduation.[49] This has brought a range of benefits to the country that are not limited to education. Australian campuses today are vibrant, multicultural communities, reflective of Australian society as a whole. However, international students have also become increasingly important as a source of untied revenue, since universities are able to charge these students high fees. Government figures show there were around 624,000 international students in Australia in 2017, a 12.7 percent increase over the previous year, though numbers varied substantially by sector and at the institutional level.[50]

The better universities have become in sourcing private income, the easier it has been for the government to withdraw public subsidies. Professor Peter Høj, vice chancellor of the University of Queensland, noted in a memo to staff: "The [2017] Federal Budget cuts—if passed—will increase the likelihood that we decide to enroll a higher percentage of international students, likely with commensurately fewer domestic students, as Federal funding for infrastructure expansion and renewal is siphoned away."[51]

Given the fragile global geopolitical situation, this is a very precarious basket in which to hold all the sector's eggs. Australia has already had direct experience of how quickly things can go wrong in international markets. A series of attacks on Indian students between 2008 and 2010 saw enrollment from that country plunge, and they are only now—seven years later—beginning to recover.[52] Nevertheless, the Australian education sector has continued to attract international students. In the four quarters to March 2018, the Australian Bureau of Statistics suggests that international education exports were worth around AUD 30.7 billion, which represents an increase of more than 10 percent over the previous period.[53]

Recruiting ever more international students is also a response to the legislative mandate that Australian universities must carry out research. As is discussed in the next section, the one-size-fits-all requirement that universities carry out both instructional and research roles creates a number of problems, including funding pressures that revenue from international students helps alleviate.

THE ONE-SIZE-FITS-ALL UNIVERSITY

The legacy of the Unified National System—whereby the higher education sector was reshaped into a uniform comprehensive university model—became enshrined in legislation in Australia in 2000.[54] By deliberately removing the distinctions between the university and advanced education sectors, the Dawkins reforms of the 1980s created a "one-size-fits-all" model, intended to bring together the best of both sectors to produce more rounded graduates. In practice, though, their adoption has also meant that government dollars have been forced to stretch further over a larger number of players. As long as Australian politicians avoid any move to enable high-quality teaching-only universities through legislative change, the flawed model will continue to challenge the sector financially. It has also obligated whichever political party is in power to fund all entities that have achieved university status as though they are active in research, even though years of research block grant funding, which is allocated in part based on past performance, calls into question the extent to which this is true.[55]

Legislatively requiring Australian universities to be research active has proven costly. Training researchers, embracing PhD students who take some eight years of study to reach the first rung on their career ladder, in addition to the basic infrastructure necessary to carry out research, is financially draining. Yet even the most competitive research-intensive institutions, those that do the heavy lifting in research and in turn consistently achieve the highest ranks in the international ranking systems, receive only partial public support. Over time this has inevitably led to a squeeze in research funding. The universities that make up Australia's Group of Eight carry out some AUD 6 billion of research each year.[56] Yet only AUD 2.8 billion of that research is supported through government funds (the equivalent of USD 2.2 billion). The remainder must be obtained through cross-subsidization from whatever other sources of funding the group can access, public or private. Given the limited quantity of government-provided funds to support domestic teaching, and an Australian culture that is not as inclined toward philanthropy as some other nations, institutions have turned to one of the few sources of untied funding available: international students.

It remains unclear if back in 1989 Dawkins understood that altering the fundamental structure of Australia's higher education sector from two reputable, well-regulated, diverse streams into a potpourri of forty relatively homogenous teaching-plus-research entities would have such compound long-term effects. He probably did not foresee that the capacity to have high-quality, globally recognized teaching-only universities would be lost when all institutions of higher education were legislatively obliged to chase rapidly declining government research dollars. Yet the idea that all institutions pursue research and teaching had become so entrenched that the 2008 Bradley Review recommended that "the Australian Government . . . [should] develop more rigorous criteria for accrediting universities . . . based around strengthening the link between teaching and research as a defining characteristic of university accreditation."[57] In other words, there was an implicit assumption about the existence of a teaching-research nexus, "despite," as one commentator has noted, "the absence of any clear evidence to support it."[58]

Early in 2017 the Turnbull government announced its intention to conduct a review of the government's higher education provider categories as part of its federal budget. This could open the door to introducing new types of universities, such as teaching-focused or even teaching-only institutions. However, it remains to be seen whether these types of institutions would be considered acceptable by the sector, even after thirty years of Dawkins's Unified National System.

ONGOING POLICY STRUGGLES AND "DEREGULATED" TUITION

In Australia 2013 was a federal election year. The incumbent, Labor prime minister Kevin Rudd, faced opposition leader Tony Abbott, a conservative politician who aggressively campaigned on the platform that years of Labor governments had left Australia's coffers seriously depleted, creating a looming "debt and deficit" disaster.[59] When Abbott's coalition party was swept into power in September 2013, he assumed that the Australian public agreed with his message. Abbott's first budget, unveiled in May 2014, heavily targeted all areas of public spending. The reason, as Treasurer Joe Hockey explained to the Australian Parliament, was that "'the age of entitlement is over. It has to be replaced, not with an age of austerity, but with an age of opportunity. [Spending should be about] spending less on consumption and more on investment so we can keep making decent, compassionate choices in the future.'"[60]

Unfortunately, there proved to be a considerable mismatch between what the Abbott government and the Australian public considered to be "entitlement." As described by Mark Triffitt from the University of Melbourne, the 2014 budget left Australia with "broken promises and quarter-truths, ill-thought through spending cuts targeting the less well-off, a cosmic-sized disconnect from public sentiment, [and] consumer confidence undermined."[61]

The budget proposal specifically targeted higher education. On the plus side, it was sufficiently brave to look at the problems in the system, but, conversely, it mainly saw the sector as an easy target for seeking budget repair in other areas.

Federal Education Minister Christopher Pyne proposed a radical overhaul of the existing funding model as part of the 2014 budget. Universities would be "deregulated." They would no longer be bound by tuition caps dictated federally; instead, they could charge students whatever fees the market would bear. The trade-off would be that the government would cut direct per-student funding for institutions of higher education by 20 percent.

These changes did not, however, address the systemic issue of the 1989 Dawkins reforms with respect to how universities were structured and mandated to conduct research. The government was still uninterested in addressing the legislative definition of an Australian university, and all institutions were still bound to carry out research. They did not see the tensions this policy created as meriting reform.

The higher education sector came out in almost unanimous support for the Pyne proposal.[62] Some did so reluctantly, but most recognized that letting institutions set their own tuition prices at least provided a way for them to recoup lost government funding. However, they still railed against the accompanying 20 percent funding cuts. As noted by Professor Ian Young, then chair of the Group of Eight and vice chancellor of the Australian National University:

> Our higher education system is unsustainable. . . .
>
> The sector has grown far more quickly than predicted by the Bradley Review. . . .
>
> Funding per student, in constant 2013 dollars, has decreased by 14 per cent over the 17-year period since 1996. . . .
>
> Under significant budget pressure the previous Labor government cut deeply into both education and research. These cuts totaled $3.5 billion. The presently proposed cuts to [the Commonwealth Grant Scheme] amount to approximately $2.8 billion over the forward estimates. The lifeline offered to universities is deregulation [the ability to set tuition at where they see fit]![63]

In the end, the 2014 budget was rejected by Parliament and ultimately cost both Joe Hockey and Tony Abbott their jobs. Pyne's 2014 proposal failed along with it.

By 2015 Australia had a new prime minister, Malcolm Turnbull, who replaced Tony Abbott mid-term. Turnbull had made an exceptionally strong public commitment to universities in his first days in power, placing a "National Innovation and Science Agenda" front and center of his platform. Universities were told how the future of the nation would rest on research, an educated population, and increasing engagement between industries and universities. But Australians were not as excited about this as their prime minister, and the 2016 federal election saw Turnbull's coalition government just scrape back into power. The majority that Abbott had won in 2013 was reduced to just one seat. The makeup of Parliament became more complex, as 23 percent of votes were cast for minor parties in what has historically been a two-party system.[64] The innovation theme was all but banished from the government's lexicon. Though it was true the government took delight in extolling the value of burgeoning education exports, it did so while ignoring the fact that its success was partly being driven by the desperation of institutions in the face of inadequate policy and funding settings.

Turnbull appointed a new education minister in Simon Birmingham, who set about trying to reassure the sector with a promise to take a "pragmatic and consultative approach to higher education policy."[65] However, not much seemed to change under the new education minister's leadership. Reports, reviews, and panels abounded to little end, and the consultation process spluttered out. And then in December 2016 the government announced it would use the Education Investment Fund, originally earmarked for university infrastructure, to instead fund the National Disability Insurance Scheme, a Labor initiative intended to provide financial support to Australians with disabilities. While admirable in intent, it had never been adequately funded and now faced an annual funding shortfall of AUD 3.7 billion (almost USD 3 billion).[66]

Funding for higher education was now being pitted directly against assistance for the disabled. To the higher education sector this was a cynical attempt to wedge it publicly, forcing it into a lose-lose situation. Then as part of the 2017 budget, the government targeted higher education for more cuts, pointing to large surpluses in university revenues as evidence that the sector was over-subsidized.[67] Large new buildings on university campuses were claimed as examples of profitable largesse. Even the media described the charges as "an unprecedented propaganda war on universities."[68]

In the second half of 2018, uncertainty remains about the future of Australian higher education reform. A bill has passed in the Australian Senate that will significantly lower student loan repayment thresholds and limit students' capacity to borrow these loans, capping lifetime maximum borrowing at AUD 150,000 (USD 129,758) for students studying medicine, dentistry, and veterinary science courses, and AUD 104,440 (USD 90,346) for other students.[69]

In late 2017, the Australian government also announced measures that will freeze per-student higher education funding at 2017 levels for two years.[70] Universities Australia has estimated that this equates to a AUD 2.1 billion funding cut to the higher education sector.[71] Even when tuition increases are permitted for bachelor level courses in 2020, increases cannot exceed the growth rate of the eighteen-to-sixty-four-year-old population (estimated at around 1.2 percent a year). Additionally, only universities that meet yet-to-be-determined performance metrics are eligible for the increase.[72]

CONCLUSION

Australia's higher education sector is enviable for a number of reasons. It is strong in teaching, research, and innovation, and in pioneering social policy such as income-contingent loans and genuine open access to higher education to people of all backgrounds. As this chapter has shown, however, some of these innovations have come at a price. Australia has had to confront a number of challenges despite the achievements of its higher education system.

Australia was right in its desire to open higher education to more students when it implemented the DDS, but the imperfect implementation has strained government finances. Job market outcomes for recent graduates have also been weaker than expected. While the Dawkins reforms of the 1980s recognized that charging students tuition is necessary to expand access, the government has stopped short of letting universities set their own tuition. This keeps costs down for students, but it constrains the revenues that universities need to provide quality education. Meanwhile, mandating that all universities follow the comprehensive model for research universities unnecessarily drives costs up and pressures universities to recruit international students.

As the recent developments in the government reveal, these consequences continue to pose ongoing policy challenges that will surely prompt reforms in the near future. A review of the government's higher education provider categories is taking place in 2018, and this could pave the way to rolling back the idea of the Unified National System and reintroducing alternative models such as teaching-only universities or high-quality polytechnics. However, Australia still remains in search of the highly skilled and innovative society once promised by Dawkins thirty years ago.

CHAPTER 8

Brazil: Expanding Access Through Private Institutions

Dante J. Salto

The expansion of higher education systems worldwide is an established trend. Global enrollment reflects mass access—even universal access—to higher education in many developed and developing countries.[1] Latin America is no exception to this trend. While public universities have played different roles in enrollment growth, in some Latin American countries—Brazil in particular—enrollment growth has occurred mostly at private higher education institutions.

Few countries in Latin America have relied as heavily on private higher education institutions to expand coverage as Brazil. Far from typical cases where this expansion took place before regulatory frameworks were put in place or where the sector faced a hostile regulatory environment, policy makers in Brazil promoted massification of the higher education system through the private sector.[2] In part, the growth of private higher education is seen as a lower-cost and convenient way to expand its capacity. In Brazil public higher education institutions are fully subsidized (i.e., tuition is free) and have a high cost structure. That makes expanding access through these institutions far more expensive for policy makers than funneling demand to the private sector. In fact, the cost to the government to educate a student in the public sector is three times higher than in the private sector.[3]

This chapter shows how the establishment of the higher education system, the role of the public sector, and policies affecting private higher education continue to shape the changing Brazilian system. It first compares trends in Brazilian higher education to global and regional trends, which includes an analysis of massification and universalization of higher education, how key policies evolved over time, and the role of private higher education.[4] The second part focuses on recent developments in the private sector, such as the legalization of for-profit colleges and universities and the sharp enrollment growth experienced by this sector that was supported by an expansion of government loans and grants. A third part discusses accountability mechanisms that policy makers put in place to address concerns about quality in private higher education. Finally, the concluding remarks highlight how the policy developments in Brazil represent trade-offs among competing options in designing a higher education system.

ENROLLMENT TRENDS IN BRAZILIAN HIGHER EDUCATION

Brazil, the largest economy in Latin America and the ninth worldwide, has a prominent higher education system.[5] Enrollment data suggest that Brazil has one of the largest higher education systems in the world, just after China, India, and the United States. Thus, it occupies the top position in enrollment figures in Latin America, enrolling 8 million students, followed by Mexico (3.4 million), Argentina (2.9 million), Colombia (2.2 million), and Chile (1.2 million).[6] However, as shown in figure 8.1, the country's ranking is quite different when considering the higher education gross enrollment rate.[7] Based on Martin Trow's classification, Chile and Argentina have reached universalization thresholds, with gross enrollment rates of 87 percent and 83 percent, respectively. Brazil joins Colombia near the middle with gross enrollment rates of 49 percent and 53 percent, respectively.[8] Mexico, at the bottom (30 percent), is experiencing slow enrollment growth; in contrast, Brazil and Colombia have experienced sharp growth since 1999.

The trends in higher education expansion highlighted in figure 8.1 are not a rarity worldwide. Globally, enrollments in higher education skyrocketed from 32 million in 1970 to more than 206 million in 2014, representing a growth of 10 percent to 34 percent.[9] This expansion has taken place despite public budgetary constraints, because governments have allowed public institutions to diversify their funding (i.e., charge tuition) or they have subsidized their growth in the private higher education sector.[10]

Even though Brazil's higher education gross enrollment rate has risen sharply in the last decades, access remains unequal. As shown in figure 8.2, only 5.4 percent of the bottom income quintile is enrolled in higher education compared to 50.3 percent of the top quintile. This is in contrast with other Latin American countries. In Chile, Argentina, and Mexico enrollment among the bottom quintile is considerably higher than in Brazil, at 27.4 percent, 17.6 percent, and 15.6 percent, respectively. The enrollment gap between the bottom and top quintiles in Brazil has widened, instead of shrunk, over time.[11]

FIGURE 8.1 Higher education gross enrollment rate in selected Latin American countries

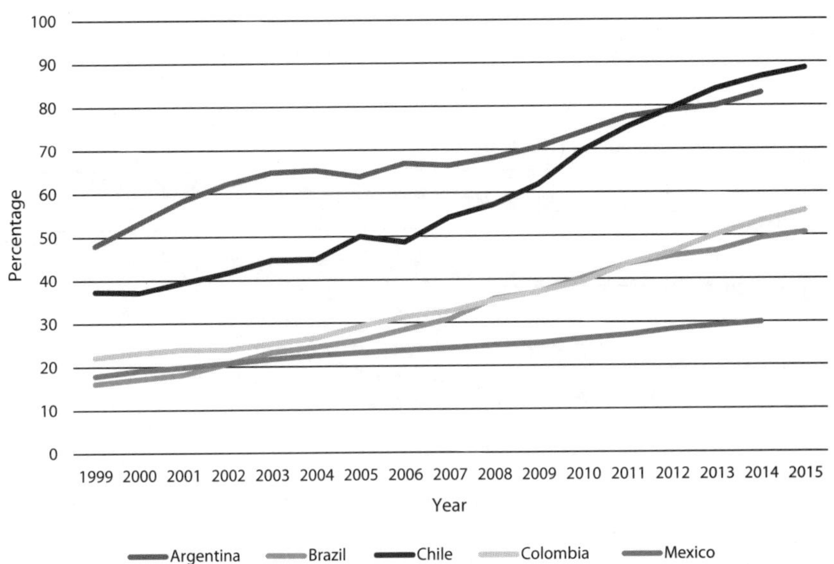

Source: Unesco Institute for Statistics (UIS), "UIS Statistics," http://data.uis.unesco.org.

Note: Missing data points are not shown (Brazil 2000, 2006, 2010; Chile 2001; Colombia 2003; Mexico 2015; Argentina 2015). For missing data, lines connect the two adjacent points to show trends over time. Argentina's 2000 value is an estimate from UIS. All of Brazil's

Reasons for such an unequal distribution are likely to be found outside higher education. Access to secondary education is far from universal in Brazil. Only 49.9 percent of those in the bottom quintile access secondary education, compared to 79.7 percent in the top quintile. This is a striking contrast to what has occurred in Argentina, Chile, and Mexico, where more than 70 percent of the bottom quintile access secondary education.[12]

In Brazil, the private sector has primarily accommodated the enrollment growth of the past decades. This sector enrolls nearly six million, or three-quarters, of students. In that regard, Brazil only comes in second place within Latin America, after Chile, where 84 percent of higher education enrollment comes from private institutions.[13]

Conventional wisdom would assume that the Brazilian mass private sector would recruit students from the bottom income quintiles. However, studies have found that public colleges and universities tend to enroll slightly more of these students than their private counterparts.[14] The reverse is true for the top quintile. Private institutions enroll a higher percentage of top quintile students than public ones. Simon Schwartzman explains that academic majors play a more decisive

FIGURE 8.2 Net enrollment rate in Brazil higher education by income quintile, selected years (1982–2014)

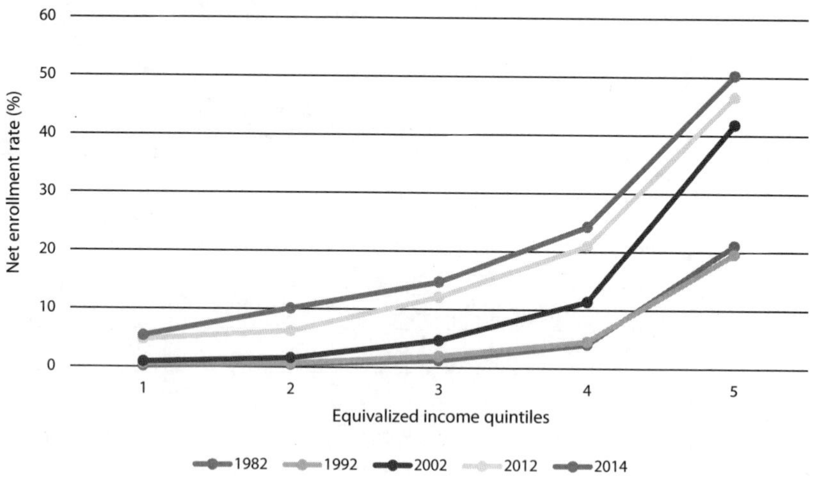

Source: Authors' calculation based on SEDLAC, 2016, www.cedlas.econo.unlp.edu.ar/wp/en/estadisticas/sedlac/estadisticas/#1496165425791-920f2d43-f84a.

Note: 2014 is added as the last data point available.

role in determining an institution's selectivity, not whether an institution is public or private. For instance, medical degree programs tend to be selective in both public and private institutions, while humanities tend to be less selective in both types of institutions.[15]

Brazil also uses several policies to restrict and limit access to higher education that interact with policies for primary and secondary school to aggravate social inequalities. To a large extent, access to the tuition-free public sector (federal and state) is limited by a national exam (National High School Exam, or ENEM).[16] Students who have attended high-quality, usually fee-charging, private secondary schools tend to perform better on that exam and therefore have higher chances of attending a selective and tuition-free public institution/program than those students who attended lower-quality primary and secondary schools.[17] Needy students who attended lower-quality schools, usually public ones, underperform on the exam and do not have more choices than attending nonselective public programs or, in a few cases, enrolling in private institutions.[18] Thus, the Brazilian educational system is not only highly stratified, but it also perpetuates social inequalities.

In an attempt to reduce the inequality gap, both Congress and the federal government have recently favored affirmative action policies and enrollment quotas. In 2010 the Congress adopted the "Statute of Racial Equality," which introduced racial quotas in education. Public institutions modified their admission criteria accordingly, but public universities at the state level (a separate category of public institutions, distinct from federal public institutions) were exempt because federal laws apply only to federal higher education institutions. Private institutions were also exempt. In 2012 the Federal Supreme Court upheld the racial quota, and that same year the federal government enacted a law that reserves 50 percent of the places at federal universities for students who attended a public school. Many of the state-level public universities, specifically those in São Paulo state, had also voluntarily incorporated affirmative action criteria into their admission processes.[19]

The percentage of students who entered through ethnic and public school quotas sharply increased after the enactment of federal laws requiring them. Table 8.1 compares the figures for 2010 and 2015. Overall, federal public institutions enroll about four times more students through quotas than they did five years earlier; state public institutions enroll twice as many. The percentage of students admitted through quotas is lower in state institutions than in federal ones due to their being exempt from the federal quotas. Although the quota policies are increasingly adopted by public higher education institutions, as shown in figure 8.2, there has not been a clear impact of the quota policies in the percentage of low-income students enrolled in higher education. This may be because the vast majority of such students are enrolled in the private sector.

EARLY YEARS AND RECENT REFORMS

Brazil is an outlier not only because of the size of its higher education system or its level of inequality but also because it is one of the youngest systems in the region. While the oldest institutions of higher learning in the Spanish Americas date back to the sixteenth and seventeenth centuries, Brazil created its first higher education institutions in the nineteenth century and its first university at the beginning of the twentieth century.[20] Historical and cultural differences between the Spanish and Portuguese colonies explain the large gap. Portugal preferred to train the colonial elites in the metropolis of the empire; in fact, the University of Coimbra remained the only Portuguese-language university worldwide during several centuries despite many attempts to create higher education institutions in Brazilian territory.[21]

TABLE 8.1 Percentage of newly admitted students through quotas (2010 and 2015)

Higher education institutions by sector	*2010 Ethnic quota*	*2015 Ethnic quota*	*2010 Public school quota*	*2015 Public school quota*	*2010 All types of quotas*	*2015 All types of quotas*
Public (federal)	3%	16%	7%	27%	9%	32%
Public (state)	4%	8%	9%	18%	14%	24%
Public (municipal)	0%	0%	1%	0%	1%	1%
Private (for-profit)	0%	0%	0%	0%	0%	0%
Private (nonprofit)	0%	0%	0%	0%	0%	0%

Source: Authors' calculation based on Instutito Nacional de Estudos e Pesquisas Educacionais Anisio Teixeira (INEP), "Microdados Censo da Educação Superior 2010 & 2015 [2010 & 2015 Higher Education Census Database]," *Portal INEP*, 2010 and 2015, http://portal.inep.gov.br/microdados.

However, as Daniel C. Levy notes, the fundamental difference between Brazil and its neighbors is not just the late starting point for higher education but how quickly the first private institutions emerged after the first public ones were established—just twelve years.[22] For instance, in countries such as Argentina, where the oldest higher education institution was established in 1613, the government did not allow the establishment of private institutions until 1958.[23] By the time the private sector created its first higher education institution in that country, the public sector had already absorbed a considerable part of the demand.[24]

Reforms in 1960 marked a sea change in Brazilian higher education. While under military dictatorship, Brazil adopted a unique version of the US higher education model. It departmentalized its universities and adopted the academic structure of bachelor's, master's, and doctorate degrees.[25] The reforms also restructured the public universities into research institutions, providing a sizable number of full-time and tenure-track positions, leaving little diversification within public sector institutions.[26] This also gave federal universities a selective admissions culture that excluded the bulk of students seeking a higher education, because they could not meet the academic qualifications.[27] By default, as shown in figure 8.3, the private sector started absorbing the "excess" student demand.

The 1960 reform, as well as policies that followed that period, consolidated a public sector with a large share of university institutions, each with full-time faculty who held doctorate degrees.[28] In contrast, most institutions in the private (nonprofit and for-profit) sector are non-university ones, and their faculty are typically part time or without doctorate degrees. Only 13 percent (roughly one million) of the students pursue technical and vocational degrees in Brazil, but most of those students enroll in the for-profit sector (58 percent), compared to 29 percent and 14 percent in the private nonprofit and public sectors, respectively.[29]

Unlike the US model, Brazil fully subsidizes the public sector. That is, students admitted are not charged tuition. The Brazilian constitution requires this as part of a broader set of provisions mandating that the government must subsidize public education. The provision limits the expansion of the public sector through alternative funding mechanisms, such as tuition fees.[30] Therefore, public institutions must rely on government funding for all of their revenues. This limitation is a critical feature, since the resource-intensive universities would require substantial investments to massify the higher education system, as other Latin American countries have already done through their public (Argentina) or public-private sectors (Chile).[31] And those are investments the Brazilian government has not been willing to make.

Argentina may offer one explanation for why Brazil opted not to absorb most of the increase in student demand through a fully subsidized public higher education system and instead did so through an increasingly subsidized private sector. The latest data show that a considerable share of faculty positions in Brazil are full time, which increases the cost structure of the institutions. At federal public institutions, 92 percent of faculty positions are full time, similar to the 76 percent of full-time faculty at state public institutions.[32] In sharp contrast, only 13 percent of the faculty positions at public institutions in Argentina are full time,[33] exposing a clear trade-off between massification of the public sector and availability of resources. Argentina fits the typical model of a mass public sector, whereas Brazil fits the typical model of a mass private sector. The latter model has been instrumental due to its capacity for extremely rapid enrollment growth.[34]

Figure 8.3 clearly shows a trend toward the consolidation of a dominant private sector in Brazil. The public sector remained a leader in higher education enrollment until 1960. In 1970 the private (nonprofit) sector already surpassed the public sector in enrollment by a small margin, and in 1980 that enrollment gap favored the private sector by almost thirty points. The latest figures (2015) show a 51 percentage point lead for the private sector over the public sector.

Except for the full subsidization of the public higher education sector, Brazil shares some commonalities with the US higher education system. In both cases the private sector was established early in the process and benefited from the massification outgrowth. Additionally, although the federal government does not subsidize the private sector supply with direct funding, it subsidizes student demand by providing students with grants and loans. To some observers, subsidizing demand was the best way to expand the system. Without the aid, the

FIGURE 8.3 Public and private enrollment shares in Brazil, selected years

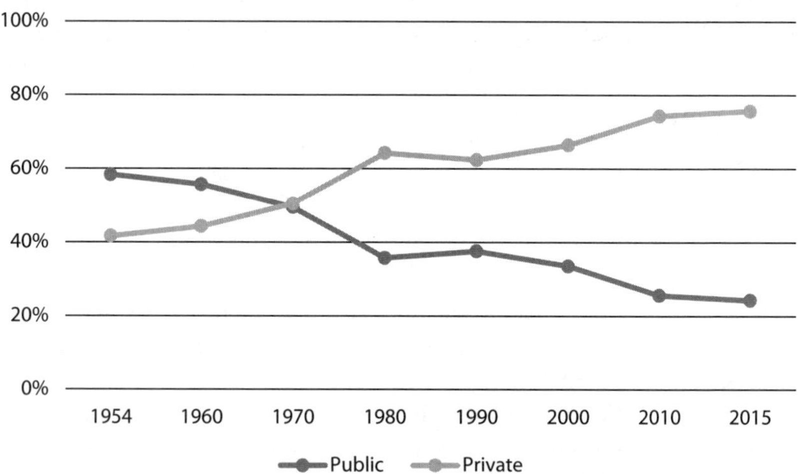

Source: Authors' calculation based on Daniel C. Levy, "Higher Education and the State in Latin America" (Chicago: University of Chicago Press, 1986); INEP, "Microdados Censo da Educação Superior 2010 & 2015 [2010 & 2015 Higher Education Census Database]," Portal INEP, 2010 & 2015, http://portal.inep.gov.br/microdados. Data from 1954 to 1970 from Levy, "Higher Education and the State in Latin America." Data from 1980 to 2014 from INEP. Systematized public-private comparison data until 2010 available at PROPHE website (http://www.albany.edu/~prophe).

Note: The figure compares the public and private sectors over time without a distinction between the private nonprofit and for-profit institutions. The main reason to focus on public versus private is that the private sector remained nonprofit only until 1999. The initial date (1954) reflects the year with the first known data on Brazilian higher education, while 2014 reflects the most recent data available.

private sector would attract few needy students, because they could not afford tuition. And because these needy students graduate from secondary education at lower rates on average than their wealthier classmates, they would also be shut out of the public universities, which tend to be selective. But there is a downside to relying on private higher education. Even if governmental incentives increase access for needier students to attend private institutions, they enter mostly teaching institutions and earn credentials that are less valued in the market than those from other professional fields.[35]

TRANSFORMING THE PRIVATE HIGHER EDUCATION SECTOR

In 1990 Brazil enrolled three of five students attending colleges and universities in the private sector. By that time many private institutions were behaving as for-profits despite a legal prohibition against doing so.[36] In other words, de jure nonprofits were de facto profiting, a typical case in private education worldwide.[37] In the late 1990s the administration of then president Fernando Henrique Cardoso wanted to take action to address this issue. He had at least three choices:

FIGURE 8.4 Enrollment in Brazilian higher education by sector

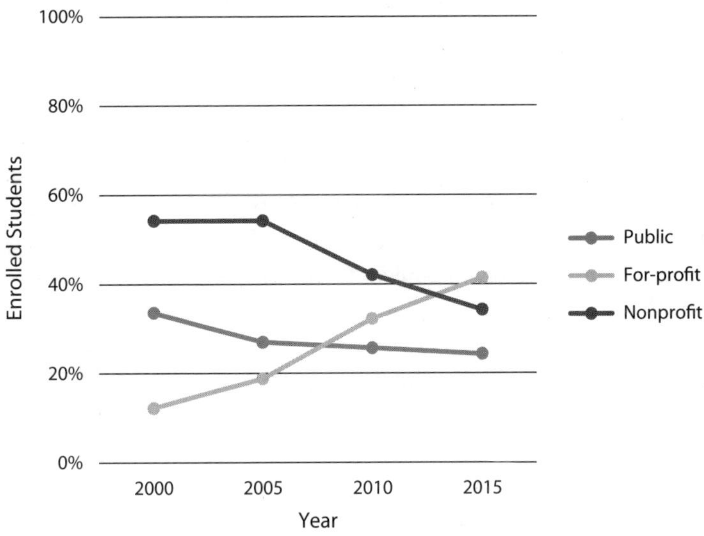

Source: Authors' calculation based on Edson de Oliveira Nunes, "Educação Superior No Brasil: Estudos, Debates, Controvérsias" [Higher Education in Brazil: Studies, Debates, and Controversies] (Rio de Janeiro: Garamond, 2012); INEP, "Microdados Censo da Educação Superior 2015 [2015 Higher Education Census Database]," Portal INEP, 2015, http://portal.inep.gov.br/microdados; PROPHE. "Data on Private Higher Education in Brazil," 2012, http://www.albany.edu/~prophe.

- continue to overlook the situation as previous administrations had done, hence, not enforcing regulation;
- enforce the legislation that prohibits profiting and penalize institutions; or
- allow institutions to be established or changed to for-profit status and collect more taxes from them.[38]

By the end of 1990s the Cardoso administration made a bold move to expand access to higher education, which many observers linked to market-friendly or "neoliberal" policies.[39] The federal government began allowing colleges and universities to operate as for-profit entities. Just six years after the decision was made, the for-profit sector had enrolled almost a million students, and by 2015 for-profit institutions enrolled more than 3 million students, surpassing the enrollment of the public and the private nonprofit sectors (which enrolled nearly 2 million and 2.5 million students, respectively). Absolute enrollment numbers moved upward for all three sectors (public, private nonprofit, and private for-profit); however, the analysis of enrollment shares by sector in figure 8.4 shows a consolidating trend: the rate of the for-profit sector growth outpaced both the public and the private nonprofit sectors. Relative enrollment growth of the for-profits meant there was a continuous decline in the other two sectors.

A CONCENTRATED MARKET

The for-profit sector in Brazil follows a pattern that is similar to its US counterpart: the consolidation of large publicly traded companies alongside smaller, sometimes family-based institutions.[40] However, Brazil departs from the US case in the distinctions between the nonprofit and the for-profit sectors. Whereas the US includes a higher number of elite and semi-elite institutions in the nonprofit sector, Brazil has only a few prestigious private institutions. In Brazil the private sector (nonprofit and for-profit) mainly behaves as a demand absorber. Thus, Brazil shows relatively similar compositions of the nonprofit and for-profit sectors, and their boundaries are blurry in features such as programs (e.g., fields of study), students (e.g., nontraditional), and faculty (e.g., full-time).[41]

Enrollment is also increasingly concentrated among a few for-profit companies. Estimates indicate that the ten largest for-profit companies enroll approximately 40 percent of students in the private sector.[42] Most of the enrollments are clustered in domestic publicly traded companies, along with some multinational corporations. One of the largest, Kroton Educacional, offers educational programs on a variety of levels, from primary to higher education, including vocational programs. In higher education the company is divided into two business segments: on-site and distance learning. The magnitude of Kroton's operations (for the entire company, not only the higher education section) could be summed up in its 2016 net income: BRL 1.86 billion (about USD 600 million).[43] Kroton's net income surpasses even large, US-based for-profit providers such as Laureate Education and Adtalem Global Education (formerly DeVry). Laureate's 2016 net income was USD 370.31 million, and Adtalem took a loss of USD 3.28 million (but in 2015 and 2017, Adtalem's net income was about USD 130 million).[44]

In 2013 Kroton merged with Anhanguera Educacional Participações, consolidating as the largest educational provider in Brazil, with the largest enrollment share in the system. Although both companies started as domestic endeavors, they are partly owned by US private-equity groups. The merger of these two companies (at the time they were the two largest Brazilian for-profits investing in higher education) created the world's largest for-profit operator by market capitalization.[45]

These publicly traded companies have gone through a series of recent mergers. After its merger with Anhanguera, Kroton attempted to buy Estácio S.A., another educational provider that plays an important role in higher education. If the antitrust approves the merger, the resulting company would own many higher education institutions across Brazil, and enrollments would reach 1.5 million students.[46] This company would represent almost 50 percent and 26 percent of student enrollment in the for-profit and private sectors, respectively.

Although Brazil is experiencing a financial (and political) crisis, the financial situation of the large for-profit companies appears to be good. While revenue has remained relatively flat comparing the 2015 and 2016 fiscal years, the net income increased by 34 percent. Some observers wonder to what extent these figures may show a trend toward declining quality of the services provided by these companies. Notably, these companies are taking advantage of the financial crisis to buy free-standing institutions or to merge with other smaller corporations.[47] Some experts caution that the expansion of large companies may reduce market competition and affect the perceived quality of the services.[48]

SUBSIDIZING PRIVATE HIGHER EDUCATION: DIFFERENT IDEOLOGIES, SIMILAR PUBLIC POLICIES

Striking as it may seem for a developing economy and a young democracy, policies aimed at private higher education have been consistent across the political spectrum despite antagonistic rhetoric. Both major political parties (and coalitions) have supported and promoted the expansion of the higher education system through the private sector, including the usually controversial for-profit sector.[49]

As noted earlier, legislation prohibits subsidizing private higher education institutions in a direct way. However, the prohibition affects only the supply side (i.e., directly providing public funds to the institutions). The federal government uses two main policy tools to funnel enrollment growth to the private sector: (1) student loan schemes aimed at students enrolling in private institutions, and (2) tax relief to those private institutions that offer scholarships to needy students. These financial mechanisms to expand access to higher education apply to both the private nonprofit and for-profit sectors.

Within the financial aid policies, student loan schemes are hardly something new in the Brazilian landscape. Levy identifies the availability of student loans in the early stages of the development of the higher education system, although these loans were much smaller in scope than the current ones.[50] In 2001 the Student Financing Fund (FIES in Portuguese) replaced the previous loan scheme, Crédito Educativo.[51]

FIES targets students enrolled in the private sector (nonprofit and for-profit) in programs that are evaluated by the Ministry of Education and Culture.[52] Although these are student loans, the funds go directly to the institution, not to the student. The debt becomes an obligation of the student to be paid to the government after graduation. Institutions may use those funds to pay federal taxes and to cover operational costs.[53] FIES rapidly became the main policy tool designed by Cardoso's administration to direct enrollment growth toward the private sector. However, due to some restrictions in the financial eligibility requirements (e.g., family income), the federal government granted only 294,000 loans during the first six years of its implementation (2004–2009), a relatively small number compared to the 2,187,000 loans granted by the government over the following six years (2010–2015). In short, applicants had difficulty showing solvency and repayment capacity, preventing them from accessing the loan programs.

President Luiz Inácio "Lula" da Silva's party platform included public policy statements that were antagonistic toward the private sector. However, as noted earlier, Lula's leftist-populist administration not only kept the loan system as it was but also enhanced it. In 2010 the federal government remodeled Cardoso's FIES program. The modifications included the reduction of the interest rate from 9 percent to 3.4 percent per year and extended the repayment grace period after graduation from six months to eighteen months.[54] Thus, the modifications to the FIES program entailed more generous and flexible terms. As figure 8.5 shows, this modification fueled rapid growth in the number of loans, reaching its peak in 2014, when the federal government issued more than seven hundred thousand loans.

Almost 40 percent of the newly enrolled students benefited from the government-backed loan scheme in 2014, in sharp contrast to 2009, the year before the Lula administration made the aforementioned modifications, when less than 5 percent of new students were covered by the FIES program. Undoubtedly, FIES has become a key policy instrument to direct enrollment growth toward the private sector. Within a context of the ongoing financial crisis that led to cuts in new loans to less than half in just one year (2014–2015), it is not clear if this enrollment growth is sustainable. In December 2014 President Dilma Rousseff's administration decided to make two major changes to FIES eligibility requirements. First, students can no longer benefit from both FIES and scholarships at the same time. Second, the amendment requires a minimum score on the National High School Exam as an eligibility requirement to apply for FIES.[55]

Private higher education institutions reacted to these changes with legal challenges.[56] Associations representing these providers claimed that this measure is

FIGURE 8.5 Number of new FIES loans (in thousands) and percentage of new students covered by FIES

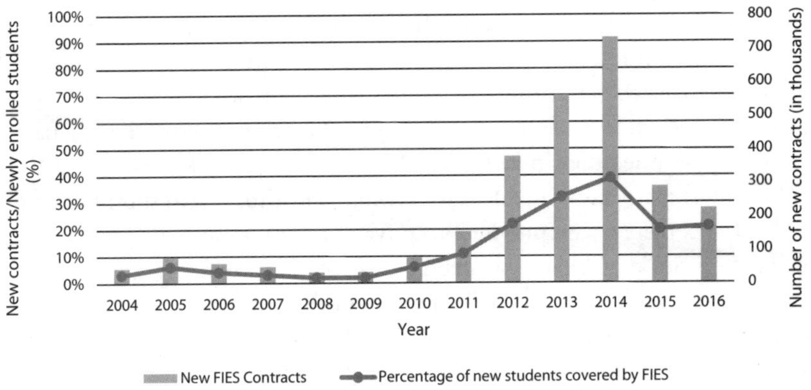

Source: Authors' translation to English from Fábio Reis and Rodrigo Capelato, "A relevância do ensino superior privado no Brasil," *Revista de Educación Superior en América Latina,* no. 1 (2016), http://rcientificas.uninorte.edu.co/index.php/edusuplatam/article/view/9430.

biased against their institutions. The government contended that modifications to the FIES program are in line with quality assurance policies. Although these changes affected the value of the share price of publicly traded companies, large for-profit companies are taking advantage of this slowdown to buy smaller companies and institutions, which have difficulty navigating the financial crisis.[57]

Aside from the government's financial difficulties, policy makers may have been prompted to modify the loan program because it increasingly shows signs of poor performance and may not be sustainable. In 2016 the Brazilian federal audit court (TCU in Portuguese) conducted an audit on the FIES program by request of the Congress. The report shows that only 51 percent of loans are current. More than a quarter of the loans (26 percent) have been delinquent for more than 360 days (officially defaulted), while the remaining 23 percent are loans that have not been paid on time up to 360 days. The audit argues that the high levels of delinquency are the result of a lack of quality control and enforcement. While the TCU recognizes that FIES student loans play a critical social role, the audit bureau highlighted the need to increase the loan program's sustainability and student accountability.[58] Brazilian repayment rates are relatively low but not atypical. For instance, in the US only 63 percent of loans are paid on time, 13 percent are in default, and 8 percent have not paid for up to 360 days. Another 15 percent are in deferment or forbearance because the borrower is having difficulty repaying.[59] In Chile, another South American country with decades of experience with student loan schemes, the share of borrowers in good standing is about 61 percent, with the delinquency rate at almost 39 percent of the borrowers, which again is quite similar to figures in Brazil and the US.[60]

Although the redevelopment of the loan scheme was meant to provide aid to an increased number of needy students, the government designed additional incentives to reach set enrollment targets. Based on what some scholars have claimed was a product of strong lobbying by the private sector, the federal government established the University for All program (widely known as PROUNI) in 2005.[61] The program provides tax benefits to institutions to subsidize student demand. Tax benefits are provided to private (nonprofit and for-profit) colleges and universities that offer scholarships to needy students who graduated from public high schools.[62] The federal government designed this program to supplement the FIES program, because many needy students were still not eligible to apply for student loans based on financial requirements.

A fundamental difference between FIES and PROUNI is that scholarships, unlike loans, do not need to be paid back. PROUNI mixes need-based and merit-based eligibility criteria. To qualify, the student's family income must not be higher than three times the minimum wage.[63] The neediest students qualify for full scholarships, and those in better socioeconomic situations receive partial scholarships. For the merit component, students can apply for PROUNI spots only if they have scored at least 450 of 1,000 points on the National High School Exam. That requirement is a quality assurance mechanism for public funding provided to private higher education.[64] It is meant to ensure that private providers are enrolling only academically prepared and qualified students. As discussed earlier, this type of requirement limits the opportunities for those most in need, because these students typically could not afford to attend high-quality private secondary schools, nor can they afford to purchase the tutoring and materials needed to prepare for the exam.

PROUNI also extended new tax benefits to for-profit private institutions in the form of broad tax exemptions if they provided scholarships to low-income students. As a result of the reforms, such institutions that offer scholarships end up with similar tax benefits as their religious, nonprofit counterparts. The private sector aggressively and rapidly responded to this new incentive. Figure 8.6 shows a sharp and steady growth in the number of PROUNI scholarships available to students in need. In PROUNI's eleven-year existence, higher education institutions have provided almost 3 million full and partial scholarships. Additionally, scholarships have increased at an average annual growth rate of 11 percent. Since this funding program is based on tax exemptions and does not involve direct payments to institutions from the government, it has endured the recent budget

FIGURE 8.6 Number of full and partial PROUNI scholarships available per year

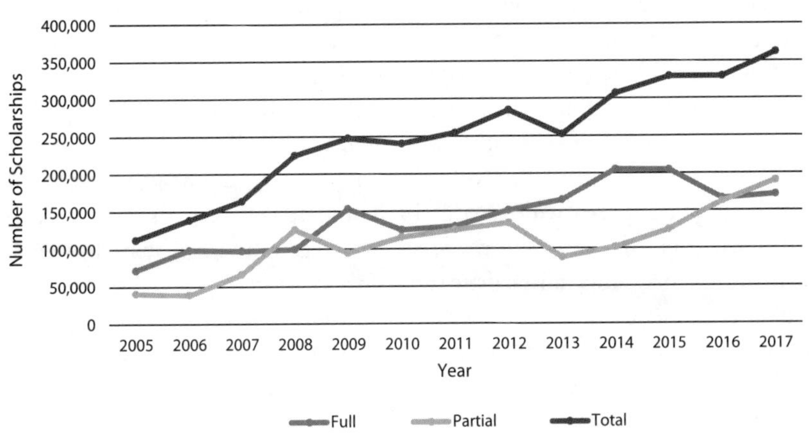

Source: Authors' calculation using Federal Ministry of Education and Culture (MEC) data, http://prouniportal.mec.gov.br/dados-e-estatisticas/9-quadros-informativos.

crisis better than FIES. While the government has cut or limited other sources of funding for higher education, policy makers have not changed the PROUNI program, and the number of scholarships available remains in an upward trend.

Together, FIES and PROUNI have reached almost three million students each, in twelve and eleven years, respectively. Although some students may have received both FIES loans and partial PROUNI scholarships (except as of 2014), the funding scheme plays a critical role in supporting the private sector's enrollment growth, which expanded from slightly more than three million students in 2005 to just over six million students in 2015. Schwartzman estimates that the federal government spends approximately BRL 2 billion (approximately USD 600 million) on FIES and PROUNI, a large sum considering the critical rhetoric from policy makers regarding private higher education in recent decades.[65]

REGULATING PRIVATE HIGHER EDUCATION THROUGH QUALITY ASSURANCE

The first formal steps toward establishing quality assurance mechanisms for higher education in Brazil date to the mid-1990s.[66] This meant a new relationship between the government and higher education institutions, which occurred against the backdrop of rapid enrollment growth, greater heterogeneity among providers, and public distrust of private higher education. The role of the government thus shifted from a benevolent to an evaluative one.[67]

The establishment of a quality assurance system follows a trend that is already in place in Latin America, where many countries have established standards, tests, and regulatory agencies.[68] Public distrust of private colleges and universities stems from the increasing diversification of the higher education systems that commonly occurs during their massification and universalization.[69] As systems grow larger, stratification of institutions is inevitable.[70] Private higher education in many countries, mostly in those where private institutions play a "demand-absorbing" role, is seen with distrust by its public counterparts.[71] This lack of trust is exacerbated when the private sector can legally adopt a for-profit status.[72] Increasingly, for-profits in Brazil are seen as controversial not only by their public counterparts but also by the nonprofit sector. Some observers even call for tighter regulation but just for for-profits, mostly regarding quality assurance.[73]

Regulation of private institutions in the Brazilian higher education system is conducted in two main ways. First, the federal government utilizes the results from the ENEM as an eligibility requirement to apply for financial aid (loans and scholarships). Second, it uses various criteria to assess the quality of programs and institutions. Within those criteria, a central one has been the Provão and its redeveloped version, the National Student Performance Exam (ENADE in Portuguese). The Provão was first established in 1995 when Congress passed a law creating the National Evaluation System, and the ENADE replaced it beginning in 2004.[74]

While US audiences may be more familiar with quality controls for *institutions* of higher education, the ENEM is focused on the quality of the prospective *students*.[75] The federal government designed this exam as a quality screen for the students that any higher education institution (public or private) may admit and to determine if those students are eligible for government aid, but only at private higher educations. Developed in 1998 and widely used by federal universities since 2009 (its redeveloped version), ENEM is a test aimed at measuring knowledge acquired during high school. Students apply to programs at federal universities in a centralized system called the Unified Selection System. Based on the ENEM score, students may request admission to most federal universities. Some federal, state, and private institutions use ENEM's results as part of their admission systems but not as the sole criterion. Some state and private institutions still use the Vestibular (an institution-based admission exam) but not as widely as in the past.

As mentioned above, the PROUNI scholarship program uses the ENEM scores as an eligibility criterion.[76] In 2014 the federal government expanded the test to the student loan program. Students must obtain a minimum score of 450 points to qualify. Almost six million students took the exam in 2014, and approximately 1.5 million of them did not reach the minimum score and thus did not qualify for any government aid.[77] Those differences widen when comparing students who attended public versus private secondary schools. Less than 10 percent of the students coming from private secondary schools failed to reach the minimum score, whereas 25 percent of the students from public secondary schools failed. To some extent this finding confirms the challenges that students who attended public secondary schools face in accessing higher education in Brazil. Typically, low-income students who attended public secondary education underperform in the exit exam and have little chance of being admitted and accessing financial aid to attend higher education. The difference in performance exacerbates income inequality between those attending public and private secondary schools and restricts higher education enrollment. In other words, enrollment growth in Brazil has been rapid, but it would have been even more so if it were not for the academic eligibility criteria imposed on low-income students.

In addition to the ENEM, the federal government administers the ENADE. As mentioned above, the ENADE replaced the long-standing student performance exam widely known as the Provão beginning in 2004. The ENADE is a nationwide assessment of students while they are attending higher education institutions in their first and final years of enrollment. This is yet another instance of Brazil preferring to focus on *student* performance for quality assurance in contrast to the US approach, which relies on *institutional* metrics. Although the ENADE is not a high-stakes exam (the results do not have any effect on the student), students must take it in order to obtain a diploma. The ultimate goal of the exam is to include information about student performance in assessing the quality of higher education institutions and specific education programs. The exam has steadily grown from including only three fields of study initially to twenty-six today. In 2001 Brazil's National Institute of Educational Studies and Research (INEP in Portuguese) was given authority to use the results of the exam (at that time the test was still the Provão) to license and renew licenses of higher education institutions and undergraduate programs.[78] However, only in extreme cases have institutions or programs lost licensing despite concerns that some private institutions continually underperform in evaluations.[79]

The federal government uses the ENADE in formulas to determine the quality of undergraduate programs and institutions. More recently, INEP has built two main indexes to determine program and institutional quality: the Preliminary Program Category and the General Program Index.[80] The former is used to assign a category to undergraduate courses and the latter, for institutions. Both result in a composite index that heavily weights ENADE scores and other institutional variables of relevance.[81] Those categories turn into program and institutional rankings from 1 to 5, with the higher number (5) signifying excellence. If a program or institution receives unsatisfactory scores (1 or 2) for more than two years in a row, the federal government may order a halt to enrollment, and the institution or program would automatically lose eligibility for federal financial aid (FIES and PROUNI). Losing eligibility for financial aid is an incremental sanction; if a college or university does not comply with recommended improvements, it is shut down. The results have led many to see scores as a ranking of programs and institutions, but policy makers argue that the intent is only to improve quality and accountability.[82]

These assessments and the rankings continue to face criticism by the academic community.[83] One problem relates to the difficulty of calculating value-added measures. Specifically, first-year students' performance cannot adequately be compared to those in the last year, since it is a different class of students.[84] Despite their methodological flaws, the government continues to use these exams and methods of scoring to reward or punish programs and institutions.

Even with the distrust of private higher education in Brazil, an analysis of the results of program evaluations shows little difference in performance between public and private (nonprofit and for-profit) sectors. This is in direct conflict with the conventional wisdom that the private sector, and mainly for-profits, inherently provides lower-quality education. In 2014 an average of 12.1 percent of the assessed undergraduate programs received underachieving categories (1 and 2), with the public sector having slightly fewer cases (9.2 percent) than the private for-profit (13.4 percent) and nonprofit (14.3 percent) institutions. A similar trend can be observed at the institution level. Sixteen percent of institutions did not reach category 3 or higher, with surprisingly similar rates in the public (15.1 percent), private nonprofit (16.4 percent), and for-profit (15.8 percent) sectors.[85] To be sure, many scholars have criticized the basis of the exam used as the main variable to define the categories. Even so, these indexes do maintain a level of legitimacy as the main policy tools employed by the federal government to determine whether a program or institution participates in financial aid programs, and the measures are widely used by other entities interested in quality.

Programs that fall into categories 1 and 2 in the preliminary evaluation are subject to a site visit from the federal government to analyze the situation and determine whether the category assigned is correct. If the result of the on-site evaluation confirms the preliminary category, then programs must commit to overcoming the deficiencies. If the underperforming programs continue underperforming in successive evaluations, the federal government may decide to halt new enrollment and limit access to financial aid. But such action is still rare. In 2014 just 2 percent of the assessed higher education programs lost their credentials, mostly programs provided by the private sector.[86] These policy tools may be useful at filtering out dubious programs from "predatory" providers, but it appears that the government is reluctant to take such action when it is warranted.

CONCLUSION

Expanding access to higher education entails risks. As policy makers pursue this goal, the higher education systems inevitably become more complex and diverse. Typically, that diversification leads to an expansion of teaching-centered institutions, generally criticized by their research-centered peers as being inherently low quality. The situation becomes even more pronounced when the growth occurs through the private sector. But as the case of Brazil shows, convenience often trumps ideological objections to expanding higher education through private providers. The private sector can more easily add capacity to reach enrollment targets with less of a public investment than expanding tuition-free public universities that have high cost structures. In Brazil, successive federal administrations (with a few exceptions) saw the private sector as a pragmatic way to expand access by providing students with a mix of loans and scholarships to attend them.

Brazil's experience in directing enrollment growth to the private sector highlights a number of important policy trade-offs that have implications for higher education policy in the US. In systems with largely uniform public sectors that fully subsidize students (i.e., by providing free tuition) and employ only full-time faculty with doctorate degrees, expanding access in the public sector is financially challenging. Adding capacity requires large government investments. In this context the private nonprofit and for-profit sectors are an expedient and less expensive way to expand higher education. But this approach is not without its own set of trade-offs—and controversy.

As expected, the expansion and diversification of higher education in Brazil raises quality concerns. In Brazil, as in many other Latin American and European countries, public institutions tend to be at the top of the quality and prestige ladder. Private institutions in Brazil, except for a few cases, focus on teaching and tend to be viewed somewhere toward the middle and bottom part of the prestige ladder. Unlike the US, where for-profits are more heavily regulated (e.g., the gainful employment regulation) than their nonprofit and public counterparts, in Brazil the same rules apply to all sectors. However, due to the legal status of Brazilian public higher education institutions, it would be impossible to shut one down based on low performance.[87] Yet government ranking results show that public universities and their programs tend to fail accountability tests at similar rates.

Perhaps the most surprising response to quality concerns among private higher education providers is Brazil's early and bold move toward considering student performance measures to evaluate programs and institutions. In addition to an evaluation that includes assessments of first- and final-year students as a way to measure outcome indicators, Brazil restricts eligibility for loans and scholarships based on student test scores. Instead of punishing programs and institutions by shutting them down, the federal government approaches regulation in incremental steps. If programs underperform, they have the chance to improve with governmental oversight from the quality assurance agency. If they do not improve within three years, they automatically lose access to federal financial aid (only programs in the private sector are sanctioned in this way).

Finally, some issues remain unresolved and are likely to shape future policy debates in Brazil. The accountability system remains centralized under one agency that many worry does not have the capacity in a growing system to sustain the incremental approach to helping low-performing institutions improve. Additionally, for-profit institutions continue to concentrate under the control of a few large companies, and this may bring more challenges to the federal government in the future as it works to maintain quality controls. Some observers are already calling for additional regulation of for-profit providers. But as this chapter shows, because private providers are uniquely situated to expand access to higher education, policy makers are likely to exercise restraint in regulating this sector.

Conclusion

Jason D. Delisle and Alex Usher

The chapters in this volume have much to add to conventional views about higher education policies abroad. They show that many features of a country's higher education system can be part of a broader set of trade-offs and policy choices. In contrast to debates in the US, which often imply that looking to other countries will reveal silver-bullet solutions, reality is much more complicated. That does not mean US policy makers cannot learn from other countries and borrow their policies. Rather, they should look to them with a broader perspective that seeks to understand and acknowledge the unintended consequences and limitations of such policies. The chapters in this volume make clear that these unintended consequences and limitations are not mere abstractions or hypotheticals. In fact, one of the key lessons is that the trade-offs policy makers must balance when implementing higher education policies show up in similar patterns across a diverse range of countries. They are more the rule than the exception. Being aware of these patterns will not only help US policy makers looking abroad to manage expectations about the merits of specific policies but will also encourage them to think carefully about how to strike the right balance among the goals that this volume shows are so often in tension.

In this concluding chapter we link themes and lessons from the chapters in this volume to specific policy debates happening today in the United States. But before proceeding to that discussion, it is helpful to establish some important facts about the US higher education system. Contrary to what is often implied in debates about reforming higher education in the US, there are many ways in which the US system is as good as, or even superior to, higher education systems in other countries. In other words, some of the impetus to look abroad in order to solve problems here in the US might be based on the faulty premise that the US is underperforming on some key metric relative to other countries. On the contrary, many countries have been striving to reach US performance levels on a range of metrics. The discussion below thus ensures that we are not looking abroad to solve a problem that does not actually exist in the US or does not exist to the extent that popular accounts would have us believe.

STRENGTHS AND WEAKNESSES OF THE US SYSTEM

Although critiques of the US system often start from the premise that higher education outcomes in the United States trail those of other countries in various ways, the available data hardly paint a negative picture. To be sure, the US system is not lacking in challenges, but it is important to understand its success as well as its failures.

Access and Attainment

The data show fairly unequivocally that the United States remains one of the top countries in ensuring *access* to higher education. The Organisation of Economic Cooperation and Development's (OECD's) *Education at a Glance 2017* shows that among major OECD countries, the US is second only to Korea in terms of the percentage of eighteen-to-twenty-year-olds enrolled in tertiary education, roughly 15 percentage points above the OECD average.[1] The United States does not have as clear an advantage when it comes to *attainment*: although 48 percent of Americans ages twenty-five to thirty-four have a tertiary credential, this is well behind countries such as Japan (60 percent), Canada (61 percent), and Korea (70 percent). That said, America trails these countries mostly in terms of attainment at the associate degree level; the American rate of bachelor's attainment still exceeds the OECD average by 5 percentage points, which is equal to Sweden and considerably ahead of Germany. The United States is clearly not as efficient in bachelor's degree production, however. Many students who start a degree fail to complete it, which means resources are spent on the education but no credential is earned. While that is a problem policy makers should be trying to solve, the country is still above average in terms of degree awards and well above average in terms of initial access to education.

Looking at access to higher education in terms of family backgrounds reveals additional strengths. Roughly half of all American students come from families with no college experience. According to the OECD, this is a greater percentage than either Germany or Finland, suggesting that despite greater financial barriers for students, the United States is performing at or above international norms in terms of ensuring that access is socially equitable.[2] One might argue that access to college in the US is still highly stratified: elite schools enroll far more students from high-income families than low-income families, while students with the lowest levels of financial, social, and cultural capital are vastly overrepresented at community colleges. Those are accurate statements, but they are not unique to the US. Other national systems have their own prestige and selectivity hierarchies that produce economic stratification in much the same way that they do in the US.

Subsidies, Student Aid, and College Prices

Where the data appear to support critics of the US system most strongly is on the issue of high prices and student debt. Nevertheless, the US achieves the relatively strong outcomes discussed above despite these relatively high tuition and debt levels. One reason those characteristics may not have the effects many assume they should is that tuition and debt are not nearly as high or unaffordable in the United States as commonly understood, nor are they much lower in other countries.

Criticisms about high tuition in the US tend to focus on outlier institutions of higher education or do not factor in generous student aid programs that flow from multiple sources. While it is true that tuition at elite private universities can reach nearly USD 40,000 annually, non-elite public universities that enroll the bulk of students attending four-year institutions charge median, in-state tuition of USD 7,835.[3] But even that amount overstates the price students actually pay. The US has a highly differentiated pricing scheme for its higher education system that provides more aid to lower-income students and less for others. Claims about high education prices in the US rarely note that students from low-income and high-income families pay very different prices to attend the same institutions.

For example, 58 percent of students from families earning less than USD 28,000 who attend in-state public universities full time pay no tuition after all sources of student aid are factored in (excluding student loans as aid).[4] While the institutions they attend charge a median in-state sticker price of USD 7,022 for tuition and fees per year, most low-income students receive enough in discounts, grants, and tax benefits to fully offset that tuition.[5] Even middle-income students attending these institutions are spared the full price. Their median net price was USD 1,241 after discounts, grants, and tax benefits are included, compared with a median in-state, full-time sticker price of USD 8,268 for the institutions they attend.[6] It is largely students from upper-middle and high-income families who pay full tuition.[7] Of course, this analysis demonstrates that US subsidies for higher education may be opaque—a fair criticism of the US relative to other countries—but they are not ungenerous.

Student Loans

When it comes to government-issued student loans, calls to adopt policies in other countries fail to acknowledge how much the US system has evolved over the last decade. Today the US already offers many of the features reformers argue it should copy from other countries, particularly those related to our income-based repayment plan. In 2009 the US implemented its first widely available plan for borrowers to repay their federal loans as a share of their incomes. Income-based repayment (IBR) is not the automatic option nor the sole repayment plan borrowers may use, as they do in other countries that use similar programs. Rather, borrowers opt in by submitting documentation of their incomes, usually their most recently filed federal income tax return. All borrowers with federal student loans are eligible for this option, under which payments are capped at 10 percent of discretionary income (defined as 150 percent of the federal poverty guidelines by household size, or about USD 18,000 for a single person). Any unpaid debt that remains after twenty years of payments is forgiven. In 2017 more loan debt was enrolled in this repayment plan (41 percent) than any of the other repaying options.[8]

Just as students in the US now have access to a generous IBR plans, the amounts they borrow for undergraduate educations are not that different from those in many other countries, nor are they as high in the US as media narratives suggest. Most news stories tend to focus on students with $50,000 or $100,000 in debt and leave the impression that every student leaves school with debt. In reality, most of these stories are about students who borrowed for graduate and professional school. Moreover, about one-third of students pursuing a four-year degree leave without debt.[9] Those who do and complete a degree leave with a median balance of $28,000.[10] That may sound high, but several studies have shown that as a share of household income, student loan payments have remained constant for decades.[11] Nevertheless, even if the debt levels are seen as too high, the universal access to IBR for government-issued loans guarantees all borrowers the same level of affordability.

Other features of the US loan system also meet or exceed what one finds in many countries. In the US loans are available for all credentials from certificates up to graduate school degrees. And there is no means test or academic requirement to qualify for government student loans. That is not the case in most other countries, where loans are limited in various ways, either by excluding students in vocational programs, by not incorporating living costs into the need assessment formula, or by having stricter requirements with respect to course loads. Another way that the US system is comparatively generous is in some of the specific features of its IBR plan. Providing borrowers with loan forgiveness after only twenty years of payments is ten years earlier than under the UK system, while Australia does not provide any loan forgiveness benefit under its income-contingent loan program. Australia also requires borrowers to make progressively higher payments as their incomes increase, but the US does not, providing relatively larger benefits to high-income borrowers.[12]

AMERICAN EXCEPTIONALISM IN HIGHER EDUCATION

The foregoing examples provide just a few snapshots of the US higher education system in comparison to peer nations. But before moving on to what—if anything—the United States should apply from international policy learning, there are unique features of the US system that may make importing policies from abroad practically or politically difficult.

The first of these is that the US spends more on its higher education system than virtually any other country in the world. With expenditures of over USD 29,300 per student on average, the US is the top-spending country in the OECD by a considerable distance, with only Switzerland (USD 27,800 per student) coming close.[13] The average across the OECD as a whole is a mere USD 16,143. The US has a similarly large advantage if we look at expenditures as a percentage of gross domestic product (GDP): at 2.7 percent the US figure is the highest of all OECD countries, with only Canada (2.6%) coming close to a similar level. The OECD average is 1.5 percent. The reason the US is able to spend more on higher education than other countries is because its institutions charge relatively high tuition. Government expenditures on higher education institutions in the US are actually below the OECD average (0.9% of GDP vs. 1.1%).[14]

Some observers might consider this a flaw in the US system, arguing that the higher spending is due to waste on lavish student amenities (climbing walls, lazy rivers, etc.) or administrative bloat. But others believe the additional funds result in higher quality institutions, more prestigious universities, broader student access, and more consumer choices. In other words, they view higher spending as a feature of US system, not a flaw. They would thus be reluctant to support reforms that threatened this perceived advantage.

There is something else the US system is buying with the extra 1.2 percent of GDP it spends on higher education, and that is the second feature that makes the US system unique. Some of that extra spending is cross-subsidizing the world's largest system of scientific research. The scale of scientific facilities and research efforts at American universities dwarfs those of other nations, which is why US universities typically dominate the major international university rankings. As Christopher Newfield has noted at some length in his book *The Great Mistake*, tuition dollars (and hence student aid dollars) are to a large extent implicitly subsidizing these research activities.[15] Thus, the answer to the question of how some foreign higher education systems manage to generate such "good" outcomes as low tuition, low debt, and so forth, is in part that universities abroad are not usually expected to fulfill a research mission along with their core educational missions. Jon Marcus makes exactly this point in the first chapter of this volume, which focuses on free college policies in Europe. US audiences tend to view the research role of universities as a positive attribute, however, and policies that rely on deemphasizing the research mission of universities to further some other goal are likely to encounter strong political resistance.

LINKING INTERNATIONAL LESSONS TO THE US

The chapters in this volume imply many lessons for contemporary debates about the US higher education system and policy reform. In the remainder of this chapter we briefly discuss three specific policy lessons that emerge throughout the volume that are relevant to US debates. The first provides lessons for US policy makers on what can be learned from student loan policies in other countries; the second focuses on tuition-free policies abroad and what they suggest for those policies in the US at both the state and federal level; finally, we discuss what policy makers can learn from the successes and challenges other countries have faced in trying to expand access to higher education, particularly to historically underrepresented groups.

Student Debt

There are a number of ways in which the chapters in this volume offer a new perspective on the US student loan program and potential reforms. Alex Usher's chapter on student loan systems shows how countries that integrate their income-based student loan programs into their income tax and payroll withholding systems offer an appealing alternative to the US approach. The US requires borrowers to opt into income-based repayment, submit documentation for their income (which is at least a year old at that point), and remember to send in monthly payments on time. As a result, many borrowers who qualify for low monthly payments—or no monthly payment at all if their income is low enough—never enroll, manage to stay enrolled, or receive loan forgiveness. In contrast, the tax collection approach in other countries is automatic, and the borrower need not worry about making the correct payments—or so it would seem.

Usher's chapter shows how borrowers in those systems still must opt into repayment by notifying their employer that they have a student loan. They must also fill out additional paperwork with employers if they hold more than one job to ensure they are not under-withholding payments. There is also a year-end process for reconciling payments to income, somewhat like the US tax filing process, that borrowers must complete themselves. A closer look at these system reveals that they are not automatic, foolproof, and free of paperwork burdens. Nor do they make it impossible for borrowers to default or underpay, as some might assume. Thus, importing this approach to the US system for loan repayment may not solve the problems many of its proponents argue that it will, such as eliminating administrative burdens and loan defaults.

Usher also reveals that countries that integrate loan collection into their tax systems have income tax reporting systems that track borrowers' incomes and payments in near-real time. New Zealand is the standout example. Such systems make reporting and tracking monthly loan payments easy for the government and the borrower. Meanwhile, the US tax collection system is set up to track such information only once a year with a delay of several months (i.e., the annual income tax filing process). That makes it a poor fit for tracking loans that accrue interest daily and for which payments are due monthly. In other words, it may be that in order to adopt other countries' tax-based collection system for student loans, the US would have to adopt their *entire income tax collection systems* to make the loan collection system work as it does in those countries. At a minimum, importing the loan collection systems would require modifications to the international models, which might water down the benefits that the reform was supposed to provide in the first place.

Another lesson that appears in several of the chapters is that loan performance (i.e., on-time repayment or full repayment) is weak in systems that allow greater access to government-sponsored loan programs. This highlights a direct tradeoff between policies that promote more open access to government aid and how likely students are to fully repay their debt. Other countries have to reckon with this tension just as the US does. There is no easy way to avoid it by adopting some countervailing policy.

For example, Dante J. Salto writes that in Brazil, where the government has promoted greater access to higher education by providing subsidized loans that students can use to attend private, mostly for-profit institutions, loan performance has become a major issue. The loans have attracted more students as policy makers have made them ever more generous, and now policy makers there worry that only about 50 percent of borrowers are current on their loans, which imposes a large cost on the government. The US, with its system of open access to student loans to attend any type of institution, including for-profit providers, shows similar repayment statistics. Only about 60 percent of borrowers are actively making payments on their loans, with most of the non-repayment occurring among students attending shorter-term programs at both public and private for-profit institutions. Brazil's response to the deteriorating loan performance has been to restrict loan access to students who achieve higher scores on a national test of academic preparedness.

In Australia, Vicki Thomson shows how the country's generous student loan program worked well when access to public universities was restricted. This meant that the government issued loans to a limited set of more academically prepared students who entered a job market that faced an artificially constrained supply of graduates. These students were more likely to repay their loans because they were likely to find jobs, work full time, and their earnings were relatively high. That dynamic was interrupted when the country eliminated the caps on how many students could enroll at public universities and in specific programs in 2012. This "demand-driven system" was meant to increase access to higher education—and it did. But as Thomson argues, these new students were less academically qualified than prior cohorts, as universities lowered standards to enroll more students, who financed their tuition with generous government-issued student loans. There is also evidence that enrollment growth was most pronounced in degree programs that were already facing slack demand in the labor market.

As a result of these and other trends, the Australian loan program has come under pressure as graduate earnings are not what they once were, raising alarms for policy makers. Lower than expected incomes among graduates means the income-contingent loan program will recoup less in payments from borrowers. In response, policy makers reduced the generosity of the loan program in 2016, requiring borrowers to begin repaying their debts at lower levels of income to shore up the system. It is another example of how restricting access in higher education can make it easier for policy makers to provide generous subsidies, in this case through the loan program, but expanding access often forces policy makers to rein in benefits.

Free College

Many of the chapters in this volume provide important lessons for those in the US who argue for free tuition at public universities, so-called free college proposals. These proposals gained prominence during the 2016 US presidential election when two Democratic candidates, Senator Bernie Sanders and Hillary Clinton each proposed a free college policy.[16] While the election results dashed those proposals, lawmakers continue to advocate for them. New York lawmakers have gone the furthest in their efforts. In 2017 they implemented a version of a free college program, the Excelsior Scholarship, for students from families earning up to USD 125,000 a year attending in-state public institutions.[17] It remains to be seen if other states will follow this example, whether New York can sustain the policy, and if free college proposals reemerge at the federal level.

Advocates for these policies often argue that other countries provide free tuition at public institutions, so the US can and should as well. This volume shows, however, that free tuition policies abroad are hardly without trade-offs and that policy makers would be wise to consider both the pros and cons.

Bruce Johnstone explains that there is a global movement away from free tuition in favor of cost-sharing, particularly as greater shares of the population seek some level of postsecondary education. He notes that the trend is most visible in developing countries. Developed countries, on the other hand, have a different problem that pushes them to adopt more cost-sharing: rising health care and pension obligations that crowd out funding for generous higher education subsidies. The US, one could argue, faces both sets of pressures, as a larger share of the population will need a credential beyond a high school diploma just as public budgets come under strain from rising Medicare, Medicaid, Social Security, and pension costs. Figure 9.1 illustrates how states used to spend much more on their public universities than on Medicaid, a trend that reversed in the 1990s, and that gap has grown nearly every year since.[18]

Jon Marcus echoes this theme when he discusses how European countries are struggling to maintain free tuition policies and are introducing fees or rolling back subsidies for living expenses. In Denmark tuition remains free, but lawmakers have cut grants for living expenses and required students to complete their programs on time in order to save costs. That is probably a sign that there is more cost cutting to come. At first glance, Germany appears to be an exception to budgetary challenges of maintaining free tuition. The German equivalent of state governments abandoned plans to charge tuition in the mid-2000s and reinstated free tuition. Yet those states have been charging students "fees" between USD 350 and USD 590 per year to offset costs. The lesson here is that free college looks increasingly unsustainable in other countries. US policy makers supporting free college proposals will need to assess how they can avoid or address the enrollment and budget trends pressuring free college abroad. Otherwise, they may need to temper their promises.

There is another trade-off in free college policies that many of the chapters in this volume illustrate. It is one that US policy makers should think about care-

FIGURE 9.1 Spending by share of state budgets (1987–2017)

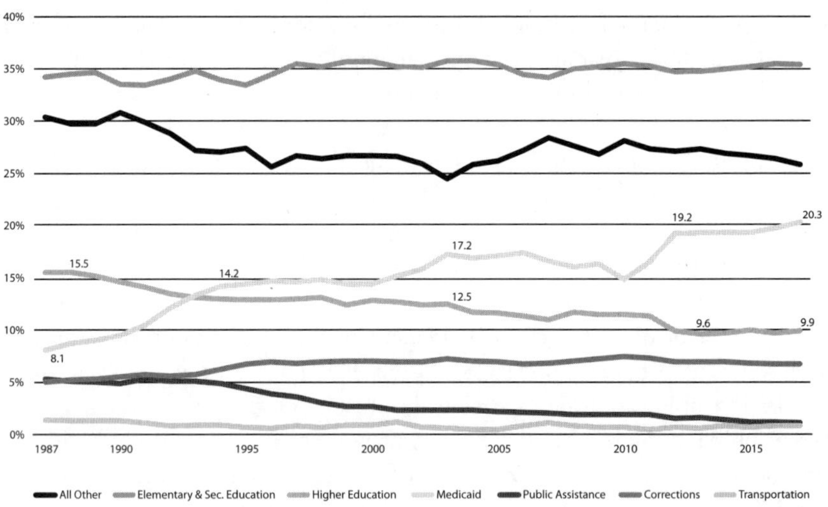

Source: American Enterprise Institute using National Association of State Budget Officers reports.

Note: Reflects state expenditures from state general funds only, which are financed largely with broad-based taxes such as income and sales taxes; expenditures financed with other dedicated revenue sources such as gasoline taxes, college tuition, federal grants, etc. are excluded.

fully because it shows how free tuition is in competition with providing greater access to higher education. That is the opposite of what free tuition is supposed to accomplish. Fully subsidizing tuition—which is done almost always exclusively at public institutions—is expensive for governments, which means something has to give for policy makers to deliver on the "free" promise. Often this trade-off takes the form of limits on the number of students who can enroll in free public institutions. And when universities have a centrally rationed number of seats to offer, they naturally skim the best students. These students also tend to be from the wealthiest families.

The chapters in this volume provide many examples of this dynamic. Vicki Thomson's discussion of the 1980s reform to the Australian higher education system that first instituted tuition was a response to exactly that pattern. Tuition was free, but it was not low-income students who were benefiting. Daniel C. Levy explains the same phenomenon, but from a different angle, in his chapter. Private institutions, frequently low-quality ones, often act as demand absorbers in systems where enrollment at public institutions is limited. The case study of Brazil offers a concrete and specific example of this effect. Selective public universities, which are fully subsidized by the government and therefore do not charge tuition, shut out students from low-income families. Private for-profit colleges are their only choice.

This problem may not manifest itself in the same way in the US given the range of quality among its public institutions, many of which have open enrollment policies. Rather, it is more likely to take the form of policy makers renaming free college a "scholarship" and imposing academic achievement requirements on students to qualify. Even when policy makers target free tuition to students below a certain income threshold in order to prevent the regressive effects seen abroad, that can still have effects on access. More selective public colleges could opt to limit their enrollment of students eligible for free tuition, because the institutions consider the government's tuition payment on behalf of the student as insufficient for covering its costs, which may be well above average. That is where another problem comes in.

Even if the US can avoid the regressive effects of free tuition seen in other countries, it may still diminish the quality of public colleges and universities. Prohibiting institutions from charging tuition or capping how much they may charge can threaten quality. That is a concern that rarely comes up in US debates about free college. But in country after country discussed in this volume, universities say that free tuition means they must rely on the government for their revenue, and lawmakers are inclined to underfund institutions, given competing budget priorities. Jon Marcus explains in his chapter how tuition-free German universities face funding shortfalls, deferred maintenance, and increasing use of temporary staff, due to their reliance on government appropriations for nearly all of their revenue. Marcus notes that Scotland is a similar case.

The case studies on Chile and Australia in this volume each reveal the same phenomenon. In Australia tuition is not free, but it is capped by the government, and in lieu of charging tuition, universities receive a funding allocation from the government. The universities say they are underfunded as a result and quality suffers. The *gratuidad* program in Chile prohibits public institutions from charging tuition for eligible students and caps tuition for students from more affluent families. Universities are funded by the government via a formula based on the *average cost* within their sector. As Andrés Bernasconi explains in his chapter, the country's most prestigious universities, which have the highest cost structures, now face budget deficits and are prohibited from raising tuition to fill the gap. Bernasconi expects they will have to cut spending, likely diminishing quality and prestige. In the US higher education system, higher spending by institutions is often associated with more prestige and quality, but research also shows that higher spending leads to more degree attainment, particularly at less selective institutions.[19] Higher dropout rates could thus be another counterintuitive effect that free college policies could bring about if adopted in the US.

Increasing Access

This volume covers a wide range of higher education systems and their design features, which makes another of the common themes somewhat surprising—and instructive for US policy audiences. A number of chapters in this volume discuss how countries aim to enroll more underrepresented students in higher education, particularly those from low-income families, but struggle to reach their goals despite employing different designs and policies. The authors identify a number of reasons for this.

One is that a country's primary and secondary education systems can have a major influence on college-going rates. Higher education policies may be ineffective in changing whatever stratification or inequities take hold in these formative years. Salto discusses how private, fee-charging elementary and secondary schools can "aggravate social inequalities" in Brazil, since wealthier families are more likely to send their children to private schools to avoid the less-equipped public system. In turn, those students receive better education, enhanced preparation for college-level qualifying exams, and have a greater chance at obtaining a seat at one of Brazil's selective public colleges. Enrollment quota policies at the postsecondary level have had little effect on breaking this connection.

In the UK the quality of primary and secondary schools is closely associated with family incomes in the neighborhood they serve, and wealthy families are able to afford elite private schools. As in the US, students who attend these high-quality schools are far more likely to enroll in the most elite institutions of higher education and subsequently go on to have the highest earnings.

Another impediment to enrollment is parental education. Several chapters describe how the level of parental education is still a strong predictor of whether their children will pursue a higher education and ultimately complete the education; this phenomenon is as true in Germany and Scandinavia as it is in the United States. As scholars of the phenomenon known as "effectively maintained inequality" have repeatedly shown over the past couple of decades, middle-class parents the world over are on the whole remarkably successful at ensuring that their children have superior access to education at all levels.[20] This is not a uniquely American phenomenon and appears to have little to do with financial factors such as fees.

CONCLUDING THOUGHTS

Higher education is among the most complex fields of policy in most countries. The ends being pursued are varied and contested. There may be general agreement that these systems serve as tools of both social and economic policy, but it is rare to find much agreement on the correct proportions. And they are embedded in larger structures—tax structures, secondary school structures, labor market structures—in such a way that a change in policy in one area often leads to cascading changes across a variety of fields. Because of such complications, transplanting policy from one country to another in higher education may be more difficult than it is in other policy fields.

Fortunately learning from policies abroad is about more than mere transplantation of policy. Studying how other countries have approached policy challenges can be an extraordinarily helpful tool in policy analysis. Such analyses not only teach alternative strategies, but they can also illuminate some hidden trade-offs in our own country's policies. Our hope is that this book will prompt policy makers and higher education scholars in the United States to learn more about international higher education policy and, in so doing, improve the quality of policy analysis and the design of new policy options.

Equally, though, our hope is that this volume will dissuade some who wish to look abroad in search of unicorns and silver bullets. Each country trades one feature or outcome in its higher education system for another in ways that suit its values and institutions. No two sets of problems, preferences, and institutions are ever exactly alike. Foreign experience can often provide insight, but it can rarely drive solutions on its own.

Notes

Introduction

1. Emma Duncan, "Excellence vs. Equity," *The Economist*, March 26, 2015, www.economist.com/news/special-report/21646985-american-model-higher-education-spreading-it-good-producing-excellence.
2. Jeffrey Selingo, "Is College Worth the Cost? Many Recent Graduates Don't Think So," *Washington Post*, September 30, 2015.
3. Tamar Jacoby, "Why Germany Is So Much Better at Training Its Workers," *The Atlantic*, October 16, 2014.
4. Bernie Sanders, "Make College Free for All," *Washington Post*, October 22, 2015.
5. Mary Clare Amselem, "When England Offered Free College, Look What Happened," *CNS News*, October 6, 2017, www.cnsnews.com/commentary/mary-clare-amselem/when-england-offered-free-college-look-what-happened.
6. Richard Murphy, Judith Scott-Clayton, Gillian Wyness, "The End of Free College in England: Implications for Quality, Enrollments, and Equity," National Bureau of Economic Research (NBER), September 2017, www.nber.org/papers/w23888.
7. Danielle Douglas-Gabriel, "Top Public Universities Are Shutting Out Poor Students, Report Says," *Washington Post*, October 26, 2017.
8. Joseph E. Stiglitz, "Equal Opportunity, Our National Myth," *New York Times*, February 16, 2013; Michele S. Moses and Laura Dudley Jenkins, "Affirmative Action around the World," *The Conversation*, November 13, 2014, https://theconversation.com/affirmative-action-around-the-world-82190.
9. For examples of this, see Paul Hockenos, "A Guide to Getting a Bachelor's Abroad," *New York Times*, November 2, 2016; Laura Krantz, "Canadian Colleges Offer US Students Lower Tuition and Trudeau Instead of Trump," *Boston Globe*, September 27, 2017; Amy Gibbons, "The Countries Offering Students Free (or Somewhat Affordable) University Education," *The Independent*, December 5, 2016.
10. Susan Dynarski, "American Can Fix Its Student Loan Crisis. Just Ask Australia," *New York Times*, July 9, 2016.
11. Peter Martin, "Nobel Prize-Winning Economist Joseph Stiglitz Says Abbott Government Budget Changes Are 'a Crime,'" *Sydney Morning Herald*, July 3, 2014, www.smh.com.au/federal-politics/political-news/nobel-prizewinning-economist-joseph-stiglitz-says-abbott-government-budget-changes-are-a-crime-20140702-3b8vb.html.
12. Universities Australia, "Higher Education and Research Facts and Figures," November 3, 2015, 17–18, www.universitiesaustralia.edu.au/australias-universities/key-facts-and-data#.WiWU-Gfo70c.

Chapter 1

1. Jan Petter Myklebust, "Agreement on Controversial Student Loan Scheme Reform," *University World News*, April 25, 2013, http://www.universityworldnews.com/article.php?story=20130425101943592.
2. Organisation for Economic Cooperation and Development (OECD), *Education at a Glance 2017*, September 12, 2017, http://dx.doi.org/10.1787/eag-2017-en.
3. Myklebust, "Agreement on Controversial Student Loan Scheme Reform."
4. Jon Marcus, "Forcing Students to Graduate 'On Time,'" *Atlantic*, June 11, 2015.
5. Jan Petter Myklebust, "Thousands of Students Protest against Study Time Cuts," *University World News*, November 28, 2013, http://www.universityworldnews.com/article.php?story=20131128170931863.
6. WeChange, "Skriv under mod lovforslaget om uddannelsesloft," April 12, 2016, https://www.wechange.dk/indsamling/uddannelsesloft-99.
7. European Students Union, "2016 Policy Paper on Public Responsibility, Governance, and Financing of Higher Education," May 2016, www.esu-online.org/?policy=2016-policy-paper-on-on-public-responsibility-governance-and-financing-of-higher-education.
8. Philip Oltermann, "Germany Axed Tuition Fees—but Is It Working Out?" *Guardian*, June 4, 2016.
9. Nick Hillman, *Keeping Up with the Germans? A Comparison of Student Funding, Internationalization, and Research in UK and German Universities* (Oxford, Eng.: Higher Education Policy Institute, September 3, 2015), www.hepi.ac.uk/2015/09/03/keeping-germans-comparison-student-funding-internationalisation-research-uk-german-universities.
10. Rose Troup Buchanan, "Last German State Abolished University Fees," *Independent*, October 4, 2014.
11. Marius Busemeyer, Philipp Lergetporer, and Ludger Woessmann, *Public Opinion and the Acceptance and Feasibility of Educational Reforms*, European Expert Network on Economics of Education, November 2016, https://publications.europa.eu/en/publication-detail/-/publication/a29f75ba-dc81-11e6-ad7c-01aa75ed71a1/language-en.
12. Interview with Ludger Woessmann, December 6, 2017.
13. OECD, *Education at a Glance 2017.*
14. OECD, "Germany," *Education at a Glance 2014: OECD Indicators*, 2014, http://www.oecd.org/edu/Germany-EAG2014-Country-Note.pdf.
15. Nils Zimmermann, "Apprenticeships Go Begging in Germany," *Deutsche Welle*, June 14, 2016, www.dw.com/en/apprenticeships-go-begging-in-germany/a-19329543.
16. U.S. Bureau of Labor Statistics, "Unemployment Rates and Earnings by Educational Attainment, 2016," www.bls.gov/emp/ep_chart_001.htm.
17. Woessmann interview.
18. OECD, "All-In Average Personal Income Tax Rates at Average Wage by Family Type for 2016," http://stats.oecd.org/index.aspx?DataSetCode=TABLE_I1.
19. Busemeyer et al., *Public Opinion.*
20. Interview with Hans de Wit, December 8, 2017.
21. German Federal Ministry of Education and Research, *Education and Research in Figures 2017*, www.bmbf.de/pub/Education_and_Research_in_Figures_2017.pdf.
22. Rachael Pells, "German Universities to Reintroduce Tuition Fees for Non-EU Students," *Independent*, December 3, 2016.

23. Joel McFarland et al., *The Condition of Education 2017*, National Center for Education Statistics, May 2017, https://nces.ed.gov/pubs2017/2017144.pdf.
24. Hillman, *Keeping Up with the Germans?*
25. German Rectors' Conference (HRK), "Funding of the Higher Education System from 2020 Onwards: Resolution by the 22nd General Meeting of the HRK," March 9, 2017, www.hrk.de/resolutions-publications/resolutions/beschluss/detail/funding-of-the-higher-education-system-from-2020-onwards.
26. Audit Scotland, *Audit of Higher Education in Scottish Universities*, July 2016, http://audit-scotland.gov.uk/uploads/docs/report/2016/nr_160707_higher_education.pdf.
27. Sue Hubble and Paul Bolton, "Higher Education Tuition Fees in England," House of Commons Library, June 25, 2018, http://researchbriefings.files.parliament.uk/documents/CBP-8151/CBP-8151.pdf.
28. Benjamin Kentish, "University Tuition Fees in England Now the Highest in the World, New Analysis Suggests," *Independent*, March 28, 2017.
29. Richard Adams and Rowena Mason, "Tuition Fee Repayment Earnings Threshold to Rise to £25,000," *Guardian*, October 1, 2017.
30. Philip Kirby, "Degrees of Debt: Funding and Finance for Undergraduates in Anglophone Countries," Sutton Trust, April 2016, http://www.suttontrust.com/wp-content/uploads/2016/04/DegreesofDebt.pdf.
31. Institute for College Access and Success, "Student Debt and the Class of 2016," September 2017, https://ticas.org/sites/default/files/pub_files/classof2016.pdf.
32. In January 2018, Oslo and Akershus University College was granted full university status, and the new university is now called Oslo Metropolitan University. For more information, see Oslo and Akershus University College of Applied Sciences "Norway Has a New University: OsloMet," January 3, 2018, www.hioa.no/eng/node_2273/Norway-Has-a-New-University-OsloMet.
33. Interview with Curt Rice, December 4, 2017.
34. Rice interview.
35. Oltermann, "Germany Axed Tuition Fees."
36. Pells, "German Universities."
37. European Students Union, "Resolution Against the Rise of Tuition Fees for International Students," May 23, 2017, www.esu-online.org/?policy=bm72-resolution-rise-tuition-fees-international-students.
38. Jan Petter Myklebust, "Rectors Oppose Proposal for Non-European Student Fees," *University World News*, November 12, 2014, www.universityworldnews.com/article.php?story=20141112155301874.
39. Oltermann, "Germany Axed Tuition Fees."
40. Rice interview.
41. Marcus, "Forcing Students to Graduate."
42. Anthon Schrader, "80,000 Citizens Are Protesting Against a New Educational Law by the Danish Government," *Business Insider Nordic*, January 4, 2017, http://nordic.businessinsider.com/80000-citizens-are-protesting-against-a-new-educational-law-by-the-danish-government-2017-1.
43. European Students Union, "2016 Policy Paper."
44. Layal Freije and Caroline Hallkvist, "Elever demonstrerer: 'Nej til skæring! Ja til læring!,'" *Politiken*, October 13, 2016, https://politiken.dk/indland/uddannelse/article5647052.ece.

45. European Students Union, "Resolution Against the Rise."
46. Belingske Business, "Studerende: SU-reform giver unge gæld i årevis," August 30, 2016, www.business.dk/oekonomi/studerende-su-reform-giver-unge-gaeld-i-aarevis.
47. Danish Ministry of Higher Education and Science, "Bank & Budget," *Study in Denmark*, http://studyindenmark.dk/live-in-denmark/bank-budget.
48. Matt Phillips, "College in Sweden Is Free but Students Still Have a Ton of Debt. How Can That Be?" *Quartz*, May 31, 2013, https://qz.com/85017/college-in-sweden-is-free-but-students-still-have-a-ton-of-debt-how-can-that-be.
49. Freije and Hallkvist, "Elever demonstrerer."
50. Gary R. Pike, George D. Kuh, and Ryan C. Massa-McKinley, "First-Year Students' Employment, Engagement, and Academic Achievement: Untangling the Relationship between Work and Grades," *Journal of Student Affairs Research and Practice* 45, no. 4 (2008): 560–82.
51. German Federal Ministry of Education and Research, *Education and Research in Figures 2017*; and German Academic Exchange Service, "Cost of Living," *Study in Germany*, www.study-in.de/en/plan-your-stay/money-and-costs/cost-of-living_28220.php.
52. Jon Marcus, "Germany Proves Tuition-Free College Is Not a Silver Bullet for America's Education Woes," *Quartz*, October 18, 2016, https://qz.com/812200/is-free-college-possible-germany-shows-there-are-downsides-to-tuition-free-college.
53. Busemeyer et al., *Public Opinion.*
54. Interview with Nathalie Schäfer, December 11, 2017.
55. Lucy Hunter Blackburn, "The Fairest of Them All? The Support for Scottish Students in Full-Time Higher Education in 2014–15," Centre for Research in Education Inclusion and Diversity, University of Edinburgh, February 2014, www.docs.hss.ed.ac.uk/education/creid/Projects/34ii_d_ESRCF_WP3.pdf.
56. de Wit interview.
57. Universities UK, *Patterns and Trends in UK Higher Education 2017*, www.universitiesuk.ac.uk/facts-and-stats/data-and-analysis/Documents/patterns-and-trends-2017.pdf.
58. Universities UK, *Working in Partnership: Enabling Social Mobility in Higher Education*, Social Mobility Advisory Group, 2016, www.universitiesuk.ac.uk/policy-and-analysis/reports/Documents/2016/working-in-partnership-final.pdf.
59. Jon Marcus, "Why Are More Poor Kids Going to College in the UK?" *Atlantic*, June 10, 2016.
60. Parliament UK, "Written Question 109016," October 23, 2017, www.parliament.uk/business/publications/written-questions-answers-statements/written-question/Commons/2017-10-23/109016.
61. Interview with Les Ebdon, December 5, 2017.
62. Marcus, "Why Are More Poor Kids Going to College?"
63. Ebdon interview.
64. Universities UK, *Working in Partnership.*
65. Universities UK, *Working in Partnership.*
66. Lucy Sherriff, "The Proportion of Poorer Students Studying at UK's Top Universities Has Fallen," *Huffington Post UK*, February 18, 2016, www.huffingtonpost.co.uk/2016/02/18/number-of-poorer-students-at-uks-top-universities-has-fallen_n_9260912.html.
67. Parliament UK, "Written Question 109016."
68. Marcus, "Why Are More Poor Kids Going to College?"

69. Richard Murphy, Judith Scott-Clayton, and Gillian Wyness, "The End of Free College in England: Implications for Quality, Enrolments, and Equity" (working paper, National Bureau of Economic Research, Cambridge, MA, September 2017), www.nber.org/papers/w23888.
70. Suzi Macpherson, "Higher Education Institutions: Subject Profile," Scottish Parliament Information Centre, September 5, 2016, www.parliament.scot/ResearchBriefingsAndFactsheets/S5/SB_16-71_Higher_Education_Institutions-_Subject_Profile.pdf.
71. German Federal Ministry of Education and Research, *Education and Research in Figures 2017.*
72. Berthold U. Wigger, quoted in Hillman, *Keeping Up with the Germans?*
73. Busemeyer et al., *Public Opinion.*
74. Woessmann interview.
75. Marcus, "Germany Proves Tuition-Free College Is Not a Silver Bullet."
76. Busemeyer et al., *Public Opinion.*
77. de Wit interview.
78. Elisabeth Hovdhaugen, "Widening Participation in Norwegian Higher Education," CFE Research, October 2013, www.hefce.ac.uk/media/hefce/content/pubs/indirreports/2013/WP,international,research/2013_WPeffectivenessNorway.pdf.
79. Hovdhaugen, "Widening Participation."
80. Rice interview.
81. German Federal Ministry of Education and Research, *Education and Research in Figures 2017.*
82. Hubble and Bolton, "Higher Education Tuition Fees in England"; and Universities UK, *Working in Partnership.*
83. Universities UK, *Patterns and Trends.*
84. Interview with Elisabeth Hovdhaugen, December 8, 2017.
85. OECD, *Education at a Glance 2017.*
86. Rice interview.
87. OECD, *Education at a Glance 2017.*
88. de Wit interview.

Chapter 2

1. D. Bruce Johnstone, "The Economics and Politics of Cost Sharing in Higher Education: Comparative Perspectives," *Economics of Education Review* 20, no. 4 (2004): 403–410; and D. Bruce Johnstone and Pamela Marcucci, *Financing Higher Education Worldwide: Who Pays? Who Should Pay?* (Baltimore: Johns Hopkins University Press, 2010), 66.
2. National Center for Education Statistics, "Digest of Education Statistics: 2015, Table 333.90," https://nces.ed.gov/programs/digest/d15/tables/dt15_333.90.asp.
3. D. Bruce Johnstone, "A Political Culture of Giving and the Philanthropic Support of Public Higher Education in International Perspective," *International Journal of Educational Advancement* 5, no. 3 (2005): 256–64.
4. D. Bruce Johnstone and Pamela Marcucci, "Financing Higher Education: Worldwide Perspectives and Lessons," Center for Comparative and Global Studies in Education, State University of New York at Buffalo, December 14, 2013, http://gse.buffalo.edu/org/inthigheredfinance/files/Recent_Publications/FinancingHigherEducation_Worldwide-PerspectivesAndLessons_Johnstone_2013.pdf.

5. In the United States, a payment to cover a portion of instructional costs is called *tuition*. In Britain, and in most of the comparative higher educational literature, the term *tuition* means instruction, and thus a payment to cover a part of instructional expenses must be called a *tuition fee*, which sounds redundant to the American ear. As this chapter is about an international comparative perspective on cost-sharing, even if meant largely for a US readership, we will generally employ the term *tuition fee* to signal the payment from parents or students to cover expenses for instruction and other institutionally provided services that benefit all students.
6. D. Bruce Johnstone, "The Costs of Higher Education: Worldwide Issues and Trends for the 1990s," in *The Funding of Higher Education: International Perspectives*, ed. Philip G. Altbach and D. Bruce Johnstone (New York: Garland Publishing, 1993).
7. D. Bruce Johnstone, "Financing Higher Education: Worldwide Perspectives and Policy Options," International Comparative Higher Education Finance and Accessibility Project, State University of New York at Buffalo, 2014, http://gseweb.gse.buffalo.edu/org/inthigheredfinance/files/Recent_Publications/Financing%20H%20Ed%20WW%20Perspectives%20and%20policy%20options%20revised.pdf.
8. D. Bruce Johnstone, "Cost Sharing in Higher Education: Tuition, Financial Assistance, and Accessibility in a Comparative Perspective," *Sociologický časopis* [Czech Sociological Review] 39, no. 3 (2003): 351–74, www.ssoar.info/ssoar/bitstream/handle/document/5638/ssoar-2003-3-johnstone-cost_sharing_in_higher_education.pdf?sequence=1.
9. Paul Bolton, "The Value of Student Maintenance Support," House of Commons Library, December 18, 2017, http://researchbriefings.files.parliament.uk/documents/CBP-7258/CBP-7258.pdf.
10. D. Bruce Johnstone, "Higher Education Finance and Accessibility: Tuition Fees and Student Loans in Sub-Saharan Africa," *Revue de l'enseignement supérieur en Afrique* [Journal of Higher Education in Africa] 2, no. 2 (2004): 11–36, www.codesria.org/IMG/pdf/2-johnstone.pdf?687/20231eb1df2afb42521d7cdc71a9b88ea39f9efa.
11. Pamela Marcucci, D. Bruce Johnstone, and Mary Ngolovoi, "Higher Educational Cost-Sharing, Dual-Track Tuition Fees, and Higher Educational Access: The East African Experience," *Peabody Journal of Education* 83, no. 1 (2008): 101–116.
12. Johnstone and Marcucci, *Financing Higher Education Worldwide.*
13. D. Bruce Johnstone, "Common Misunderstandings about the Financing of Higher Education World Wide," *Peking University Education Review* 2 (2013): 36–45.
14. D. Bruce Johnstone, *Student Loans in International Perspective: Promises and Failures, Myths and Partial Truths*, State University of New York at Buffalo, January 2001, www.researchgate.net/profile/D_Johnstone/publication/247662572_Student_Loans_in_International_Perspective_Promises_and_Failures_Myths_and_Partial_Truths/links/557c318308aeb61eae2360a9/Student-Loans-in-International-Perspective-Promises-and-Failures-Myths-and-Partial-Truths.pdf.
15. Johnstone, "Cost Sharing in Higher Education."
16. Johnstone and Marcucci, *Financing Higher Education Worldwide.*
17. Christine Mulhern, Richard R. Spies, Matthew P. Staiger, and D. Derek Wu, *The Effects of Rising Student Costs in Higher Education: Evidence from Public Institutions in Virginia*, Ithaka S+R, March 4, 2015, www.sr.ithaka.org/wp-content/uploads/2015/08/SR_Report_Effects_of_Rising_Student_Costs_in_Higher_Education_Virginia_030415.pdf.

18. Author's calculations using the National Postsecondary Student Aid Study (NPSAS), 1996–2012.
19. Beth Akers and Matthew M. Chingos, *Game of Loans: The Rhetoric and Reality of Student Debt* (Princeton, NJ: Princeton University Press, 2016), 30.
20. D. Bruce Johnstone, "The US Higher Education System: An Introduction for International Students and Scholars," Center for Comparative and Global Studies in Education, State University of New York at Buffalo, April 2014, http://gse.buffalo.edu/org/inthigheredfinance/files/Recent_Publications/USHigherEdfor%20International StudentsScholars2014.pdf.
21. Johnstone, "Higher Education Finance and Accessibility."
22. National Center for Education Statistics, "Digest of Education Statistics: 2016, Table 317.10," https://nces.ed.gov/programs/digest/current_tables.asp.
23. Private nonprofit degree-granting institutions in New York State prepare 52 percent of all bachelor's degrees, 71 percent of master's degrees, and 79 percent of doctoral and advanced professional degrees.
24. Council for Aid to Education, "Colleges and Universities Raise Record $40.30 Billion in 2015," press release, January 27, 2016.
25. College Board, "Trends in Student Aid," 2016, https://trends.collegeboard.org/sites/default/files/2016-trends-student-aid.pdf.
26. College Board, "Trends in Student Aid," 2016.
27. D. Bruce Johnstone, "Making Student Loans Work in Africa," *International Journal of African Higher Education* 2 (2015): 55–67, https://ejournals.bc.edu/ojs/index.php/ijahe/article/view/9256/8309.

Chapter 3

1. This chapter's 2010 data come from the first comprehensive dual-sector data set on higher education. See www.prophe.org/en/data-laws. For detailed analysis of the global and regional dimensions, see Daniel C. Levy "Global Private Education: An Empirical Profile of its Size and Shape," *Higher Education* (January 2018),https://doi.org/10.1007/s10734-018-0233-6.
2. To some variable degree not yet sufficiently clear to the author, Taiwan and Singapore could be added to the chapter's references to Japan and South Korea as being unusual in the (relatively) developed world for their private colleges and universities. Both Taiwan's and Singapore's private shares are over 60 percent.
3. In contrast to Japan and South Korea, in the US private versus public size and which sector would be dedicated more to elite or mass functions was not a central government policy issue. See World Bank, *Higher Education: The Lessons of Experience* (Washington, DC: World Bank, 1994).
4. One argument often made in favor of ending public monopoly and allowing at least some private colleges and universities (or private branch campuses of foreign universities, as in Greece) has been that in the absence of such institutions, more students will study abroad. Basic historical debates over allowing private higher education pitted claimed advantages of uniform public standards, quality assurance, accountability, and national sovereignty versus claimed advantages of enhanced choice, competition, and access.
5. If US states look outside their boundaries when contemplating state policy for private higher education, they look much more to other US states than to other countries.

6. Daniel C. Levy, *Higher Education and the State in Latin America: Private Challenges to Public Dominance* (Chicago: University of Chicago Press, 1986).
7. For example, Indonesia's Bogor School of Tourism, not in the country's top one thousand institutions, and Brazil's nonprofit Unified Institute of Higher Education in Goiás state and for-profit Anhanguera Faculty of Technology of São Bernardo in wealthy São Paulo state.
8. And even where private remains the minority sector, its largest subsector is almost always non-elite (e.g., China, Malaysia, Portugal, and Poland).
9. BRICS is an acronym for the association of Brazil, Russia, India, China, and South Africa, five countries with notable commonalities in their emerging national economies.
10. Such policy challenges increasingly arise with cross-border education. This education is usually non-elite, providing access and aspiring to offer some specific status or skill advantage. The sending institution is almost always from the developed world (especially the US, UK, and Australia) and itself not non-elite; the host, almost always from the developing world. Whether the sender institution is public or private at home, it functions like a private institution in its cross-border presence.
11. Status varies all the way from demand-absorbers toward possibly elite (as with some engineering schools or leading German professional schools; e.g., in law). Examples of French business and management schools would include the PSB Paris *School* of *Business* (formerly ESG Management School) and ISG International Business School, and for engineering, the ECE Paris–Graduate School of Engineering. A singular institution such as the Stockholm School of Economics, privately established and still mostly privately funded, has long enjoyed high status but in a limited set of fields. See Moris Triventi and Paolo Trivellato, "Does Graduating from a Private University Make a Difference? Evidence from Italy," *European Journal of Education* 47, no. 2 (2012): 260–76.
12. Mashood Shah and George Brown, "The Rise of Private Higher Education in Australia: Maintaining Quality Outcomes and Future Challenges," *Proceedings of AUQF2009: Internal and External Quality Assurance: Tensions and Synergies*, no. 19 (July 2009): 143–50, http://citeseerx.ist.psu.edu/viewdoc/download?doi=10.1.1.147.6337&rep=rep1&type=pdf.
13. That the striking demographic stagnation in Japan and South Korea has not yet undermined private *share* is partly a tribute to the strength of these non-elite subsectors as not being overwhelmingly demand-absorbing.
14. Weisbrod Burton, *The Nonprofit Economy* (Cambridge, MA: Harvard University Press, 1994); and Walter W. Powell and Richard Steinberg, eds., *The Nonprofit Sector* (New Haven, CT: Yale University Press, 2006).
15. Several Islamic countries have public as well as private religious institutions; both types confront religious institutions' trade-offs about how to hold the line or secularize. Islamic countries split on whether they allow identity institutions for minority groups.
16. The religious higher education revival, with surges of Evangelical and Islamic identity, is only faint in developed compared to developing countries. See Joel A. Carpenter, Nicholas S. Lantinga, and Perry L. Glanzer, eds., *Christian Higher Education: A Global Reconnaissance* (Grand Rapids, MI: William B. Eerdmans Publishing, 2014).
17. Thus, students often face trade-offs between the benefits of the highest status degree and the benefits of more personalized attention. The private Waseda offers tuition waivers

to students who have been admitted to Japan's top research university, the University of Tokyo.

18. Victor E. Ferrall, *Liberal Arts at the Brink* (Cambridge, MA: Harvard University Press, 2011).
19. Some elite efforts are cross-border as with New York University's Abu Dhabi or Russia's Smolny College granting dual degrees from Bard and St. Petersburg State University.
20. Simon Marginson, "Imagining Ivy: Pitfalls in the Privatization of Higher Education in Australia," *Comparative Education Review* 41, no. 4 (1997): 460–80.
21. BPP, originally founded by Alan Brierley, Richard Price, and Charles Prior, is a private higher education institution with sites located across the United Kingdom, most prominently in London. BPP first obtained degree-awarding powers in 2007, was granted university college status in 2010, and finally was awarded university status in 2013. For more information, see BPP University, www.bpp.com/about-bpp/bpp-university.
22. Levy, *Higher Education and the State*.
23. Daniel C. Levy, "East Asian Private Higher Education: Reality and Policy," http://siteresources.worldbank.org/INTEASTASIAPACIFIC/Resources/EastAsianPrivateHigherEducation.pdf; World Bank, *Pakistan—Higher Education Policy Note : An Assessment of the Medium-Term Development Framework*, 2006, http://documents.worldbank.org/curated/en/766731468284381395/pdf/372470PK0white1er01410200601PUBLIC1.pdf.
24. Asena Caner and Cagla Okten, "Higher Education in Turkey: Subsidizing the Rich or the Poor?" (working paper, Institute for the Study of Labor, Bonn, Germany, 2012), http://ftp.iza.org/dp7011.pdf.
25. The general reality of private-public distinctiveness is especially valid sectorally, allowing that particular institutions deviate.
26. The generalization about the limited government role in the creation of private higher education holds more strongly for Latin America, Africa, and Eastern Europe than for the Asian and Arab regions. Moreover, it is not mostly as if government attempts to create a private sector or botches attempts, or that it seeks to create an elite private university and winds up with a non-elite one; it is less that results fall short of plan than that activities are not mostly undertaken through government plans. Daniel C. Levy, "The Unanticipated Explosion: Private Higher Education's Global Surge," *Comparative Education Review* 50, no. 2 (May 2006): 217–40.
27. David Levi-Faur, "The Global Diffusion of Regulatory Capitalism," *ANNALS of the American Academy of Political and Social Science* 598, no. 1 (2005): 12–32; and Peter A. M. Maassen and Frans A. van Vught, "An Intriguing Janus-Head," *European Journal of Education* 23, nos. 1/2 (1988): 65.
28. Burton R. Clark, *The Higher Education System: Academic Organization in Cross-National Perspective* (Berkeley, CA: University of California Press, 1983).
29. Of course, this compartmentalization of distinctiveness is only one possibility. Rather distinctive characteristics may also reinforce one another, as with product-oriented institutions' governance structure and employment linkages.
30. In the developing world, for-profit institutions are especially prevalent in Asia (e.g., Indonesia, Philippines) and Africa (Ethiopia, South Africa). Legal for-profit institutions in Latin America thrive in Brazil and Peru; in Mexico and much of that region "for-profit"

institutions flourish largely through legally nonprofit institutions that function in arguably for-profit ways. In Central and Eastern Europe some countries permit for-profit higher education, while others do not.

31. A contrary view might highlight an excess publicness, as US for-profits depend so heavily on public funds while engaging in practices contrary to public interests, with disproportional impact on students with low socioeconomic status.
32. In 2017 public Purdue University bought for-profit Kaplan Learning (for one dollar), seeking to offset decreased state funding and expand its online and adult education presence. The acquisition fits patterns of both privatizing the public sector and blurring private-public distinctions.
33. At an extreme, states like Virginia and Michigan have pondered the formal legal privatization of their public flagships. See Marian Wang, "Breaking Away: Why Several Top Public Universities Are Going Private," *Pacific Standard,* October 21, 2013, https://psmag.com/education/breaking-away-several-top-public-universities-going-private-68007.
34. There is a parallel to where US charter schools aim to provide an educationally superior alternative and to apply pressure for reform in the remaining public mainstream.
35. Private higher education remains the politically easier route to privateness even when supplementary public money is added over time. As with public loans for private college and university students, the pertinent policy trade-off is to give some public money to keep viable a private education sector that remains a comparatively private alternative to a basically public-funded public sector. A broader policy case can be made that allowing private higher education a wide berth where privateness is warranted can leave the public sector freer and fitter to concentrate on functions where publicness is especially warranted. See Claudio de Moura Castro and Daniel C. Levy, "Higher Education in Latin America and the Caribbean: Strategy Paper," Inter-American Development Bank, December 1997.
36. John S. Whitehead, *The Separation of College and State: Columbia, Dartmouth, Harvard, and Yale* (New Haven, CT: Yale University Press, 1973).
37. Roger L. Geiger, *Private Sectors in Higher Education: Structure, Function, and Change in Eight Countries* (Ann Arbor: University of Michigan Press, 1986).
38. Market dynamics are so dynamic to the US public sector that they get reproduced even as the sector takes on new forms and mass functions, as occurs with competition among community colleges or for federal research money.
39. Maassen and van Vught, "Intriguing Janus-Head"; and Clark, *Higher Education System.*
40. Both sectors, by providing differentiation, in effect allow students and other private stakeholders more space in which to weigh trade-offs and choose for themselves than in public standardized systems, where more trade-offs are governments' to weigh (for the system and its stakeholders).
41. In the British *Times* rankings, US private and public institutions are tied at thirty-one each, and in the Shanghai rankings, public institutions lead those that are private forty to thirty-one.
42. Although the free tuition movement has incremental characteristics, both because financial need assistance is already substantial and because practical programs like New York governor Andrew Cuomo's Excelsior Scholarship Plan include eligibility stipulations, the end goal of free public higher education is what animates the Democratic base.

43. Whereas attacking public tuition is a policy option in only some countries, as such tuition is absent in others, a sudden increase in public admissions is a populist policy option almost everywhere and it, too, puts private sector enrollment size at risk.
44. It was not just a unique private sector but a unique higher education system more broadly that Burton Clark keenly feared being at risk where increased government roles jeopardized US distinctiveness. See Burton R. Clark, "The Benefits of Disorder," *Change* 8, no. 9 (1976): 31–37.
45. Internationally inspired reform in recent decades has involved considerable "Americanization," including (1) two important sectors rather than just an important public sector and (2) a public sector with privateness, differentiation, and competition across institutions, and internally centralized, autonomous institutions. Although the US was itself a significant borrower when infusing the research function, the key US private-public dynamics highlighted in this chapter are best seen as having evolved fundamentally in a domestic political, economic, and cultural milieu. See Daniel C. Levy, *To Export Progress: The Golden Age of University Assistance in the Americas* (Bloomington: Indiana University Press, 2005); and Heinz-Dieter Meyer, *The Design of the University: German, American, and "World Class"* (New York: Routledge, 2017).

Chapter 4

1. Phillips Exeter Academy, "Major Financial Aid Initiative Announced Today: A Free Exeter Education to Those with Need," News and Events, November 7, 2007.
2. James Heckman, "The Economics of Inequality: The Value of Early Childhood Education," *American Educator* 35, no. 1 (2011): 31–35.
3. Richard Breen and John. H. Goldthorpe, "Class, Mobility and Merit—The Experience of Two British Birth Cohorts," *European Sociological Review* 17, no. 2 (2001): 81–101.
4. John Rawls, *A Theory of Justice* (Harvard, MA: Harvard University Press, 1971).
5. Compare with Plato, *Republic*, trans. George M. A. Grube and C. David C. Reeve (Indianapolis: Hackett Publishing, [380 BC] 1992).
6. Basil Bernstein, *Class, Codes, and Control* (London: Routledge and Kegan Paul, 1971); Pierre Bourdieu and Jean-Claude Passeron, *Reproduction in Education, Society, and Culture* (London: Sage Publications, 1977); and James Coleman, "Social Capital in the Creation of Human Capital," *American Journal of Sociology* 94 (1988): S95–S120.
7. David L. Featherman, F. Lancaster Jones, and Robert M. Hauser, "Assumptions of Social Mobility Research in the US: The Case of Occupational Status," *Social Science Research* 4, no. 4 (1975): 329–60, https://doi.org/10.1016/0049-089X(75)90002-2.
8. Adrian E. Raftery and Michael Hout, "Maximally Maintained Inequality: Expansion, Reform, and Opportunity in Irish Education, 1921–75," *Sociology of Education* 66, no. 1 (1993): 41–62.
9. Stephan Vincent-Lancrin, "The Reversal of Gender Inequalities in Higher Education," Organisation for Economic Cooperation and Development (hereafter, OECD), November 18, 2008, http://dx.doi.org/10.1787/9789264040663-en.
10. Samuel R. Lucas, "Effectively Maintained Inequality: Education Transitions, Track Mobility and Social Background Effects," *American Journal of Sociology* 106, no. 6 (2001): 1642–90.
11. Central Bureau of Statistics Israel, "Statistical Abstract of Israel 2014," www.cbs.gov.il/reader/shnaton/shnatone_new.htm?CYear=2014&Vol=65&CSubject=19.

12. Ayala Hendin and Dalia Ben-Rabi, *The Access Plan for Higher Education of Arab, Druze, and Circassians: Preliminary Findings from an Evaluation Study of the Implementation of the Student Support Services*, Myers-JDC-Brookdale Institute [in Hebrew], 2015, https://brookdale.jdc.org.il/wp-content/uploads/2018/01/741-16_eng_summary.pdf.
13. Ayala Hendin, Dalia Ben-Rabi, and Faisal Azaiz, "Framing and Making of Access Policies: The Case of Palestinian Arabs in Higher Education in Israel," in *Access to Higher Education: Theoretical Perspectives and Contemporary Challenges*, ed. Anna Mountford-Zimdars and Neil Harrison (London: Routledge, 2017).
14. Sarab Abu-Rabia-Queder and Khaleb Arar, "Gender and Higher Education in Different National Spaces: Female Palestinian Students Attending Israeli and Jordanian Universities," *Compare* 41, no. 3 (2011): 353–70, http://dx.doi.org/10.1080/03057925.2010.545200.
15. Philip Kasinitz, John H. Mollenkopf, and Mary C. Waters, *Becoming New Yorkers: Ethnographies of the New Second Generation* (New York: Russell Sage Foundation, 2004).
16. Ann Jardine, "Widening Access in a Vast Country," in Mountford-Zimdars and Harrison, *Access to Higher Education.*
17. Maia Chankseliani, "Rural Disadvantage in Georgian Higher Education Admissions: A Mixed-Methods Study," *Comparative Education Review* 57, no. 3 (2013): 424–56.
18. Richard Breen, "Educational Expansion and Social Mobility in the 20th Century," *Social Forces* 89, no. 2 (2010): 365–88; and OECD, "Knowledge and Skills for Life. First Results from PISA 2000," 2001, www.oecd.org/edu/school/programmeforinternationalstudentassessmentpisa/33691620.pdf.
19. OECD, "Income Inequality Update," November 2016, www.oecd.org/social/OECD2016-Income-Inequality-Update.pdf.
20. OECD, "Education Policy Outlook Finland," November 2013, www.oecd.org/edu/EDUCATION%20POLICY%20OUTLOOK%20FINLAND_EN.pdf. The PISA (Programme for International Student Assessment) test is a standardized test given to fifteen-year-olds.
21. Jon Marcus, "Forcing Students to Graduate 'On Time,'" *Atlantic*, June 11, 2015.
22. Nadine Ketel, Edwin Leuven, Hessel Oosterbeek, and Bas van der Klaauw, "The Returns to Medical School in a Regulated Labor Market: Evidence from Admission Lotteries" (working paper, Amsterdam School of Economics Research Institute, Amsterdam, Netherlands, 2012), https://pure.uva.nl/ws/files/1601728/115751_377659.pdf.
23. Peter Stone, "Access to Higher Education by the Luck of the Draw," *Comparative Education Review* 57, no. 3 (2013): 577–99.
24. Chris Hamnett and Tim Butler, "Distance, Education, and Inequality," *Comparative Education* 49, no. 3 (2013): 317–30.
25. Eric A. Hanushek, John F. Kain, and Steve G. Rivkin, "New Evidence about *Brown v. Board of Education*: The Complex Effects of School Racial Composition on Achievement," *Journal of Labor Economics* 27, no. 3 (July 2009): 349–83.
26. Fiona Millar, "School Admission: Is a Lottery a Fairer System?" *Guardian*, March 14, 2017.
27. Anna Mountford-Zimdars, *Meritocracy and the University: Selective Admission in England and the United States* (London: Bloomsbury, 2016).
28. Yossi Shavit, Richard Arum, and Adam Gamoran, eds., *Stratification in Higher Education: A Comparative Study* (Stanford, CA: Stanford University Press, 2007).

29. Further education colleges historically educated students in courses that were not part of a degree program. However, in recent years these institutions have started offering higher education degree courses, often accredited by partnering universities (known as "HE in FE"). In 2009, 172,000 students were enrolled in higher education courses in further education colleges; see Eve Rapley, "HE in FE—Past, Present, and Future," *Journal of Pedagogic Development* 2, no. 2 (2012), www.beds.ac.uk/jpd/volume-2-issue-2/he-in-fe-past,-present-and-future; and Education and Training Foundation, "Introduction," www.et-foundation.co.uk/supporting/support-practitioners/he-in-fe.
30. Vikki Boliver, "Are There Distinctive Clusters of Higher and Lower Status Universities in the UK?," *Oxford Review of Education* 41, no. 5 (2015): 608–627.
31. National Vocational Qualifications (NVQs) are on-the-job training programs available to both students and workers. NVQ programs allow participants to earn money and earn a qualification while working, similar to US apprenticeship programs. NVQs vary in levels of competency, where a level 1 NVQ is the most introductory and a level 5 NVQ is most advanced. Similarly, BTEC programs are a vocational-focused qualification. BTECs encompass a wide variety of subjects from engineering to arts and can be used for eligibility for higher education. For more information, see Michael Young, "National Vocational Qualification in the United Kingdom: Their Origins and Legacy," International Labour Office, Geneva, 2010, http://www.ilo.org/wcmsp5/groups/public/---ed_emp/---ifp_skills/documents/genericdocument/wcms_145934.pdf; and Tess Reidy, "Will Taking a BTEC Help or Hinder Your University Application?," *Guardian*, July 21, 2015, www.theguardian.com/education/2015/jul/21/will-taking-a-btec-help-or-hinder-your-university-application.
32. Independent Schools Council, 2018, www.isc.co.uk/research.
33. Carole Leathwood, "A Critique of Institutional Inequalities in Higher Education," *Theory and Research in Education* 2, no. 1 (2004): 31–48.
34. Student Loans Company, "Student Loans in England: Financial Year 2015–16, Statistical First Release," www.slc.co.uk/media/7594/slcsfr012016.pdf.
35. Office for Fair Access, "Frequently Asked Questions," www.offa.org.uk/press/frequently-asked-questions.
36. Gill Wyness, "Deserving Poor: Are Higher Education Bursaries Going to the Right Students?," *Education Sciences* 6, no. 1 (2015), doi:10.3390/educsci6010005.
37. These percentages exclude students enrolled at further education colleges. For more information, see Higher Education Statistical Agency (UK), "Non-Continuation Rates (Including Projected Outcomes), Introduction," March 2017, www.hesa.ac.uk/data-and-analysis/performance-indicators/non-continuation.
38. These percentages exclude students enrolled at further education colleges.
39. Vikki Boliver, "Exploring Ethnic Inequalities in Admission to Russell Group Universities," *Sociology* 50, no. 2 (2016): 247–66.
40. Anthony F. Heath, Catherine Rothon, and Elina Kilpi, "The Second Generation in Western Europe: Education, Unemployment, and Occupational Attainment," *Annual Review of Sociology* 34 (August 2008): 211–35.
41. Yaojun Li and Anthony Heath, "Minority Ethnic Men in British Labour Market (1972–2005)," *International Journal of Sociology and Social Policy* 28, nos. 5/6 (2008): 231–44.
42. Anna Mountford-Zimdars et al., "Causes of Differences in Student Outcomes," Higher Education Funding Council for England (HEFCE), July 23, 2015, https://ore.exeter.

ac.uk/repository/bitstream/handle/10871/31891/HEFCE2015_diffout.pdf?sequence=1&isAllowed=y.

43. Universities UK, "Graduate Employment (2014–15)," www.universitiesuk.ac.uk/facts-and-stats/Pages/higher-education-data.aspx.
44. Paul Wakeling and Gillian Hampden-Thompson, *Transition to Higher Degrees across the UK: An Analysis of National, Institutional, and Individual Differences*, Higher Education Academy, April 2013, www.heacademy.ac.uk/system/files/transition_to_higher_degree_across_the_uk_0.pdf.
45. Andrea Abbas, Paul Ashwin, and Monica McLean, "The Influence of Curricula Content on English Sociology Students' Transformations: The Case of Feminist Knowledge," *Teaching in Higher Education* 21, no. 4 (2016): 442–56; Arnaud Chevalier and Gavan Conlon, "Does It Pay to Attend a Prestigious University?" (working paper no. 848, Institute for the Study of Labor (hereafter, IZA), Bonn, Germany, 2003); Harriet Bradley et al., "The Paired Peers Project Year 3 Report," University of Bristol, 2013, www.bristol.ac.uk/media-library/sites/spais/migrated/documents/report.pdf; and Francis Green, Golo Henseke, and Anna Vignoles, "Private Schooling and Labour Market Outcomes," *British Educational Research Journal* 43, no. 1 (2017): 7–28.
46. Michael Hout, "Social and Economic Returns to College Education in the United States," *Annual Review of Sociology* 38 (2012): 379–400.
47. Philip Kirby, "Levels of Success: The Potential of UK Apprenticeships," Sutton Trust, 2014, www.suttontrust.com/wp-content/uploads/2015/10/Levels-of-Success3.pdf.
48. Patrick de Hahn, "It's harder than it's ever been to get into the Ivy League," *USA Today*, April 5, 2017.
49. Hout, "Social and Economic Returns"; and Richard Arum and Josipa Roksa, *Academically Adrift: Limited Learning on College Campuses* (Chicago: University of Chicago Press, 2011), 272.
50. Hout, "Social and Economic Returns."
51. Sylke V. Schnepf, "Inequalities in Secondary School Attendance in Germany" (working paper, Southampton Statistical Sciences Research Institute, Southampton, UK, 2003), https://eprints.soton.ac.uk/id/eprint/212; Christian Dustmann, Patrick A. Puhani, and Uta Schönberg, "The Long-Term Effects of Early Track Choice" (working paper no. 7897, IZA, Bonn, Germany, 2014), http://ftp.iza.org/dp7897.pdf; and Jürgen Baumert et al., eds., *PISA 2000: Basiskompetenzen von Schülerinnen und Schülern im internationalen Vergleich* [PISA 2000: Basic Competencies of School Students in an International Comparison] (Opladen, Germany: Leske and Budrich, 2001).
52. Daniele Checchi and Luca Flabbi, "Intergenerational Mobility and Schooling Decisions in Germany and Italy: The Impact of Secondary School Tracks," *Rivista di Politica Economica* 103, no. 3 (2013): 7–60.
53. Private primary and secondary schools have been a growing sector in Germany, so their share of students is now larger than in England, although state subsidies mean that fees are nominal or low (monthly fees of EUR 10–300 are common), giving the German private school sector a broader social base than in England. For more information, see Steffen Hillmert and Marita Jacobs, "Selections and Social Selectivity on the Academic Track: A Life-Course Analysis of Educational Attainment in Germany," *Research in Social Stratification and Mobility* 28, no. 1 (2010): 59–76, https://doi.org/10.1016/j.rssm.2009.12.006.

54. David Gordon Smith, "German Universities 'Share Blame' for Problems," *Spiegel Online*, August 15, 2012, www.spiegel.de/international/germany/press-review-on-bologna-process-education-reforms-a-850185.html.
55. Hillmert and Jacobs, "Selections and Social Selectivity."
56. *Spiegel Online*, "Studenten: Wer das Studium abbricht – und warum," July 29, 2015, www.spiegel.de/lebenundlernen/uni/welche-studenten-ihr-studium-abbrechen-und-warum-a-1045486.html.
57. Ulrich Heublein, "Student Drop-Out from German Higher Education Institutions," *European Journal of Education* 49, no. 4 (2014): 497–513.
58. Eurostat 2017, "Tertiary Education Statistics," June 2017, http://ec.europa.eu/eurostat/statistics-explained/index.php/Tertiary_education_statistics.
59. Lower Saxony was the last state to remove tuition, in the 2014–2015 school year, although some fees still exist. See Nick Hillman, *Keeping Up with the Germans?: A Comparison of Student Funding, Internationalisation, and Research in the UK and German Universities*, Higher Education Policy Institute, September 2015, www.hepi.ac.uk/wp-content/uploads/2015/09/HEPI-Keeping-Up-WEB.pdf.
60. German Federal Statistical Office, "BAföG Statistics 2015: 870,000 Recipients of Training Assistance in Germany," press release, August 11, 2016, https://www.destatis.de/EN/PressServices/Press/pr/2016/08/PE16_278_214.html.
61. Katja Bosse, "Nach der Uni an den Tresen—Wie finanziere ich mein Studium?," ZEIT Campus, 2017, www.zeit.de/campus/2017/02/studienfinanzierung-kredit-nebenjob-bafoeg-stipendien-ratgeber.
62. Bernd Kramer, "Deutschland im OECD-Vergleich," *Spiegel Online*, November 24 2015, www.spiegel.de/lebenundlernen/job/oecd-studie-nur-wenige-studenten-halten-bis-zum-abschluss-durch-a-1064253.html.
63. Achim Schmillen and Heiko Stüber, "Lebensverdienst nach Qualifikation—Bildung lohnt sich ein Leben lang," IAB-Kurzbericht, 2014, http://doku.iab.de/kurzber/2014/kb0114.pdf.
64. Steffen Hillmert and Marita Jacob, "Social Inequality in Higher Education: Is Vocational Training a Pathway Leading To or Away from University?," *European Sociological Review* 19, (2003): 319–34; and Yossi Shavit and Walter Müller, "Vocational Secondary Education: Where Diversion and Where Safety Net?," *European Societies* 2 (2000): 29–50.
65. Paul Samuelson, "The Pure Theory of Public Expenditure," *Review of Economics and Statistics* 36, no. 4 (1954): 387–89; Simon Marginson, "Higher Education and Public Good," *Higher Education Quarterly* 65, no. 4 (2012): 411–33.
66. Anna Mountford-Zimdars et al., "Framing Higher Education: Questions and Responses in the British Social Attitudes Survey 1983–2010," *British Journal of Sociology of Education* 34, nos. 5/6 (2013): 792–811.
67. Samuel Bowles and Herbert Gintis, *Schooling in Capitalist America: Educational Reform and the Contradictions of Economic Life* (New York: Basic Books, 1976); Steven G. Brint and Jerome Karabel, *The Diverted Dream: Community Colleges and the Promise of Educational Opportunity in America, 1900–1985* (New York: Oxford University Press, 1989); and Raftery and Hout, "Maximally Maintained Inequality."
68. Ralph H. Turner, "Sponsored and Contest Mobility and the School System," *American Sociological Review* 25 (1960): 855–67.

Chapter 5

1. Robert Henry, *The History of Great Britain*, vol. 6 (London: Harding and Lepard, 1823), 280.
2. Frederick Maurice Powicke and Alfred Brotherston Emden, *The Universities of Europe in the Middle Ages by the Late Hastings Rashdall*, vol. 2 (Oxford: Clarendon Press, 1936).
3. Jenny Adams, "The History of Student Loans Goes Back to the Middle Ages," *The Conversation*, March 23, https://theconversation.com/the-history-of-student-loans-goes-back-to-the-middle-ages-56326.
4. Sven-Eric Reiterberg and Allan Svensson, "The Importance of Financial Aid: The Case of Higher Education in Sweden," *Higher Education* 12, no. 1 (1983): 89–100, https://link.springer.com/article/10.1007/BF00140274.
5. Jamil Salmi, "Student Loans in an International Perspective: The World Bank Experience," World Bank, January 1, 2003, http://siteresources.worldbank.org/INTLL/Resources/student_loans.pdf.
6. World Bank, "Financing Education in Colombia," 2015, http://treasury.worldbank.org/bdm/pdf/Case_Study/Colombia_ICETEX_customlending_2015.pdf.
7. Theresa M. Scanlon, *Student Aid in Western Germany 1945–1971: A Study with Particular Reference to the Honnef Scheme* (Koln: Kommision bei Bohlau, 1993).
8. Salmi, "Student Loans."
9. The College Cost Reduction and Access Act of 2007 enacted income-based repayment (IBR) plans, but they didn't take effect until July 1, 2009. See The Institute for College Access and Success (TICA), "Fair and Manageable Loan Payments," https://ticas.org/initiative/fair-and-manageable-loan-payments.
10. In Chile, needy students in who seek admission to colleges that are part of the Council of Rectors of Chilean Universities (CRUCh) are eligible for the Programa de Credito con Aval del Estado (CAE), while similar students in private institutions have access to the Fondos Solidarios de Credito Universitario (FSCU). Both are income-contingent, but the maximum payment as a percentage of income is lower in the former, as is the number of years before loan forgiveness occurs.
11. Age limits apply to students at the time they begin their studies.
12. The UK offers a variant of this in that it has a multiple allowance system based on geography and residency (i.e., whether one lives at home and whether one is based in London), but it is still not an individualized need-assessment system.
13. Australia's system is technically a deferred contribution rather than a loan, but for most purposes the loan terminology makes sense.
14. William J. Bennett, "Our Greedy Colleges," *New York Times*, February 18, 1987.
15. The Bennett Hypothesis, named after Education Secretary William Bennett, argues that increasing financial aid eligibility has allowed colleges to raise tuition.
16. Milton Friedman, "The Role of Government in Education." From Economics and the Public Interest, ed. Robert A. Solo, copyright 1955 by the Trustees of Rutgers College in New Jersey. https://la.utexas.edu/users/hcleaver/330T/350kPEEFriedmanRoleOfGovttable.pdf.
17. Friedman, "Role of Government in Education," 11.
18. HECS was introduced through the Higher Education Funding Act of 1988. In 1996 the Higher Education Budget Statement revised HECS to reflect lowered income thresholds for repayment and exempted repayments for borrowers with dependents on Medi-

care. The 1996 reform also introduced undergraduate merit-based scholarships, which did not need to be repaid. See Graduate School of Education at the University of Buffalo, "Higher Education Finance and Cost-Sharing in Australia," http://gse.buffalo.edu/org/inthigheredfinance/files/Country_Profiles/Australia/Australia.pdf; and Parliament of Australia, "The Higher Education Contribution Scheme," August 12, 2003, www.aph.gov.au/About_Parliament/Parliamentary_Departments/Parliamentary_Library/Publications_Archive/archive/hecs#Majorchange.

19. Locally, loans for cost-of-living expenses are called "maintenance loans."
20. In the US, for example, the repayment rate through an income-based repayment plan applies only to income above a certain threshold. In 2018, for a household of two, that threshold is USD 24,690. In Australia, however, the repayment rate is applied to all income as soon as a borrower's income reaches a certain level, creating a type of "cliff effect" where monthly payments suddenly jump.
21. Loan forgiveness occurs in the US after twenty years of on-time payments. Individuals who borrowed for graduate school before July 1, 2014, were eligible for the Revised Pay as You Earn (REPAYE) program, which offered loan forgiveness after twenty-five years of on-time repayments. Borrowers who qualify for public service loan forgiveness receive loan forgiveness after ten years of repayment.
22. EU students at UK universities are eligible for UK student assistance, but their borrowing makes up only about 0.3 percent of the total loan portfolio.

Chapter 6

1. A total of 113,393 beneficiaries of 2016 gratuidad carried over their benefit to 2017. The rest either dropped out or graduated. See Ministerio de Educación, 2017, *Resultados de asignación y renovación gratuidad, becas y créditos, 31 de mayo de 2017, Minuta actualizada al 14 de junio*, División de Educación Superior, 2017. The author would like to thank the Higher Education Division of Chile's Ministry of Education for sharing with me their minutes for press releases used in 2016 and 2017.
2. Throughout this chapter, an exchange rate of USD 1 = CLP 670 is used, which is a rough average of the value of the dollar in Chilean pesos during the Bachelet administration. See Federal Reserve Bank of St. Louis, "National Currency to US Dollar Spot Exchange Rate for Chile," accessed March 1, 2018, https://fred.stlouisfed.org/series/CCUSSP02CLM650N. Myriam Bustos, "Expansion of Gratuity in 2018 Will Cost an Additional $217 Billion," *La Tercera*, 2017, www.latercera.com/noticia/ampliacion-gratuidad-2018-costara-217-mil-millones-adicionales/amp.
3. Pilar Galleguillos Carvajal et al., "Reforma a la Educación Superior: Financiamiento Actual y Proyecciones," Dirección de Presupuestos, Gobierno de Chile, November 2016, www.dipres.gob.cl/572/articles-154341_doc_pdf.pdf.
4. José Joaquín Brunner, *Informe sobre la educación superior en Chile* (Santiago, Chile: FLACSO, 1986).
5. Andrés Bernasconi and María Paola Sevilla, "Against All Odds: How Chile Developed a Successful Technical and Vocational Sector in Postsecondary Education," in *Responding to Massification: Differentiation in Postsecondary Education Worldwide*, ed. Philip G. Altbach, Liz Reisberg, and Hans de Wit (Chestnut Hill, MA: Boston College Center for International Higher Education, 2016).

6. Alfonso Muga, "Estadísticas sobre la evolución del sistema de educación superior en Chile: 1980–1992," in *Informe de la Educación Superior 1993*, Foro de la Educación Superior (Santiago, Chile: Talleres Gráficos Constitución, 1993).
7. Ministry of Education of Chile, "Compendio Histórico de Educacion Superiór," 2016, www.mifuturo.cl/index.php/estudios/estructura-compendio.
8. I use "public" and "state" interchangeably to denote ownership by the state. See law no. 20.910, Create Fifteen State Technical Training Centers, www.leychile.cl/Navegar?idNorma=1088775.
9. Converted using purchasing power parity exchange rates.
10. Alex Solis, "Credit Access and College Enrollment," *Journal of Political Economy* 125, no. 2 (2017): 562–622, https://eml.berkeley.edu/~saez/course131/solis.pdf.
11. Organisation for Economic Cooperation and Development (OECD) and World Bank, *La Educación Superior en Chile*, Revisión de Políticas Nacionales de Educación, 2009, www7.uc.cl/webpuc/piloto/pdf/informe_OECD.pdf.
12. OECD, "Reviews of National Policies for Education: Tertiary Education in Chile," OECD and World Bank, 2009, http://siteresources.worldbank.org/EDUCATION/Resources/278200-1269619804461/LAC_P106874_ChileOECDWB.FULL.pdf.
13. Commission for Student Financing for Higher Education, "Analysis and Recommendations for the Student Financing System," March 2012, http://media.biobiochile.cl/wp-content/uploads/2012/03/Informe-Comision-Ayuda-Estudiantil_marzo_2012.pdf.
14. OECD, *Education at a Glance 2016: OECD Indicators*, 2016, www.oecd.org/edu/education-at-a-glance-19991487.htm.
15. Cristián Bellei, Cristian Cabalín, and Víctor Orellana, "The 2011 Chilean Student Movement against Neoliberal Educational Policies," *Studies in Higher Education* 39, no. 3 (2014): 426–40, http://dx.doi.org/10.1080/03075079.2014.896179; and Andrés Bernasconi, "Policy Path Dependence of a Research Agenda: The Case of Chile in the Aftermath of the Student Revolt of 2011," *Studies in Higher Education* 39, no. 8 (2014): 1405–16, http://dx.doi.org/10.1080/03075079.2014.950448.
16. Cristián Larroulet and Pedro Montt, "Políticas educativas de largo plazo y acuerdo amplio en educación: el caso chileno," in *¿Fin de Ciclo? Cambios en la Gobernanza del Sistema educativo*, ed. Sergio Martinic and Gregory Elacqua (Santiago, Chile: Ediciones Pontificia Universidad Católica de Chile and UNESCO, 2010).
17. Bellei, Cabalín, and Orellana, "Chilean Student Movement."
18. Atria also produced numerous columns and opinion pieces in this period, which were highly influential among student leaders, as one of them, Giorgio Jackson, declared in his prologue to a 2012 book by Atria, noting that he kept underlined and annotated opinion articles by Atria in his backpack during the 2011 upheaval. Fernando Atria, *Mercado y ciudadanía en la educación* (Santiago, Chile: Editorial Flandes Indiano, 2007); and Fernando Atria, "¿Qué educación es 'pública'?" in *Ecos de la revolución pingüina*, ed. Cristián Bellei, Dante Contreras, and Juan Pablo Valenzuela (Santiago, Chile: UNICEF, 2010).
19. This means students coming from families from the bottom seven income deciles.
20. Since the government would now be paying via transfers in lieu of the students, caps were put in place to prevent institutions from raising tuition beyond current levels.
21. Author's translation from Michelle Bachelet, "Chile de todos. Programa de gobierno de Michelle Bachelet 2014–2018," October 2013, http://michellebachelet.cl/programa; notes 19 and 20 added to original.

22. Alberto Arenas de Mesa and Michelle Bachelet Jeria, "Mensaje de S.E. la Presidenta de la Republica con el que Inicia un Proyecto de Ley de Reforma Tributaria que Modifica el Sistema de Tributacion de la Renta e Introduce Diversos Ajustes en el Sistema Tributario" (speech, Camara de Diputados de Chile, April 1, 2014), www.camara.cl/pley/pdfpley.aspx?prmID=9500&prmTIPO=INICIATIVA; and Sergio Granados Aguilar, "Informe Financiero Sustitutivo," Ministerio de Hacienda, August 11, 2014, www.economiaynegocios.cl/noticias/pdf/hacienda.pdf.pdf.
23. That is, students coming from families from the bottom six income deciles.
24. Author's translation and from Cooperativa, "Educación: Bachelet anunció gratuidad en 2016 para el 60 por ciento más vulnerable," May 21, 2015, www.cooperativa.cl/noticias/pais/politica/discurso-21-de-mayo/educacion-bachelet-anuncio-gratuidad-en-2016-para-el-60-por-ciento-mas/2015-05-21/100526.html; note 23 added to original.
25. Galleguillos Carvajal et al., "Reforma a la Educación Superior."
26. See *Historia de la Ley 20.882*, p. 665, in Biblioteca del Congreso Nacional de Chile, www.bcn.cl.
27. In a March 2016 interview, the Minister of Education said (in my translation): "because we don't want profit making in terms of distribution of earnings with resources that are public." Fernando Abarca Back, "En entrevista exclusive con Radio U. de Santiago, ministra de Educacion aborda aspectos asociados a la gratuidad," Universidad de Santiago de Chile, March 10, 2016, www.usach.cl/news/entrevista-exclusiva-radio-u-santiago-ministra-educacion-aborda-aspectos-asociados-la-gratuidad.
28. Author's translation from Prensa Presidencia, "Presidenta Bachelet: 'Habrá gratuidad para la educación superior en las instituciones universitarias o técnicas que tengan convenios con el Estado,'" https://prensa.presidencia.cl/comunicado.aspx?id=6000.
29. Rol no. 2935-15 CPT, www.tribunalconstitucional.cl/descargar_sentencia.php?id=3200.
30. Galleguillos Carvajal et al., "Reforma a la Educación Superior."
31. Law no. 20.890, www.leychile.cl/Navegar?idNorma=1085782.
32. Flavia Cordella and Pablo Cádiz, "The Points of the Agreement That Untangled the Short Law of Gratuity in the Senate," T13, December 23, 2015, www.t13.cl/noticia/politica/gobierno-negocia-acuerdo-destrabar-ley-corta-gratuidad.
33. Rosario Alvarez, "Adimark: Reforma Educacional sube aprobación tras implementación de la gratuidad," *La Tercera*, February 3, 2016, www.latercera.com/noticia/adimark-reforma-educacional-sube-aprobacion-tras-implementacion-de-la-gratuidad.
34. "Encuesta Cadem: Sólo tres de cada 10 chilenos apoya que la gratuidad universitaria sea universal," *EMOL*, July 11, 2016, www.emol.com/noticias/Nacional/2016/07/11/811889/Encuesta-Cadem-3-de-cada-10-chilenos-se-inclina-por-entregar-la-gratuidad-universal.html.
35. Ministerio de Educación, "Informe duración real y sobreduración de carreras o programas generación titulados y graduados 2012–2016," Servicio de Información de Educación Superior, December 2016, http://analisis.umag.cl/documentos/duracion_real_sobreduracin_sies_2016.pdf.
36. Ministerio de Educación, *Gratuidad 2016 y 1° asignación 2017*, División de Educación Superior, April 13, 2017.
37. The exact number of eligible institutions is hard to pin down, because while the accreditation requirement is easy to verify, compliance with the nonprofit clause requires digging into the statutes and by-laws of each private university.

38. Ministerio de Educación, *Minuta Análisis del Efecto de la Gratuidad 2016 en el Acceso a Beneficios de Estudiantes de Primer Año*, División de Educación Superior, July 19, 2016.
39. Law no. 20.981, www.leychile.cl/Navegar?idNorma=1098001.
40. *EMOL*, "Encuesta Cadem."
41. Ministerio de Educación, "Conoce las instituciones adscritas a Gratuidad," December 16, 2016, www.gratuidad.cl/2016/12/16/universidades.
42. Alonso Bucarey, "Who Pays for Free College? Crowding Out on Campus" (job market paper, Massachusetts Institute of Technology, Cambridge, Massachusetts, 2018), http://economics.mit.edu/files/14234.
43. OECD, "Reviews of National Policies for Education: Tertiary Education in Chile," OECD and World Bank, 2009, http://siteresources.worldbank.org/EDUCATION/Resources/278200-1269619804461/LAC_P106874_ChileOECDWB.FULL.pdf.
44. Ministry of Education of Chile, *Minuta Análisis del Efecto de la Gratuidad 2016 en el Acceso a Beneficios de Estudiantes de Primer Año.*
45. Carlos Peña and Eduardo Silva S.J., "Una gratuidad sin reforma," *El Mercurio*, March 27, 2017, www.elmercurio.com/blogs/2017/03/27/49870/Una-gratuidad-sin-reforma.aspx.
46. Comisión Presidencial Ciencia para el Desarrollo de Chile, *Un sueño compartido para el futuro de chile. Informe a la Presidenta de la República, Michelle Bachelet*, July 2015, www.economia.gob.cl/cnidweb/wp-content/uploads/sites/35/2015/07/Informe-Ciencia-para-el-Desarrollo.pdf.
47. The National Socio-Economic Characterization Survey (CASEN) is administered by the Chilean Ministry of Social Development to evaluate the effect of government programs. For more information, see Ministry of Finance, "CASEN Survey" Government of Chile, www.hacienda.cl/english/documents/statistics/casen-survey.html; and Harald Beyer and Loreto Cox, "Gratuidad de la educación superior: una política regresiva," *Puntos de Referencia*, no. 337 (October 2011), www.cepchile.cl/cep/site/artic/20160304/asocfile/20160304095625/pder337_LCox_HBeyer.pdf.
48. Ministerio de Educación, *Minuta Análisis del Efecto de la Gratuidad.*

Chapter 7

1. Academic Ranking of World Universities, "Academic Ranking of World Universities 2016," www.timeshighereducation.com/students/news/shanghai-ranking-academic-ranking-world-universities-2016-results-announced.
2. Throughout this chapter, an exchange rate of USD 1 = AUD 1.156 is used, which is the approximate value of the five-year and ten-year historical average of the dollar in Australian dollars. See OFX Group, "Historical Exchange Rates," www.ofx.com/en-au/forex-news/historical-exchange-rates. Simon Birmingham, "International Student Sector Smashes Records," media release, February 22, 2017, https://www.senatorbirmingham.com.au/international-student-sector-smashes-records-2.
3. Australian Government, "HELP, SSL, ABSTUDY SSL, TSL and SFSS Repayment Thresholds and Rates," Australian Taxation Office, www.ato.gov.au/Rates/HELP,-TSL-and-SFSS-repayment-thresholds-and-rates.
4. Organisation for Economic Cooperation and Development (OECD), "Australia," *Education at a Glance 2016: OECD Indicators*, www.keepeek.com/Digital-Asset-Management/oecd/education/education-at-a-glance-2016/australia_eag-2016-41-en#page2.

5. "Employment rate" refers to bachelor's degree graduates in full-time employment as a proportion of bachelor's degree graduates available for full-time employment. See Graduate Careers Australia, "GradStats: Employment and Salary Outcomes of Recent Higher Education Graduates," December 2015, www.graduatecareers.com.au/wp-content/uploads/2015/12/GCA_GradStats_2015_FINAL.pdf.
6. Australian Government, "Budget Savings (Omnibus) Act 2016," Federal Register of Legislation, 2016, www.legislation.gov.au/Details/C2016A00055.
7. Parliament of Australia, "Higher Education Support Legislation Amendment (Student Loan Sustainability) Bill 2018," www.aph.gov.au/Parliamentary_Business/Bills_Legislation/Bills_Search_Results/Result?bId=r6051.
8. Commonwealth of Australia, "Higher Education Standards Framework (Threshold Standards) 2015," October 7, 2015, www.legislation.gov.au/Details/F2015L01639; and Leo Goedegebuure et al., "A Framework for Differentiation," in *Visions for Australian Tertiary Education*, ed. Richard James, Sarah French, and Paula Kelly, University of Melbourne, February 2017, http://melbourne-cshe.unimelb.edu.au/__data/assets/pdf_file/0006/2263137/MCSHE-Visions-for-Aust-Ter-Ed-web2.pdf.
9. John S. Dawkins, *Higher Education: A Policy Statement* (Canberra: Australian Government Publishing Service, 1988).
10. Dawkins, *Higher Education.*
11. Dawkins, *Higher Education.*
12. Goedegebuure et al., "Framework for Differentiation."
13. Andrew Norton, "Mapping Australian Higher Education 2016," Grattan Institute, August 2016, https://grattan.edu.au/wp-content/uploads/2016/08/875-Mapping-Australian-Higher-Education-2016.pdf.
14 Gavin Moodie, "Civilisation as We Don't Know It: Teaching Only Universities," *The Conversation*, June 30, 2014, https://theconversation.com/civilisation-as-we-dont-know-it-teaching-only-universities-28505.
15. See recommendations 2 and 4 of the Bradley Review. Recommendation 2 was modified by the Labor government upon adoption to have a target date of 2025. See Denise Bradley, Peter Noonan, Helen Nugent, and Bill Scales, *Review of Australian Higher Education: Final Report*, Australian Department of Education and Training, December 2008, www.voced.edu.au/content/ngv%3A32134.
16. David Kemp and Andrew Norton, *Review of the Demand Driven Funding System Report*, April 13, 2014, 9, Australian Department of Education and Training, https://docs.education.gov.au/node/35537.
17. Australian Department of Education and Training, "Higher Education Statistics Collection," https://www.education.gov.au/higher-education-statistics.
18. Tim Dodd, "While the Numbers Steady, Dropout Rate Remains a Concern," *The Australian*, November 14, 2017, www.theaustralian.com.au/higher-education/while-the-numbers-steady-dropout-rate-remains-a-concern/news-story/83e8fde8f742fdf91ef11a71f69f9ec4.
19. Kemp and Norton, *Review of the Demand Driven System.*
20. Commonwealth of Australia, *Budget 2017-18: Portfolio Budget Statements 2017-18: Budget Related Paper No. 1.5*, Department of Education and Training, 2017, https://docs.education.gov.au/system/files/doc/other/education_and_training_portfolio_budget_statements_2017-18_full_print.pdf.

21. Graduate Careers Australia, "GradStats: Employment and Salary Outcomes," 2015, http://www.graduatecareers.com.au/wp-content/uploads/2015/12/GCA_GradStats_2015_FINAL.pdf.
22. Ibid.
23. Joshua Healy, "Graduating into a Weak Job Market: Why So Many Grads Can't Find Work," *The Conversation*, July 29, 2016, https://theconversation.com/graduating-into-a-weak-job-market-why-so-many-grads-cant-find-work-45222.
24. Kemp and Norton, *Review of the Demand Driven System*.
25. Healy, "Graduating into a Weak Job Market"; Edmund Tadros and Katie Walsh, "Too Many Law Graduates and Not Enough Jobs," *Australian Financial Review*, October 22, 2015, www.afr.com/business/legal/too-many-law-graduates-and-not-enough-jobs-20151020-gkdbyx; and Glyn Davis, "Election or Not, Graduate Outcomes and Better Regulation Are the Key," *The Australian*, June 29, 2016, www.theaustralian.com.au/higher-education/opinion/election-or-not-graduate-outcomes-and-better-regulation-are-key/news-story/e12f8e0dc14a8cf8d1147614bcde1d40.
26. Tadros and Walsh, "Too Many Law Graduates"; and Davis, "Election or Not."
27. Peter Noonan, "Modelling Increased Tertiary Participation in Australia," Mitchell Institute, May 24, 2017, www.mitchellinstitute.org.au/presentations/tertiary-participation-in-australia; and Adam Creighton and Simone Fox Koob, "TAFE Graduates Have Better Jobs Prospects, New Research Finds," *The Australian*, May 22, 2017, www.theaustralian.com.au/higher-education/tafe-graduates-have-better-jobs-prospects-new-research-finds/news-story/6d91bba571fc9400ef751b4bbb0fa137.
28. Toli Papadopoulos, "Overqualified and Underemployed: Meet Australia's Graduates," *The Australian*, July 12, 2014, www.theaustralian.com.au/business/business-spectator/overqualified-and-underemployed-meet-australias-graduates/news-story/6c4b36b7fd7b00117be43dadb3f7b048.
29. Attrition rate given is for all commencing bachelor's students at Table A providers. See Australian Department of Education and Training, "Higher Education Statistics Collection," 2016.
30. Universities Australia, "Higher Education and Research Facts and Figures," November 2015, www.universitiesaustralia.edu.au/australias-universities/info-for-students#.WpbenGfkDj4; and Andrew Norton, "HELP for the Future: Fairer Repayment of Student Debt," Grattan Institute, March 2016, https://grattan.edu.au/wp-content/uploads/2016/03/968-HELP-for-the-future1.pdf.
31. Norton, "HELP for the Future."
32. Tim Dodd, "We Are Told We Need More Scientists but Science Grads Struggle for Jobs," *Australian Financial Review*, February 14, 2016, www.afr.com/leadership/careers/jobs/we-are-told-we-need-more-scientists-but-science-grads-struggle-for-jobs-20160208-gmovql.
33. Davis, "Election or Not."
34. Graduate Careers Australia, "GradStats: Employment and Salary Outcomes of Recent Higher Education Graduates," December 2008, www.graduatecareers.com.au/wp-content/uploads/2012/01/gca001224.pdf.
35. Graduate Careers Australia, "GradStats," 2015.
36. Emma Alberici, "Students Should Contribute to Their Own Education," *Lateline*, May 20, 2014, www.abc.net.au/lateline/content/2014/s4008642.htm.

37. John Ross, "Students' False Hope on Jobs," *The Australian*, March 5, 2014, www.theaustralian.com.au/higher-education/students-false-hope-on-jobs/news-story/362034b4faf7c359d160b7f3ec7a4f85; and Tim Dodd, "Vocational Education Is a Better Pathway to a Job Than a University Degree, New Report Finds," *Australian Financial Review*, May 21, 2017, www.afr.com/leadership/vocational-education-is-a-better-pathway-to-a-job-than-a-university-degree-new-report-finds-20170519-gw8rdn.
38. Kemp and Norton, *Review of the Demand Driven System.*
39. Dan Conifer and Michael McKinnon, "University, Vocational Training Debts to Skyrocket Costing Budget Billions, Documents Show," ABC News, April 6, 2016, www.abc.net.au/news/2016-04-06/higher-education-debts-to-skyrocket-costing-budget-billions/7302062.
40. Parliament of Australia, *Higher Education Loan Programme: Impact on the Budget*, Parliamentary Budget Office, April 6, 2016, www.aph.gov.au/About_Parliament/Parliamentary_Departments/Parliamentary_Budget_Office/Publications/Research_reports/Higher_Education_Loan_Programme.
41. Ibid.
42. Parliament of Australia, "Higher Education Support Legislation Amendment (Student Loan Sustainability) Bill 2018," www.aph.gov.au/Parliamentary_Business/Bills_Legislation/Bills_Search_Results/Result?bId=r6051.
43. Domestic students can defer all tuition repayments until they begin earning above a certain income threshold. However, it should be noted that HELP payments to universities are brokered by the government on behalf of students only until such time as they are repaid through the taxation system. HELP payments should not, therefore, be considered public funding.
44. Note that in this context "Canberra" refers to the federal government. See Glyn Davis, "Why I Support the Deregulation of Higher Education," *The Conversation*, January 28, 2015, https://theconversation.com/glyn-davis-why-i-support-the-deregulation-of-higher-education-36766.
45. Universities Australia, "Unis and Students Have Done Their Bit for Budget Repair: Almost $4 Billion since 2011," April 24, 2017, www.universitiesaustralia.edu.au/Media-and-Events/media-releases/Unis---students-have-done-their-bit#.WVB0B8YRV1O.
46. Bernard Lane, "Senate Told $2.8bn Higher Education Savings May Push Another 5 Universities into Deficit," *The Australian*, October 4, 2017, www.theaustralian.com.au/higher-education/senate-told-28bn-education-investment-fund-cut-may-mean-deficit-for-10-universities/news-story/06bb95ec8aee2d0f509114c2c7d2361e.
47. Department of Education, Employment and Workforce Relations, *Higher Education Base Funding Review: Final Report [Lomax-Smith Review*], October 2011, www.voced.edu.au/content/ngv%3A49506.
48. Tim Dodd, "John Dawkins Says His University Reforms Are 'Completely Out of Date,'" *Australian Financial Review*, September 25, 2016, www.afr.com/leadership/john-dawkins-says-his-university-reforms-are-completely-out-of-date-20160924-grnt3e.
49. Alison Moodie, "Australia: Long History of International Higher Education," University World News, March 6, 2011, www.universityworldnews.com/article.php?story=20110305121304874.
50. Australian Government, "End of Year Summary of International Student Enrolment Data—Australia—2017," Department of Education and Training, https://internation-

aleducation.gov.au/research/International-Student-Data/Documents/MONTHLY%20 SUMMARIES/2017/International%20student%20data%20December%202017%20 detailed%20summary.pdf.

51. Peter Høj, memo to staff at the University of Queensland, May 2017, quoted in Julie Hare, "Unis Not Forced to Choose: IEAA," *The Australian*, May 15, 2017, https://www.theaustralian.com.au/higher-education/unis-not-forced-to-choose-ieaa/news-story/3d428b670fbba5f3854484883fe196a7.
52. James Bennett, "India No Longer Fears Racial Attacks on Its Students in Australia," *ABC News*, April 7, 2017, www.abc.net.au/news/2017-04-07/india-no-longer-fears-students-at-risk-of-racial-attacks/8424124.
53. Australian Bureau of Statistics, International Trade in Goods and Services, Australia (Cat no: 5368.0), April 2018, www.abs.gov.au/AUSSTATS/abs@.nsf/DetailsPage/5368.0Apr%202018?OpenDocument.
54. Goedegebuure et al., "Framework for Differentiation."
55. Goedegebuure et al., "Framework for Differentiation."
56. The Group of Eight universities are (in order of establishment): University of Sydney (1850), University of Melbourne (1853), University of Adelaide (1874), University of Queensland (1909), University of Western Australia (1911), Australian National University (1946), University of New South Wales (1949), and Monash University (1958).
57. Bradley et al., *Review of Australian Higher Education*, xxi.
58. Goedegebuure et al., "Framework for Differentiation," 9.
59. Tony Abbott, "Tony Abbott's Campaign Launch Speech: Full Transcript," *Sydney Morning Herald*, August 25, 2013, www.smh.com.au/federal-politics/federal-election-2013/tony-abbotts-campaign-launch-speech-full-transcript-20130825-2sjhc.html.
60. Quoted in Michelle Grattan, "Federal Budget 2014: The Days of Borrow and Spend Must Come to an End," *The Conversation*, May 13, 2014, https://theconversation.com/federal-budget-2014-the-days-of-borrow-and-spend-must-come-to-an-end-26627.
61. Mark Triffitt, "Three Tests the 2015 Federal Budget Must Pass," *The Conversation*, May 4, 2015, https://theconversation.com/three-tests-the-2015-federal-budget-must-pass-39797.
62. Stephen Parker, "Letting the Market Rip Will Suck the Soul Out of Universities," *The Conversation*, May 2, 2014, https://theconversation.com/letting-the-market-rip-will-suck-the-soul-out-of-universities-26216.
63. Ian Young, "Deregulation—Where to from Here?" *The Age*, July 14, 2014, www.theage.com.au/comment/deregulation--where-to-from-here-20140714-zt6lq.
64. Lachlan Harris and Andrew Charlton, "The Tipping Point in Australian Politics: Is the End of the Two Party System Near?" *Sydney Morning Herald*, March 18, 2017, www.smh.com.au/comment/the-tipping-point-in-australian-politics-is-the-end-of-the-twoparty-system-near-20170317-gv097u.html.
65. Kylar Loussikian, "Simon Birmingham Rethinks Uni Reforms, Promises to Consult," *The Australian*, September 23, 2015, www.theaustralian.com.au/higher-education/simon-birmingham-rethinks-uni-reforms-promises-to-consult/news-story/0b57c32783ee7574be1991627fa745fd.
66. Julie Hare and Rick Morton, "$3.7bn Hole in NDIS Funding after Transfer of Education Money Fails," *The Australian*, January 13, 2017, www.theaustralian.com.au/national-affairs/health/37bn-hole-in-ndis-funding-after-transfer-of-education-money-fails/news-story/c1245559a618008c53242bc01d520d4c.

67. Tim Dodd, "Simon Birmingham Attacks University Vice Chancellors' $1m Salaries," *Australian Financial Review*, May 1, 2017, www.afr.com/news/policy/budget/simon-birmingham-attacks-university-vicechancellors-1m-salaries-20170501-gvw3lg.
68. Dodd, "Simon Birmingham Attacks."
69. Parliament of Australia, "Higher Education Support Legislation Amendment (Student Loan Sustainability) Bill 2018," www.aph.gov.au/Parliamentary_Business/Bills_Legislation/Bills_Search_Results/Result?bId=r6051.
70. Michael McGowan, "Coalition's $2.2bn Education Cut Unfairly Targets the Poor, Universities Say," *Guardian*, December 19, 2017, www.theguardian.com/australia-news/2017/dec/19/coalitions-22bn-education-cut-unfairly-targets-the-poor-universities-say.
71. Universities Australia, "Graduate Contributions and the Impacts of the Funding Freeze," May 2018, www.universitiesaustralia.edu.au/Media-and-Events/submissions-and-reports/Graduate-contributions-and-the-impacts-of-the-funding-freeze/Graduate-contributions-and-the-impacts-of-the-funding-freeze.
72. Mark Warburton, "Universities Get an Unsustainable Policy for Christmas," *The Conversation*, December 20, 2017, https://theconversation.com/universities-get-an-unsustainable-policy-for-christmas-89307.

Chapter 8

1. Martin Carnoy et al., *University Expansion in a Changing Global Economy: Triumph of the BRICs?* (Stanford, CA: Stanford University Press, 2013); and Simon Marginson, "The Worldwide Trend to High Participation Higher Education: Dynamics of Social Stratification in Inclusive Systems," *Higher Education* 72, no. 4 (2016): 413–34, https://doi.org/10.1007/s10734-016-0016-x.
2. Daniel C. Levy, "The Unanticipated Explosion: Private Higher Education's Global Surge," *Comparative Education Review* 50, no. 2 (2006): 217–40, https://doi:10.1086/500694; and Daniel C. Levy, "Public Policy for Private Higher Education: A Global Analysis," *Journal of Comparative Policy Analysis: Research and Practice* 13, no. 4 (2011): 383–96, https://doi:10.1080/13876988.2011.583107.
3. Simon Schwartzman, "The National Assessment of Courses in Brazil," in *Public Policy for Academic Quality: Analyses of Innovative Policy Instruments*, ed. David D. Dill and Maarja Beerkens (Dordrecht, Netherlands: Springer, 2010), 293–312.
4. Martin Trow (1973) classifies higher education systems worldwide based on their gross enrollment ratio. The latest classification update (Trow 2007) establishes that those higher education systems that enroll less than 15 percent of the typical student age cohort (18–25) are considered elite systems; mass higher education systems enroll between 16 percent and 50 percent; and universal systems are those that enroll more than 50 percent of the relevant age cohort. See Martin Trow, "Problems in the Transition from Elite to Mass Higher Education" Carnegie Commission on Higher Education, 1973, www.eric.ed.gov/ERICWebPortal/detail?accno=ED091983; and Martin Trow, "Reflections on the Transition from Elite to Mass to Universal Access: Forms and Phases of Higher Education in Modern Societies since WWII," in *International Handbook of Higher Education*, ed. James J. F. Forest and Philip G. Altbach, Springer International Handbooks of Education 18 (Dordrecht, Netherlands: Springer, 2007), 243–80.
5. International Monetary Fund, "World Economic Outlook Database April 2017," 2017, www.imf.org/external/pubs/ft/weo/2017/01/weodata/index.aspx.

6. UN Educational, Scientific, and Cultural Organization's Institute for Statistics (UIS), "UIS Statistics," 2014, http://data.uis.unesco.org.
7. "Gross enrollment ratio" refers to the total enrollment in higher education (International Standard Classification of Education levels 5 to 8), regardless of age, expressed as a percentage of the total population of the five-year age group following on from leaving secondary school.
8. Martin Trow, "Problems in the Transition"; and Trow, "Reflections on the Transition."
9. UIS, "UIS Statistics."
10. Daniel C. Levy, *Higher Education and the State in Latin America* (Chicago: University of Chicago Press, 1986); Levy, "Unanticipated Explosion"; Daniel C. Levy, "The Global Growth of Private Higher Education," *The Global Growth of Private Higher Education: ASHE Higher Education Report* 36 (2010): 121–33; and Levy, "Public Policy for Private Higher Education."
11. Center for Distributive, Labor, and Social Studies (CEDLAS) and World Bank, "Socio-Economic Database for Latin America and the Caribbean (SEDLAC)," 2016, http://sedlac.econo.unlp.edu.ar.
12. CEDLAS, "Socio-Economic Database."
13. Program for Research on Private Higher Education (PROPHE), "Data on Private Higher Education in Chile," www.prophe.org/en/data-laws/national-databases.
14. Carnoy et al., *University Expansion*; and Clarissa Eckert Baeta Neves, Leandro Raizer, and Rochele Fellini Fachinetto, "Access, Expansion, and Equity in Higher Education: New Challenges for Brazilian Education Policy," *Sociologias* 3, no. SE [Selected Edition] (2007): 1–24.
15. Simon Schwartzman, "Masificación, Equidad y Calidad—Los Retos de La Educación Superior En Brasil—Análisis Del Período 2009–2013 [Massification, Equity, and Quality—Challenges to Brazilian Higher Education, 2009–2013 Analysis]," in *Políticas de Educación Superior En Iberoamérica, 2009–2013* [Higher Education Policy in Ibero-America, 2009–2013], ed. José Joaquín Brunner and C. Villalobos (Santiago, Chile: Universidad Diego Portales, 2014), 199–248.
16. There are federal, state, and municipal higher education institutions in Brazil. The large majority of the public institutions are universities, and most of them depend on the federal and state government, with just a small number of municipal institutions. Federal and state higher education institutions offer tuition-free education. See Elizabeth Balbachevsky, "Brazilian Higher Education: Converging Trajectory Patterns in a Diverse Institutional Environment," in *Biographies and Careers throughout Academic Life*, ed. Jesús F. Galaz-Fontes, Akira Arimoto, Ulrich Teichler, and John Brennan (Dordrecht, Netherlands: Springer, 2016), 31–45.
17. Tristan McCowan, "Expansion without Equity: An Analysis of Current Policy on Access to Higher Education in Brazil," *Higher Education* 53 (2007): 579–98, http://doi:10.1007/s10734-005-0097-4.
18. In sharp contrast to the US educational system, primary and secondary education provided by the private sector tends to be of better quality than public schools. McCowan judges the situation as an "anomaly," since it is reversed at the higher education level, where most prestigious institutions are located in the public sector with a few exceptions (usually Catholic universities) in the private sector.
19. Schwartzman, "Masificación, Equidad y Calidad," 199–248.

20. Levy, *Higher Education and the State.*
21. Levy, *Higher Education and the State.*
22. Levy, *Higher Education and the State.*
23. The National University of Cordoba (Argentina) was founded by the Jesuits in 1613, and thus cannot strictly be considered a public university since its inception. In 1820 the Cordoba province governor provincialized it, and shortly after the enactment of the 1853 national Constitution (first Constitution of Argentina), the national government nationalized it in 1856. The time span between the provincialization of the National University of Cordoba and the establishment of the first private university in Argentina is still considerably longer than in Brazil.
24. Levy, *Higher Education and the State.*
25. Robert E. Verhine, "Pós-Graduação No Brasil E Nos Estados Unidos: Uma Análise Comparativa [Graduate Studies in Brazil and in the United States: A Comparative Analysis]," *Educação* 31 (May 2008): 166–72.
26. Levy, *Higher Education and the State*; and Simon Schwartzman, *A Space for Science: The Development of the Scientific Community in Brazil* (University Park: Pennsylvania State University Press, 1991).
27. Carlos Benedito Martins, "A Reforma Universitária de 1968 E a Abertura Para O Ensino Superior Privado No Brasil [The 1968 Reform and the Opening of Doors to Private Higher Education in Brazil]," *Educação E Sociedade* 30 (2009): 15–35.
28. Although the Brazilian system does not have a formal university and non-university distinction, scholars make that differentiation based on the level of research and autonomy granted to different types of institutions. There are no differences, however, in the types of degrees granted by university and non-university institutions.
29. Dante J. Salto, "To Profit or Not to Profit: The Private Higher Education Sector in Brazil," *Higher Education* 75, no. 5 (2018), 809–825, https://doi.org/10.1007/s10734-017-0171-8, first published August 2, 2017.
30. Andrés Bernasconi, "Constitutional Prospects for the Implementation of Funding and Governance Reforms in Latin American Higher Education," *Journal of Education Policy* 22, (2007): 509–29; and Levy, *Higher Education and the State.*
31. Adriana Chiroleu and Mónica Marquina, "Democratisation or Credentialism? Public Policies of Expansion of Higher Education in Latin America," *Policy Reviews in Higher Education* 1, no. 2 (2017): 139–60, http://doi:10.1080/23322969.2017.1303787; and José Joaquín Brunner and Daniel Andrés Miranda, eds., *Educación Superior En Iberoamérica. Informe 2016* [Higher Education in Ibero-America. 2016 Report] (Santiago, Chile: Centro Interuniversitario de Desarrollo (CINDA), 2016), www.cinda.cl/documentos-y-publicaciones/libros.
32. National Institute of Educational Studies and Research Anísio Teixeira (INEP), "Microdados Censo Da Educação Superior [Higher Education Census Database]," *Portal INEP*, 2014, http://portal.inep.gov.br/microdados.
33. Secretaria de Politicas Universitarias (SPU), *Anuario de Estadísticas Universitarias 2013* [University Statistics Yearbook 2013] (Buenos Aires: SPU, 2013), http://informacionpresupuestaria.siu.edu.ar/DocumentosSPU/Anuario_2013.pdf.
34. Roger L. Geiger, *Private Sectors in Higher Education* (Ann Arbor: University of Michigan Press, 1986).
35. McCowan, "Expansion without Equity," 579–98.

36. The behavior of legal nonprofit institutions before the legislation allowing for-profits was often related to stretching the intent of the law.
37. Kevin Kinser and Daniel C. Levy, "For-Profit Higher Education: U.S. Tendencies, International Echoes," in *International Handbook of Higher Education*, ed. James J. F. Forest and Philip G. Altbach, Springer International Handbooks of Education, vol. 18 (Dordrecht, Netherlands: Springer, 2006), 107–20; and Kevin Kinser and Dante J. Salto, "For-Profit Higher Education," in *Encyclopedia of International Higher Education Systems and Institutions*, ed. Jung Cheol Shin and Pedro Teixeira (Dordrecht, Netherlands: Springer Netherlands, 2017), 1–7.
38. Unlike the US, private nonprofit higher education institutions in Brazil pay taxes. There are two types of nonprofits in Brazilian higher education: (1) religious and communitarian and (2) philanthropic. The former pay slightly more taxes than the latter. In all nonprofit cases, the tax rate is considerably lower than that applied to for-profit organizations.
39. Eunice R. Durham, "Higher Education in Brazil: Public and Private," in *The Challenges of Education in Brazil*, ed. Colin Brock and Simon Schwartzman (Didcot, Eng.: Symposium, 2004); Edson de Oliveira Nunes, *Educação Superior No Brasil: Estudos, Debates, Controvérsias* [Higher Education in Brazil: Studies, Debates, and Controversies] (Rio de Janeiro: Garamond, 2012); and Helena Sampaio, "O Setor Privado de Ensino Superior No Brasil: Continuidades E Transformações [The Private Sector in Brazilian Higher Education: Continuities and Transformations]," *Revista Ensino Superior Unicamp*, no. 3 (2011): 28–43.
40. Kevin Kinser, *From Main Street to Wall Street: The Transformation of for-Profit Higher Education: ASHE Higher Education Report* (San Francisco: Association for the Study of Higher Education, 2006).
41. Salto, "To Profit or Not to Profit."
42. Fábio Reis and Rodrigo Capelato, "A relevância do ensino superior privado no Brasil," *Revista de Educación Superior en América Latina* 0, no. 1 (2016), http://rcientificas.uninorte.edu.co/index.php/edusuplatam/article/view/9430.
43. Conversion rate used is US$1 = BZ$3.483, which is the 2016 annual average value of the dollar in terms of Brazilian reals (not seasonally adjusted). See Federal Reserve Bank of St. Louis, "Brazil/U.S. Foreign Exchange Rate," https://fred.stlouisfed.org/series/DEXBZUS; *Financial Times*, "Kroton Educacional S.A. (KROTY)," https://markets.ft.com/data/equities/tearsheet/summary?s=KROT3:SAO; and Yahoo Finance, "Kroton Educacional S.A. (KROTY)", https://finance.yahoo.com/quote/KROTY/financials.
44. *MarketWatch*, "Adtalem Global Education Inc.," https://www.marketwatch.com/investing/stock/atge/financials; and *MarketWatch*, "Laureat Education Inc. CI A," https://www.marketwatch.com/investing/stock/laur/financials.
45. Joe Leahy, "Brazil Education Groups in $2.5bn Tie-Up," *Financial Times*, April 22, 2013, www.ft.com/content/fab10e34-ab8b-11e2-ac71-00144feabdc0.
46. Reis and Capelato, "A relevância do ensino superior privado no Brasil."
47. Marcelo Knobel, "In Brazil the For-Profit Giants Keep Growing," *World View—Inside Higher Ed*, July 18, 2016, www.insidehighered.com/blogs/world-view/brazil-profit-giants-keep-growing.
48. Vera Lûcia Jacob Chaves, "Expansão Da Privatização/Mercantilização Do Ensino Superior Brasileiro," *Educação & Sociedade* 31, no. 111 (2010): 481–500; Knobel, "In Brazil

the For-Profit Giants Keep Growing"; and Marcelo Knobel and Robert Verhine, "Brazil's For-Profit Higher Education Dilemma," *International Higher Education*, no. 89 (Spring 2017): 23–24, https://ejournals.bc.edu/ojs/index.php/ihe/article/view/9843/8625.

49. Dante J. Salto, "Brazil: A For-Profit Giant," *International Higher Education*, no. 74 (June 4, 2014): 21–22, https://doi.org/10.6017/ihe.2014.74.5471; Dante J. Salto, "The Crucial Presence of Private Higher Education in Latin America," *International Higher Education*, no. 87 (Fall 2016): 24–25, https://ejournals.bc.edu/ojs/index.php/ihe/article/viewFile/9510/8478; and Salto, "To Profit or Not to Profit."
50. Levy, *Higher Education and the State*.
51. Both Crédito Educativo and FIES (Fundo de Financiamento Estudantil) are federal, publicly available loans targeted to students in need. In addition to these programs, higher education institutions and private companies and banks offer loans to students.
52. The next section addresses the relationship between financial aid and quality assurance mechanisms.
53. Schwartzman, "Masificación, Equidad y Calidad."
54. Schwartzman, "Masificación, Equidad y Calidad."
55. Donna Bowater, "For-Profits in Brazil Fight Rule Change," *Times Higher Education*, February 12, 2015, www.timeshighereducation.com/news/for-profits-in-brazil-fight-rule-change/2018420.article.
56. Bowater, "For-Profits in Brazil."
57. Bowater, "For-Profits in Brazil"; and Knobel, "In Brazil the For-Profit Giants Keep Growing."
58. TCU, "Relatório de Auditoria: Fundo de Financiamento Estudantil [Audit Report: Student Financing Fund]," Tribunal de Contas da União, 2016, http://portal.tcu.gov.br.
59. National Student Loan Data System (NSLDS), "Direct Loan Portfolio by Loan Status," 2016, https://studentaid.ed.gov/sites/default/files/fsawg/datacenter/library/PortfoliobyLoanStatus.xls.
60. Marco Kremerman, Alexander Páez, and Benjamín Sáez, "Endeudar para gobernar y mercantilizar: El caso del CAE [Indebt to Govern and Commodify: The Case of CAE]," Fundación Sol, April 20, 2016, www.fundacionsol.cl/estudios/endeudar-gobernar-mercantilizar-caso-del-cae.
61. Cristina Helena Carvalho, "O PROUNI No Governo Lula E O Jogo Político Em Torno Do Acesso Ao Ensino Superior [The PROUNI in Lula's Administration and the Political Game around Access to Higher Education]," *Educação & Sociedade* 27, no. 96 (2006): 979–1000, http://repositorio.unicamp.br/bitstream/REPOSIP/24519/1/S0101-73302006000300016.pdf; Cristina Helena Carvalho and Francisco Luiz Lopreato, "Finanças Públicas, Renúncia Fiscal E O ProUni No Governo Lula [Public Finances, Fiscal Renouncement, and the PROUNI in the Lula Government]" 16, no. 40 (2005): 93–104, www.scielo.br/scielo.php?script=sci_arttext&pid=S0101-73302006000300016; Afrânio Mendes Catani, Ana Paula Hey, and Renato de Sousa Porto Gilioli, "PROUNI: Democratização Do Acesso Às Instituições de Ensino Superior?," *Educar Em Revista*, no. 28 (December 2006): 125–40, doi:10.1590/S0104-40602006000200009; and Afrânio Mendes Catani and Renato Porto Gilioli, "O Prouni Na Encruzilhada: Entre a Cidadania E a Privatização [PROUNI at a Crossroad: Between Citizenship and Privatization]," *Linhas Críticas* 11 (2005): 55–68, www.redalyc.org/pdf/1935/193520514005.pdf.
62. Schwartzman, "Masificación, Equidad y Calidad."

63. Schwartzman, "Masificación, Equidad y Calidad."
64. The next section addresses the relationship between quality regulation and public funding for private higher education.
65. Conversion rate used is US$1 = BZ$3.336, which is the 2015 annual average value of the dollar in terms of Brazilian reals (not seasonally adjusted). See Federal Reserve Bank of St. Louis, "Brazil/U.S. Foreign Exchange Rate," https://fred.stlouisfed.org/series/DEXBZUS; Schwartzman, "Masificación, Equidad y Calidad."
66. Except for graduate education. The Coordination for the Improvement of Higher Education Personnel (CAPES), created in 1951, is the agency in charge of evaluating and funding graduate-level education. See Verhine, "Pós-Graduação No Brasil E Nos Estados Unidos."
67. José Joaquín Brunner, "Universidad, Sociedad Y Estado [University, Society, and State]," *Educación Superior Y Sociedad* 1, no. 107 (1990): 17–23, http://nuso.org/media/articles/downloads/1874_1.pdf; Guy Neave, "The Evaluative State Reconsidered," *European Journal of Education* 33, no. 3 (1998): 265–84; Martin Trow, "Trust, Markets, and Accountability in Higher Education: A Comparative Perspective," *Higher Education Policy* 9, no. 4 (1996): 309–24, https://cshe.berkeley.edu/sites/default/files/publications/rop.trow.trust.1.96.pdf.
68. María José Lemaitre and María Elisa Zenteno, eds., *Aseguramiento de la calidad en Iberoamérica. Educación Superior. Informe 2012* [Quality Assurance in Ibero-America. Higher Education. 2012 Report]," Centro Interuniversitario de Desarrollo (CINDA), 2012, www.cinda.cl/wp-content/uploads/2014/02/Aseguramiento-de-la-calidad-en-Iberoam%C3%A9rica-2012.pdf; Guillermo Ferrer, *Educational Assessment Systems in Latin America: Current Practice and Future Challenges* (Washington, DC: Partnership for Educational Revitalization in the Americas (PREAL), 2006); María José Lemaitre, "Accountability in Latin America: Focusing on Quality Assurance and Funding Mechanisms," in *Accountability in Higher Education: Global Perspectives on Trust and Power*, ed. Bjørn Stensaker and Lee Harvey (New York: Routledge, 2011), 133–56; and Dante J. Salto, "Education in Latin America and the Caribbean: Systems and Research," in *International Encyclopedia of the Social and Behavioral Sciences*, 2nd ed., ed. James D. Wright (Oxford, Eng.: Elsevier, 2015), 178–84.
69. Marginson, "Worldwide Trend"; and Trow, "Trust, Markets, and Accountability."
70. Marginson, "Worldwide Trend."
71. Levy, *Higher Education and the State.*
72. Kinser and Levy, "For-Profit Higher Education"; Kinser and Salto, "For-Profit Higher Education."
73. Maria H. de Magalhães Castro, "Higher Education Policies in Brazil: A Case of Failure in Market Regulation," in *Higher Education in the BRICS Countries*, ed. Simon Schwartzman, Rómulo Pinheiro, and Pundy Pillay (Dordrecht, Netherlands: Springer, 2015); Knobel and Verhine, "Brazil's For-Profit Higher Education Dilemma."
74. Robert E. Verhine, Lys Maria Vinhaes Dantas, and José Francisco Soares, "Do Provão Ao ENADE: Uma Análise Comparativa Dos Exames Nacionais Utilizados No Ensino Superior Brasileiro [From the National Course Exam (Provão) to ENADE: A Comparative Analysis of National Exams Used in Brazilian Higher Education]," *Ensaio: Avaliação E Políticas Públicas Em Educação* 14, no. 52 (2006): 291–310, doi:10.1590/S0104-40362006000300002.

75. In Brazil the federal government oversees public federal and private higher education institutions. The National Institute of Educational Studies and Research (INEP in Portuguese), an agency linked to the Ministry of Education and Culture, centralizes the evaluation of the education system, except graduate education. Some critics note that a central regulatory agency has limited capacity within an increasingly large and complex system in a federal country. See Castro, "Higher Education Policies in Brazil"; and Schwartzman, "Masificación, Equidad Y Calidad."
76. Simon Schwartzman, "Admission to Higher Education in Brazil: The ENEM Debacle," *World View—Inside Higher Ed*, November 7, 2010, www.insidehighered.com/blogs/the_world_view/admission_to_higher_education_in_brazil_the_enem_debacle.
77. INEP, "Microdados ENEM [ENEM Database]," *Portal INEP*, 2014, http://portal.inep.gov.br/microdados.
78. INEP, "Microdados ENEM."
79. José Dias Sobrinho, "Avaliação E Transformações Da Educação Superior Brasileira (1995–2009): Do Provão Ao Sinaes," *Avaliação: Revista Da Avaliação Da Educação Superior* 15, no. 1 (2010): 195–224, doi:10.1590/S1414-40772010000100011.
80. Helio Radke Bittencourt, Alam de Oliveira Casartelli, and Alziro César de Morais Rodrigues, "Sobre O Índice Geral de Cursos (IGC) [About the General Program Index]," *Avaliação* 14, no. 3 (2009): 667–82, http://dx.doi.org/10.1590/S1414-40772009000300008.
81. Besides student performance, the institutional variables/dimensions include percentage of faculty with a PhD, percentage of full-time faculty, infrastructure, and materials in undergraduate and graduate programs.
82. These types of categories are easily interpreted as de facto rankings, even when the aim is to improve performance. "Regulation-for-competition" (Jordana and Levi-Faur) is the term used by regulatory experts to explain the role of government (intended or unintended) in promoting competition by reducing information asymmetry in the quasi-market. This type of regulation is prevalent in many countries. For instance, Argentina uses a similar approach to the categorization (and ranking) of graduate programs based on the accreditation process. See Jacint Jordana and David Levi-Faur, *The Politics of Regulation: Institutions and Regulatory Reforms for the Age of Governance* (Cheltenham, Eng.: Edward Elgar Publishing, 2004); Dante J. Salto, "Attractive Carrots, Bland Sticks: Organizational Responses to Regulatory Policy in Argentine Graduate Education," *Studies in Higher Education* (March 15, 2017): 1–13, https://doi.org/10.1080/03075079.2017.1301415; and Dante J. Salto, "Quality Assurance through Accreditation: When Resistance Meets over-Compliance," *Higher Education Quarterly* 72, no. 2 (2018): 78–89, https://doi.org/10.1111/hequ.12151, first published November 15, 2017.
83. José Dias Sobrinho, "La Educación Superior En Brasil: Principales Tendencias Y Desafíos," *Avaliação: Revista de Avaliação da Educação Superior* 13, no. 2 (June 2008); Dias Sobrinho, "Avaliação E Transformações Da Educação Superior Brasileira (1995-2009)"; Simon Schwartzman, "O Enigma Do ENADE," 2005, www.schwartzman.org.br/simon/enade.pdf; and Verhine, Dantas, and Soares, "From the National Course Exam (Provão) to ENADE."
84. Simon Schwartzman, "O Enigma Do ENADE."
85. INEP, "Microdados ENADE."
86. Bowater, "For-Profits in Brazil."
87. Castro, "Higher Education Policies in Brazil."

Conclusion

1. Organisation for Economic Cooperation and Development (OECD), *Education at a Glance 2017: OECD Indicators*, https://read.oecd-ilibrary.org/education/education-at-a-glance-2017_eag-2017-en#page1.
2. OECD, *Education at a Glance 2017.*
3. Farran Powell, "10 Most, Least Expensive Colleges," *U.S. News & World Report*, September 12, 2017. Median tuition at less selective public universities was calculated by the authors using the US Department of Education National Postsecondary Student Aid Study (2018), https://nces.ed.gov/surveys/npsas.
4. Authors' calculation, US Department of Education, Student Aid Study (2018).
5. Authors' calculation, US Department of Education, Student Aid Study (2018).
6. Middle income is defined here as students from families with household incomes between USD 27,502 and USD 113,211 in 2014, which are the second and third income quartiles for dependent undergraduate students enrolled in 2015–2016. In other words, half of students who are still dependents of their parents enrolled in the 2015–2016 year had family incomes between USD 27,502 and USD 113,211, which are the 25th percentile to the 75th percentile of the income distribution, respectively. Statistics include dependent and independent students. Authors' calculation, US Department of Education, Student Aid Study (2018).
7. Authors' calculation, US Department of Education, Student Aid Study (2018).
8. Authors' calculation, US Department of Education Federal Student Aid Office, "Federal Student Loan Portfolio," 2017, https://studentaid.ed.gov/sa/about/data-center/student/portfolio.
9. Authors' calculation, US Department of Education, Student Aid Study (2018).
10. Authors' calculation, US Department of Education, Student Aid Study (2018).
11. Beth Akers and Matthew M. Chingos, *Game of Loans: The Rhetoric and Reality of Student Debt* (Princeton, NJ: Princeton University Press, 2016).
12. This results from a unique provision in the US income-based repayment program. It effectively includes two types of maximum monthly repayment calculations: one based solely on income and the other based on the ten-year fixed amortization rate for a borrower's original loan balance. The repayment cap ensures that a borrower will always pay a rate that is lower than, or equal to, the rate on the ten-year repayment plan. Once a borrower's income is high enough that he no longer qualifies for reduced payments under IBR, payments will represent a declining share of income.
13. OECD, *Education at a Glance 2017.*
14. OECD, *Education at a Glance 2017.*
15. Christopher Newfield, *The Great Mistake: How We Wrecked Public Universities and How We Can Fix Them* (Baltimore: Johns Hopkins University Press, 2016).
16. Hillary Clinton's plan was to make college "debt-free" by 2021—students with parents making less than USD 125,000 would be able to attend any in-state public four-year institution and not pay any tuition. Community colleges would also become free for all students, and her plan would also allow borrowers to refinance their loans. Bernie Sanders's plan was to make all public colleges tuition free, regardless of income. His plan would also cut current loan interest rates and allow generous refinancing options for borrowers. Both Clinton and Sanders have specifically stated that their plan would be "fully paid for" by eliminating certain tax loopholes, but what we have learned from other

countries is that good intentions do not translate into actual policy. When public spending inevitably failed to keep up with rising enrollment demands, cutbacks would have to be made and access and quality would suffer. In particular, Sanders would "legislate" that universities couldn't limit access, but this is what has happened in every other country with free college. See Office of Hillary Rodham Clinton, "Making College Debt-Free and Taking on Student Debt," https://www.hillaryclinton.com/issues/college; and Bernie Sanders, "It's Time to Make College Tuition Free and Debt Free," https://berniesanders.com/issues/its-time-to-make-college-tuition-free-and-debt-free.

17. To be eligible, a student must be a resident of New York state, take thirty credits per academic year, attend a State University of New York or City University of New York school, and continue to live in New York for at least four years after graduation. The grant is switched to a loan if any of the eligibility requirements are violated. See New York State, "Tuition Free Degree Program: The Excelsior Scholarship," www.ny.gov/programs/tuition-free-degree-program-excelsior-scholarship.
18. Authors' calculation, National Association of State Budget Officers, "State Expenditure Report," 2015, www.nasbo.org/mainsite/reports-data/state-expenditure-report.
19. David J. Deming and Christopher R. Walters, "The Impact of Price Caps and Spending Cuts on U.S. Postsecondary Attainment" (working paper, National Bureau of Economic Research, Cambridge, MA, August 2017), http://www.nber.org/papers/w23736.
20. The concept of effectively maintained inequality comes from Samuel R. Lucas. See Samuel R. Lucas, "Effectively Maintained Inequality: Education Transitions, Track Mobility, and Social Background Effects," *American Journal of Sociology* 106, no. 6 (2001): 1642–90.

Acknowledgments

We express our sincerest thanks to the authors for their contributions as well as their patience throughout the editing process. We are grateful for the discussants who attended an August 2017 conference at the American Enterprise Institute (AEI), where the authors presented early drafts of their work. Their feedback and insights helped shape what became the final versions of the chapters in this volume.

We are also indebted to the steadfast support of AEI and its president, Arthur Brooks. The Bill and Melinda Gates Foundation generously provided financial support for this project as well. This book would not exist without the tireless efforts of the staff at AEI—in particular, Cody Christensen, for his work managing this project, and Rooney Columbus, who helped set the project in motion. Rick Hess, director of Education Policy Studies at AEI, provided invaluable guidance throughout the project; Andrew Kelly, senior vice president for strategy and policy at the University of North Carolina system and former director of AEI's Center on Higher Education Reform, had the initial insight to recognize that such a project could make an important contribution to the education policy dialogue.

Finally, we express our gratitude to the Harvard Education Press team, particularly director Douglas Clayton and editor-in-chief Caroline Chauncey, both of whom offered skillful and timely guidance throughout the course of this project.

About the Editors

Jason D. Delisle is a resident fellow at the American Enterprise Institute (AEI), where he works on higher education financing with an emphasis on student loan programs. Delisle started his career on Capitol Hill, first in the office of Representative Thomas Petri, then as an analyst for the US Senate Committee on the Budget. His work has led him to study the history and mechanics of federal student loans and other financial aid policies and to recommend budget process reforms for rules covering financial risk in government programs, including working on fair-value accounting for loan programs. Before joining AEI, Delisle served as director of the Federal Education Budget Project at New America, where he worked to improve the quality of public information on federal funding for education and the support of well-targeted federal education policies. He was also an informal adviser on higher education reform for Governor Jeb Bush's 2016 presidential campaign. Delisle has written for a variety of publications, including *Bloomberg View*, the *Wall Street Journal*, and the *Washington Post*. He has also appeared on numerous national television and radio programs, including Fox Business, National Public Radio, and the *PBS NewsHour*. Delisle has a master's of public policy in budget and public finance from George Washington University and a bachelor of arts degree in government from Lawrence University.

Alex Usher is the president of Higher Education Strategy Associates. An internationally recognized expert in student financial aid and quality measurement in postsecondary education, Usher has authored numerous groundbreaking studies in higher education. In addition to his years of work on higher education in Canada, his recent work spans Asia, Europe, and Africa. In his former role as director of Educational Policy Institute Canada (EPI Canada), Usher managed the Measuring the Effectiveness of Student Aid project for the Millennium Scholarship Foundation, a four-year $4 million research project to investigate the long-term effects of student aid, and is the author of the project's Final Report, appearing in early 2010. In 2002 and 2004, Usher coauthored (with Sean Junor) *The Price of Knowledge*, a volume considered the standard reference on student finance in Canada. More recently he has written the theme document for UNESCO Europe's decennial meeting on higher education, "Ten Years Back and Ten Years Forward: Developments and Trends in Higher Education in Europe Region." He sits on a variety of advisory, supervisory, and editorial boards in Canada, Europe, and Asia. Prior to joining the Educational Policy Institute in 2003 and founding Higher Education Strategy Associates, Usher served as the director of research and program development at the Canada Millennium Scholarship Foundation. From 1996 to 1998 he served as a researcher and lobbyist for the Association of Universities and Colleges of Canada, and before that he was the first national director of the Canadian Alliance of Student Associations. Usher holds degrees from McGill University and Carleton University.

About the Contributors

Andrés Bernasconi is an associate professor at the School of Education at the Pontificia Universidad Católica de Chile. He has also served there as vice dean of the school (2015–2016), and director of its research center, CEPPE (2013–2015). Prior to this role he was a vice rector (2007–2012) and a professor (2005–2012) at Universidad Andrés Bello. A lawyer with a master's degree in public policy from Harvard University and a PhD in Sociology of Organizations from Boston University, his research, writing, and consulting work specialize on regulation of higher education, the academic profession, and universities as organizations.

Bruce Johnstone is Distinguished Service Professor of Higher and Comparative Education Emeritus at the State University of New York at Buffalo and director of the International Comparative Higher Education Finance and Accessibility Project. His principal scholarship is in higher education finance, governance, and policy formation in domestic and international contexts. He has led World Bank studies in Morocco, Romania, Kenya, and the East Caribbean states and has conducted conferences on cost-sharing in Tanzania, Kenya, the Czech Republic, Russia, and China. Johnstone holds bachelor's and master's degrees from Harvard and a PhD from the University of Minnesota.

Daniel C. Levy is a Distinguished Professor in the Department of Educational Policy and Leadership of the University at Albany. His research has focused on international higher education policy, related nonprofit sectors, and Latin American politics. He has authored seven books and over one hundred articles. His *Building the Third Sector* (University of Pittsburgh Press, 1996) won the 1997 prize for best book in nonprofit and voluntary action research. He has lectured on all major continents and consulted widely for leading international and other agencies. Levy is the founder and director of PROPHE (Program for Research on Private Higher Education), a global scholarly network.

Jon Marcus is a higher education editor at the Hechinger Report. He has written about higher education for the *Washington Post*, *USA Today*, *Time*, the *Boston Globe*, and *Washington Monthly*. He is also North America higher education correspondent for the *Times* (UK) *Higher Education* magazine and contributed to the book *Rein-*

venting Higher Education (Harvard Education, 2011). His Hechinger coverage has won national awards from the Education Writers Association, and he was a finalist for an award for beat reporting from the New York chapter of the Society of Professional Journalists. Marcus holds a master's degree from Columbia University's Graduate School of Journalism and a bachelor's degree from Bates College.

Anna Mountford-Zimdars is the academic director of the Centre for Social Mobility at the University of Exeter, England. She leads a team of academics using qualitative, quantitative, and theoretical tools in researching education-based social mobility. The center looks to answer key questions around higher education admissions, support during university, and transitions into employment. Anna has published widely in peer-reviewed journals; spoken in the UK, US, and across Europe; and her work has informed national and international policy discussions. Her monograph "Meritocracy and the University" was published in 2016.

Dante J. Salto is a postdoctoral fellow at the Consejo Nacional de Investigaciones Científicas y Técnicas (CONICET) Universidad Nacional de Cordoba (UNC-Argentina) and a lecturer in Educational Policy and Planning at UNC-Argentina. He earned a PhD and a MSc in educational administration and policy studies from the State University of New York at Albany (SUNY), and a Licenciatura in education from the Universidad Nacional de Cordoba. His research interest focuses on Latin American and Argentine higher education policy in a comparative perspective, mainly on issues at the intersection of quality assurance policy, regulation, public and private distinctions, privatization, and internationalization.

Vicki Thomson is the chief executive of the Group of Eight. Prior to this role she was executive director of the Australian Technology Network of Universities (ATN). Thomson's diverse background covers print and electronic journalism, politics, issues management, and the higher education sector. She has an extensive media, political, and policy background, and was chief of staff to John Olsen, premier of South Australia. She is a board member of the Australia-China Council and a member of the Australian government's New Colombo Plan Steering Group.

Index